Santuario Virgen de la Cabeza

Bailén

Linares

Andújar

Úbeda

Baeza

El Moral

MURCIA

Jaén

Peal de Becerro

Huéscar

Vélez-Blanco

Pozo Alcón

Cúllar-Baza

Alcaudete

Alcalá la Real

Guadahortuna

Vélez-Rubio

Sierra Harrana

Baza

Águilas

Guadix

Tijola

Loja

Río Genil

Granada

Lacalahorra

Los Gallardos

La Vega

Sierra Nevada

Alhama de Granada

Alpujarras

Santa Fe de Mondújar

Tabernas

Dúrcal

Níjar

Lanjarón

Ugíjar

Los Millares

Punta de los Muertos

Vélez-Málaga

Sierra de Tejeda

Nerja

Sierra de Gádor

Almería

Las Negras

Torre del Mar

Almuñécar

Cabo de Gata

aga

Roquetas

Cabo de Gata

olinos

d   e   l

a

t

MAR MEDITERRÁNEO

Chu...

Castle

Cloister

Archaeological site

National border

Regional border

Provincial border

Provincial capital

National park

0   N   15 km

ANDALUSIA

ART & ARCHITECTURE

ANDALUSIA

Brigitte Hintzen-Bohlen

KÖNEMANN

Frontispiece:
View of the Hall of Columns in the Mezquita in Córdoba

© 1999 Könemann Verlagsgesellschaft mbH
Bonner Straße 126, D-50968 Cologne

Art and Publishing Director: Peter Feierabend
Project Management: Ute Edda Hammer
Assistant: Kerstin Ludolph
Layout: Wilhelm Schäfer, Köln
Picture Research: Monika Bergmann
Cartography: Astrid Fischer-Leitl, München;
Frese, München; Rolli Arts, Essen
Production: Mark Voges
Lithography: Digiprint, Erfurt

Original Title: Kunst & Architektur Andalusien
©2000 for this English edition
Könemann Verlagsgesellschaft mbH
Bonner Straße 126, D-50968 Cologne

Translation from German: Helen Atkins, Maia Costa, Fiona Hulse, Anthony Vivis
Editing: Lilian Bernhardt
Typesetting: Divis GmbH, Gesellschaft für visuelle Kommunikation
Project Management: Kristin Zeier
Production: Ursula Schümer
Printing and Binding: Sing Cheong Printing Co. Ltd., Hong Kong
Printed in China

ISBN 3-8290-2657-9

10 9 8 7 6 5 4 3 2 1

Table of Contents

Seville, Cathedral of Santa María

Huelva, City Wall

View of Cádiz

Ronda

Almería, Alcazaba

Granada, Alhambra

Olive grove

Córdoba, Mezquita

Santillas del Mar

Andalusia — Europe's Orient

Cádiz — enchanting clarity,
Granada, a weeping river wreathed in mystery,
Roman and Moorish Córdoba cloaked in silence,
Singing Málaga,
Golden Almería,
Jaén, glistening silver,
Huelva, a shore lined with caravels,
and — Seville.
(Antonio Machado)

Andalusia, transfigured in 19th-century guidebooks as "Europe's Orient," has a uniqueness in its art and culture incomparable to anywhere else on earth. This uniqueness results from it being located where several very different civilizations meet. From earliest times, this area has always been the gateway through which conquerors from many different countries have reached Spain. Phoenicians, Carthaginians, Greeks, Celts, Romans, Visigoths, Berbers, and Arabs have all invaded the country, mingling with the original population and leaving their vestiges behind them. This is where several prehistoric cultures originated, it is where the legendary realm of Tartessos was located, and where Phoenicians, Greeks, and Carthaginians set up centers of trade. Under the Romans the province, called Baetica, was first governed as a unified whole, and they imposed a

Granada, The Alhambra, Sala de los Reyes

civilization and infrastructure whose influences are still felt today. Further, they brought in an official language: Latin. Andalusia has the Vandals to thank for its name. The Vandals, along with migrating Alani and Suevi, roamed the country plundering and laying waste. Al-(V)andaluz (land of the Vandals) was what the Arabs later called it. Under the Visigoths Christianity became the state religion. The greatest impact on the country was made by the almost 800 years of Arab rule, during which Andalusia experienced not only its political and cultural high-points but also its most lasting influence. In the cities of Andalusia the Moslem conquerors established great mosques and universities, as well as schools and libraries open to the public, all of which helped Andalusia develop into one of the great intellectual centers of Europe. It is thanks to Arab scholars that classical philosophy and culture were preserved and developed. Here also were laid the foundations of modern scientific disciplines, such as medicine, physics, geography, mathematics, and astronomy. Music and poetry were regarded highly at royal courts. Arts and handicrafts, all of which can still point to Arabic or Islamic origins, were strongly encouraged. Thanks to a complex method of irrigation, a variety of canal-systems, windmills, water wheels, and recently introduced varieties of crops,

Granada, Bañuelo de los Axares o del Nogal

agriculture expanded rapidly. While Europe was languishing in the depths of the Middle Ages, a far superior culture was thriving in Andalusia. With its climate of total tolerance, it enabled Moslems, Christians and Jews to live peacefully together; and by transmitting classical and oriental knowledge it prepared Europe's passage into the modern world. Andalusia's most famous structures date from these centuries – the Mezquita, the city of palaces, Medina al-Zahara, the Giralda, and the Alhambra, as well as the numerous Arab bathhouses.

Christian Andalusia

However, Christians from the North continually kept invading the country – the dense network of defensive strongholds is only partial evidence of the constant conflicts between Moors and Christians. After the successful outcome of the *Reconquista* (Reconquest) in 1492 Andalusia turned Catholic and became part of the Spanish empire. Neither Jews nor Moors had any further place in this state, which finally extinguished their cultures completely. Thus the period of great cathedral-building began, extending into the 18th century, but starting much later than in the rest of Europe. These cathedrals can be seen in all major cities – a monumental sign of Christian victory over an erstwhile Moorish empire. Those nobles who took part in the Reconquista settled in Andalusian cities, founded churches and built imposing palaces. The Christians contrasted the splendid style of Moorish architecture, featuring ornate, ornamental decoration, with the "European" Renaissance style. The palace of Charles V on the Alhambra, with its clearly laid-out facade, the Casa Pilatos in Seville, and the cathedrals of Jaén and Granada are exquisite examples of this period. Yet Sevillean architecture proves at the same time that the period of Christian conquest, seen from the viewpoint of cultural history, did not mark a complete break. Arabic traditions of architecture and decoration were continued and merged with new Christian forms by Moorish craftspeople, now employed by Christian patrons. *Azulejos* (colored glazed tiles), stucco-decoration and *artesonado* (ornamented wood) ceilings are to be found in many churches and aristocratic residences of that period. The most famous example of this Mudéjar style, is the magnificent palace of King Pedro I, the Cruel, in Seville. As the Gothic style was being replaced with the Renaissance style, stylistic anomalies such as the Isabellesque and Plateresque styles began emerging. These continue the tradition of stylistic pluralism within Spanish art. Under the Habsburgs

Christopher Columbus takes his leave of the Catholic monarchs. Contemporary illustration.

(1516-1700) Spain grew into a world-empire, and during the Conquista, as the American continents were being discovered and conquered, it ruled an enormous colonial area and had untold wealth at its disposal. Conflicts with other European powers increased. From the late 16th century on, defeats and territorial losses contributed to a gradual dwindling of power. World economic crises and plague epidemics worsened the situation. Quite independently, however, in the 17th century art and literature thrived splendidly, allowing Andalusia to experience the *Siglo de Oro* (Golden Age). The Baroque era marked the region's final period of glory. In the course of the Counter-Reformation, many monasteries and churches were built and provided with magnificent retables, numerous oil-paintings and life-size *pasos* (figures from the Passion). In the cities of Seville and Granada important schools for painters and sculptors were established.

Cortés receiving the representatives of the Aztecs. Madrid, Muséo América

The Poorhouse of Spain

The decline began in the 19th century – with wars, disputes about who should succeed to the throne, and the loss of the colonies. In the 20th century, the Civil War (1936-1939) and Franco's dictatorship (1936-1975) made Andalusia deteriorate into the poorhouse of Spain, with underdeveloped industry and high unemployment. The virtual absence of an architectural or artistic legacy speaks volumes. Although tourism and a flourishing agriculture give present-day Andalusia important economic strengths, they are not sufficient to resolve the problems of unemployment. An almost feudal social structure which has persisted since the Reconquista – almost half the land is owned by only about four percent of the population – and an immense number of poverty-stricken day-laborers characterize Andalusia's economic problems today. The lack of mineral resources in the southeast and the Sierra Morena, areas which have few industrial or technological centers, exacerbates the problem. As a result, the 1950s and 1970s saw huge waves of emigration. Nearly two million Andalusians left the country in order to work in the North or abroad. Nevertheless, for some time now Andalusia has not been a poor region. Nowadays it is a politically self-confident and economically thriving region, which was given fresh economic impetus by the World Exhibition of 1992.

A Country of Contrasts

Apart from its cultural heritage, Andalusia is also fascinating for its rich variety of different kinds of landscape, which are sometimes downright contradictory. Separated from the high plateau of Castile by the jagged Sierra Morena mountain range, the region lying between the North and the West is intersected by the "great river," the Guadalquivir. Within its broad river-basin lie extensive plains and areas of fertile fields. The Coto de Doñana, which has been designated a nature reserve and has one of the largest bird sanctuaries in Europe, is found within the river's estuary. Not far from the coast runs the mountain chain of the Baetic Cordillera with a low mountain range in the western part, whose sierras have charmingly dense vegetation. The high mountains of the Sierra Nevada occupy the eastern area, where you can find snow-capped peaks until early summer. In this area Mount Mulhacén is situated. At 11,421 feet (3,481 meters), it is the highest mountain on the Spanish mainland. On the fertile coastal strip of the Costa del Sol there is a desert-like landscape in the vicinity of Almería. Here, you will find the Cabo de Gata, a nature reserve

Angels at Prayer, 16th century. London, British Library

with very rare plants, a flamingo-sanctuary, and bird nesting areas. At the eastern edge of the Sierra Nevada lies the only naturally evolved desert in Europe. And there is yet another contrast marking out the Andalusian landscape. Near Tarifa, at the most southerly point in Europe, the Atlantic and Mediterranean meet. Here, the mild climate of the Mediterranean Sea turns into the changeable, harsh Atlantic climate.

Andalusia, one of the 17 *comunidades autónomas* (autonomous communities) in Spain, with a surface area of over 33,500 square miles (87,000 square kilometers) and around seven million inhabitants, is afflicted with a great many clichés. Among

Sierra Nevada

other things, it is the homeland of Carmen and Don Juan, as well as the land of flamenco and bullfighting, of sherry, olives, and lemons, of pious pilgrimages and exuberant celebrations, of Arab palaces and cool patios. Such images, often evident in the nightly enthusiastic descriptions of 19th century travelers, are quoted nowadays by package-tour managers, to increase this sun-drenched country's allure. In reality, however, they are only part of the picture. Andalusia is fascinating for its contrasts – in terms of culture, landscape, and society. Travel through Andalusia and you will encounter both Moorish palaces and Christian cathedrals, harsh mountainscapes and fertile plains, illiterates and great poets, modern cities as well as white-washed mountain villages with no electricity or running water, motorcycle races as well as bullfights – it is a list that could continue forever. Anyone traveling

Cabo de Gata

to Andalusia will have a great many expectations due to the descriptions he or she has heard and read. Ultimately, perhaps, these expectations will not be fulfilled. For Andalusia does not reveal itself completely at the first glance, offering a fully-rounded picture. The visitor needs time to get to know Andalusia. One needs to keep rediscovering the country time after time, by visiting places and localities which offer a different perspective, a new viewpoint, every time one is there. Whether you are looking at royal palaces or defensive strongholds, mosques or churches, high-rise blocks in the suburbs or winding little alleyways in historic centers, magnificently laid-out gardens or flower-bedecked patios – Andalusia contains a wealth of contrasting images, which make it one of the most intriguing cultural and natural landscapes in Europe.

The Province of Seville

Seville

When people talk about Seville they usually mean the city, because this proud, exquisite capital city dominates the surrounding province, with its extensive fields and small towns. Seville, the largest city in Andalusia, still thrives on the renown of times past. For over 200 years during the Age of Discoveries, the Rio Guadalquivir made this city the gateway to the New World, and simultaneously helped it develop into an important trading center. Seville is linked in people's minds with flamenco, Carmen, Don Juan, and the famous Barber. But it is also associated with a combination of passion and exuberance during the *Semana Santa* (Holy Week) or the *Feria de Abril*, which takes place during the Easterweek and is well known outside the borders of Andalusia. Today this Andalusian city, with its population of 700,000 people, is the seat of the autonomous community's parliament and government. Bleak new suburbs contrast with the beautiful *barrios* (districts) of the Old Town, in which one is constantly coming across cultural monuments that date from past centuries. The city is wellknown for the innumerable orange-trees which line its broad streets. Especially in spring, these trees waft their unique fragrance through the city, whilst somehow surviving the often chaotic traffic. Seville's history is briefly summed

Seville, Torre del Oro, older view

Seville, Alcázares Reales, carved wooden door

up above one of the old city gates: "Hercules built me, Caesar surrounded me with walls and towers, royal holiness made me welcome." The origins of the city are believed to date back to the second century B.C., when Iberians founded the settlement of Hispalis. This was later taken over by the Phoenicians and Carthaginians, and, during the second Punic War, it fell into Roman hands. In 206 B.C. Scipio Africanus founded the nearby settlement of Itálica, which is now one of the most interesting excavation sites in Spain. North of Seville, in Mulva, there are further vestiges of Roman settlement. In 45 B.C., during the war against Pompey, Caesar enclosed Hispalis in defensive ramparts

Azulejos showing a view of Seville, taken from an 18th-century engraving

and raised it to the status of *Colonia Iulia Romana* (Roman Colony of Julius [Caesar]). Its harbor became important for the export of goods to Rome – especially olive oil, which was transported in amphorae. Under the Visigoths, who from A.D. 461 onwards ruled the city after the Vandals and Suevi, Seville had a major personality in St. Isidor (556-636). This famous archbishop, who succeeded his brother, St. Leander, in this position, gave religion and philosophy a great boost by compiling an encyclopedic book on ancient and Christi-

an culture. He was also Head of the School of Seville. In 712 Moors occupied the city, but Ishbiliya, as the city was then called, remained overshadowed by Córdoba until the collapse of the Caliphate. It was not until 1023 that the city became the magnificent capital of one of the Taifa kingdoms ruled by the Abbadides. Their King al-Mutamid built one of the earliest palaces on the site of the present-day Alcázar. In 1091 the city fell into the hands of the fundamentalist Almoravides, who were succeeded by the Almohade monarchs in

1145. During this period Seville was extended into a residential city and experienced its first period of glory – to which the Giralda, the minaret of the former mosque, and the Torre del Oro still bear witness. In 1248, in the course of the Reconquest, Ferdinand III, the Holy, conquered the city after a siege lasting several months and expelled the entire Moorish population. Like his son and successor, Alfonso X, the Wise, he granted Seville many economic privileges. From then on, Seville always remained a bastion of fidelity to the crown. In return, Alfonso X honored the city with the title *No Majeda Do* (She did not let me down), and these words still appear on Seville's coat-of-arms. Later Christian rulers also liked being there, and in the 14th century King Pedro the Cruel, had Moorish artisans build his residence, the Alcázar. However, for the Jews living in Seville, life was terrible

Seville, the Giralda

Adolf Schroedter: Don Quijote Reading in His Armchair, 1834.
Oil on canvas, 54.5 x 46 cm

transacted. This international city was the point of connection between the Old and New World, so it was here that trading concerns from all over Europe established themselves. Spanish galleons brought vast quantities of gold and silver from the colonies to Seville, which, with 150,000 inhabitants, was the third-largest city in the western world at that time. It was not until the 17th century that Seville's economic power began to crumble. The devastating plague epidemic of 1649 was followed in 1680 by Seville losing its place as the center of maritime trade. In 1717, because the Guadalquivir was silting up more and more, Seville had to cede its monopoly of trade with America to Cádiz. Yet despite sustaining this economic loss, in the 17th century the city experienced a cultural heyday, producing a plethora of famous painters and sculptors, whose works of art adorn the city's numerous churches and monasteries. Many of them, such as Diego Velázquez and Francisco de Zurbarán, were summoned to the royal court in Madrid. Also during this period the poet Miguel de Cervantes, imprisoned in the royal

under the Christians. After the pogrom of 1391, in 1480 the first Court of the Inquisition began its activities there.

The city's period of greatest glory started with the discovery of the New World. Seville became the headquarters of the Casa de Contratación, the state trading and finance authority, and thus the sole center where trade with overseas colonies was

Gustave Doré, Don Quijote, 1863, Woodcut.

dungeons of Seville, began his illustrious novel, Don Quijote.

Seville recovered slowly from the far-reaching economic crisis, which was further exacerbated by the severe damage due to the devastating earthquake of 1755. One positive note was struck in 1929 by the Ibero-American Exhibition, but Franco's dictatorship in the following decades stifled all attempts to increase urban develop-

ment. A brilliant new start was expected from the large-scale World Exhibition of 1992 which, like Columbus's voyage of discovery 500 years before, was meant to mark the dawn of a new age. Partly as a result of the Exhibition, all the cultural monuments were restored, and the infrastructure of the whole region was brought up to the highest possible standard. Sadly, expectations proved too high.

Seville

Museo de Bellas Artes,
Calle Alfonso XII, p. 98

Cathedral of Santa María, Plaza
Virgen de los Reyes, p. 28

Hospital de la Caridad,
Calle Temprado, p. 66

Torre del Oro,
Paseo de Cristóbal
Colón, p. 72

Palacio de San Telmo,
Avenida de Roma,
p. 73

Palacio Español,
Plaza de España, p. 82

Casa de Pilatos,
Plaza de Pilatos, p. 86

Iglesia de San Salvador,
Plaza del Salvador, p. 88

Giralda, Plaza
Virgen de los
Reyes, p. 46

Alcázares Reales,
Plaza del Triunfo, p. 48

Universidad, Antigua Fábrica de
Tabacos, Calle San Fernando, p. 80

Also worth seeing:

The Cathedral of Santa María

On July 8 1401 the Cathedral Chapter of Seville decided they would "build a church so exquisite that no other would compare with it, so large and in such a style that all those who finally see it can't help thinking we must have been mad!" The new building was justified by the fact that the old mosque which had served as a cathedral ever since Ferdinand III had reconquered the city in 1248, was already showing signs of collapse and would not withstand the next earthquake. That said, it is likely that the proud city of Seville wanted to surpass that symbol of the Spanish church, the cathedral of Toledo. Sure enough, the cathedral of Seville is the largest Gothic church in the world, and its dimensions are exceeded only by St. Peter's in Rome and St. Paul's Cathedral in London.

A year or two later, the canons put their promise into effect. The Almohadic mosque, which had once comprised seventeen naves, was demolished. Of the church's Moorish predecessor, only the Giralda, the erstwhile minaret, and a few remnants in the Patio de los Naranjos, survived. The name of the architect in charge is still unknown. The design can possibly be attributed to Alonso Martínez, who, as long ago as 1386, had received the commission to design a new church. Scarcely a century after building work had started, namely in 1506, this immense project – the first cathedral in Andalusia – was finished. This was seen as a monumental sign of the Christian kings' success, for, a few years earlier, they had conquered the last remaining Moorish enclave, the kingdom of Granada. However, a mere five years later the dome collapsed, and Juan Gil de Hontañón built the characteristic fan and stellar vault which marks a transition to the Renaissance. During the Renaissance and the Baroque periods further extensions were carried out that made the cathedral a multifarious architectural whole. With its roofs and domes supported by a wealth of arched buttresses, as well as the Giralda towering over it, this cathedral dominates the whole area and still induces gasps of incredulous astonishment. Théophile Gautier responded in a similar way when he visited the church in 1840: "The real *pièce de résistance* in Seville is its cathedral, a building you observe with amazement even if you've already seen the cathedrals in Burgos or Toledo and the Mezquita in Córdoba.... It is a hollowed-out mountain, an upturned valley. In the central nave, which is so high you get vertigo, the Notre Dame in Paris could go for a walk with head held high. Columns as thick as towers, which look so fragile you shiver, rise up from the floor and hang down from the vaults like stalactites in a giant's cave."

The Cathedral of Santa María

Unlike the great French royal churches, which follow a classical basilica-pattern with three or four naves as well as a classical choir-gallery, the Cathedral of Seville follows a pattern of its own, characteristic of cathedrals in Spain. It is conceived as a hall-like basilica and is contained within a rectangular groundplan, which is presumably based on Moorish mosques. The cathedral's five naves have a total length of approximately 413 feet (126 meters). The central nave, the side-aisles, and the chapels situated between the retaining walls, attain a breadth – unequaled in any other church – of about 269 feet (82 meters). The placing of the *coro* (choir) and the *Capilla Mayor* (Main Chapel) in the central nave to the east and west of the dome, conveys the impression of a colossal, self-contained body which is not unlike an enormous treasure house. Later extensions completed the Gothic groundplan. Thus, in the eastern apse, Charles V had the *Capilla Real* (Royal Chapel) built over an older chapel. In the 16th century the *Sacrista Mayor* (Main Sacristy) and the chapter-house were built. They are both located on the south side. Then, in the 17th and 18th centuries, the baroque administration complex was added on the southwest side.

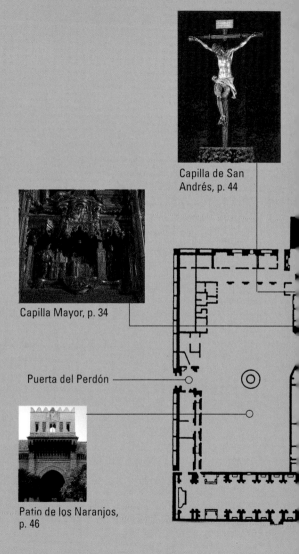

Capilla de San Andrés, p. 44

Capilla Mayor, p. 34

Puerta del Perdón

Patio de los Naranjos, p. 46

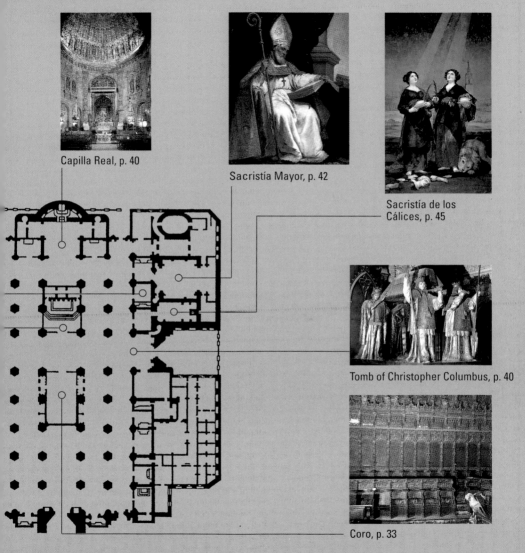

Capilla Real, p. 40

Sacristía Mayor, p. 42

Sacristía de los Cálices, p. 45

Tomb of Christopher Columbus, p. 40

Coro, p. 33

Interior View Looking West

"Everything is austere and majestic, as if we had left the real world and found ourselves in a massive grotto, furnished by a giant familiar with geometry, symmetry, and order." (Fernando Chueca Goitia)

Inside the church viewers experience a characteristic of Spanish cathedrals – an attempt to create a greater sense of spaciousness. Despite the colossal height – about 116 feet (35.5 meters) in the central nave and transepts, 78 feet (24 meters) in both the double side aisles – the most striking impression is of seemingly infinite space. Only the centrally positioned choir contrasts with this impression. The octagonal bases of the monumental compound piers, whose sides have been hollowed out are of special interest. Magnificent Gothic groined vaults with ribs separating the cells, cover the ceiling, which is illuminated by 16th century stained glass windows from the Renaissance period.

A Glance at the Vaults

After the dome collapsed in 1511, Juan Gil de Hontañón began rebuilding work in 1515. Unlike the straightforward vaulting in the naves, the dome and the adjacent bay have been decorated with richly ornamented fan and stellar vaulting. This area clearly shows the change in style that has taken place in just a few years.

Coro

The combination of Gothic, Mudéjar, and Plateresque elements in the carving and marquetry work on the stalls of the choir which, according to the inscription on the rear of the royal throne, were executed by Nufro Sánchez in 1478, makes it among

the most exquisite in southern Spain. The 117 stalls have been carved out of oak and fir with inlays of different types of wood. The upper section contains the sedilia for the clergy, and the lower section the sub-sedilia for the prebendaries. On the back-rests of the lower stalls the original Giralda is depicted. Relief scenes from the Bible adorn the headrests, and vices and sins are shown on the misericords. The upper stalls have been completed in similar fashion. They are surmounted by arches borne by wooden statuettes. In turn, they are supporting a baldachin of filigree carvings, depicting small figures.

Capilla Mayor, Main Retable (with a detail)

With a width of 59.7 feet (18.2 meters) and a height of 91.2 feet (27.8 meters), the high altar, which was designed and begun by the Flemish sculptor Pieter Dancart in 1482, is the largest in Spain. It took almost 100 years for the whole altar composition to be completed. The carving – of walnut, larch, and chestnut – takes the form of a triptych, surmounted by a baldachin and closed by a crossbeam. Within an ornately decorated architectonic frame the retable comprises 45 groups of figures, each one of which – except for the reliefs on the predella – measure 10.7 square feet (one square meter). In the central section the lives of Jesus and Mary are depicted, whilst the two wings show scenes of the Creation and Paradise. The predella depicts scenes from the lives of Sevillean saints as well as views of the city. One of the most interesting of these contemporary testimonies is the representation of the eastern facade of the cathedral with the Giralda. Therefore, we can see how the first lantern looked before it collapsed, as well as the Giralda in its Moorish form. The top section is comple-

ted by a Pietà with the twelve apostles beside it, as well as a crucifixion group in the soaring decoration on the retable. The individual reliefs are divided by several pilasters, on each of which a small sculpture has been placed. To give the effect of correct perspective, the upper figures are larger, so that, when seen from below, they do not appear smaller. The wealth of figures led the Englishman, Henry Vollam, to oberve that "the whole population of a medium-sized Gothic city was gathered here."

Seville and Chess

The downfall of the powerful caliphate of Córdoba in the early 11th century led to the proliferation of many small domains which were to give the country a new, albeit brief, period of glory. In Spanish history these petty Muslim kingdoms are known as *taifas* (from the Arabaic *ta'ifa*, meaning "stock, grouping," and the petty kings are called *reyes taifas*. The collapse of Omaiyade hegemony in Córdoba did not jeopardize the development of the sciences or the arts, as the kings continued to compete to have the best artists, poets and scholars at their courts. Even so, the political consequences were catastrophic. Although Christian rulers had never dared to rebel against the power of Córdoba, they now found it quite easy to take steps against the *taifas*, which were always squabbling among themselves.

Among the frequently short-lived petty states the dynasty of the Abbadides, who had created a largish kingdom for themselves, stood out in the history of Seville. In 1068, al-Mutamid succeeded to his father's throne and held court magnificently. He was a great poet and a strong

Moors playing chess. Chessbook of Alfonso the Wise, 1283. Madrid, El Escorial, Library

A Christian knight as a guest in a Moorish knight's tent playing chess.
Chessbook of Alfonso the Wise, 1283. Madrid, El Escorial, Library

supporter of literature, thus attracting poets and scholars to his palace, where they hoped to find a secure income in turbulent times. Among them was Ibn Ammar, who was born in Sicily and whose superb verse al-Mutamid admired profoundly. The poet, who had known the king since childhood, became his closest confidant and was given the post of Vizier at the court, where the art of poetry was considered an official's supreme virtue. Al-Mutamid, praised by a biographer as the "most generous, most popular, and most powerful of all the petty kings," was also successful in military pursuits through which he was able to add several neighboring kingdoms to his empire, including the formerly powerful Córdoba. Yet Al-Mutamid's greatest weakness was that he was not strong enough to fight the powerful king in the North,

Alfonso VI, who forced him to pay considerable sums in tribute.

King Alfonso VI, after battling several years to succeed Ferdinand I, inherited his father's dominion over Castile, Léon, and Galicia in 1072. Alfonso, who called himself *imperator totius Hispaniae* (ruler over all Spain), soon attacked Zaragoza, Granada, Seville, and Bajadoz, forcing the kings to pay larger and larger sums in tribute. His strategy was to weaken his enemies economically until they would submit to him voluntarily. When, in 1078, he marched a huge army against Seville in order to conquer the Abbadide kingdom, the city looked as if it would fall. However, Ibn Ammar saved the day by subterfuge. His weapon was the knowledge that Alfonso was keen a chess-player.

Accordingly, he had an exquisite chess set made of ebony, aloe, and sandal wood, inlaid with gold. On behalf of his master Al-Mutamid, he went to the tent of the Christian king, who

Chess pieces and chessboard. Islamic, 13th/14th century. Granada, The Alhambra

received him with every honor due to him. The king had already heard a lot about him, and considered him one of the most capable men in Spain. After one of his courtiers had told the king about the magnificent chess set, he invited Ibn Ammar to show him the exquisite set and play a game with him on it. The Vizier agreed, but on one condition: if he were to lose, the board and pieces would belong to the king. However, if he were to win, Alfonso must grant him one request. Alfonso didn't know which way to turn. On the one hand, he wanted the beautiful chess set to be his, but on the other, his sense of responsibility as king made him reluctant to take such a risk. But some of the king's courtiers, whom Ibn Ammar had bribed, were able to talk him into it. Their reasoning was: "If you win, you will gain the most beautiful chess set a king ever possessed; and if you lose, we are here to teach the Moors some manners if he makes a preposterous request." So the tale goes that Alfonso let himself be persuaded to play a game, which he eventually lost. Ibn Ammar, who was a chess master, checkmated him. When the King asked the Vizier what request he wished to make, Ibn Ammar asked him to withdraw his troops from the borders of Seville. Alfonso complained to his courtiers: "This is exactly what I was afraid of, and you made me do it." Even so, he kept his word. And so Seville was saved once again.

In fact, the game of chess to which Seville owes its salvation is still played to this day, according to the same rules. The game of chess originated in Persia and was brought to Spain by way of the Arab countries, and thence to central Europe. To the Arabs the pieces were nothing less than two opposed armies. Originally, the Queen stood for the Vizier (the Persian *fersam* was adapted into the Castilian *ferza*, the Provençal *fierce* and finally the *vierge*, the Virgin, which became transmuted into the Queen. The bishops were the elephants which, along with the (mounted) knights and the castles (rooks),

Chess figures cut from polished rock crystal, Moorish Spain, 12th/13th century. Osnabrück, Cathedral treasures

made up the heavily armed soldiers. In the front rank stood the pawns – the lightly armed troops. The game's principal figure is the *shah* (the Arab word for "king," taken from Persian) and to defeat him is the object of the game. The way to defeat the king is to "checkmate" him. This expression comes from the Persian *ash-shah-mat*, and means "the king is dead." Consequently, chess is known as the sport of kings, because players of the game, like rulers in real life, must always make the right choice. From the wealth of possibilities each move presents, players must choose only one. If they decide on the wrong move, they will be pushed into a corner and their room for maneuver will be limited. It is thus obvious that, just like a king, chess players must exercise clear-sightedness and wisdom if they want to be successful.

Arabian prince and his entourage playing chess, Chessbook from Alfonso the Wise, 1283. Madrid, El Escorial, Library

The Tomb of Christopher Columbus

In the center of the southern transept we find the tomb of the great explorer, Christopher Columbus, which was completed in 1900. Columbus is supposed to have said in his will that he wished to be buried on the Caribbean island of Santo Domingo. On his death in Valladolid in 1506, he was initially interred in the Capuchin monastery in Seville. After requests from his grandson's wife, Charles V finally granted the deceased's wish, though there is no record of the corpse having been transferred. This will always remain a point of contention between Spain and the colony. At the church fathers' behest a commission went to Santo Domingo in 1795, taking the first available urn with them in order to transport it to Cuba. In 1892 this same urn found its way from there back to Seville. However, since the real urn was excavated from Santo Domingo in 1877, it now seems highly unlikely that the sarcophagus borne by four extremely large heralds – representing the four kingdoms of Spain – contains the mortal remains of Columbus. However the inscription states the opposite: "When the island of Cuba gained independence from its motherland, Spain, Seville received the remains of Christopher Columbus, and the city councilors had this monument erected."

Capilla Real

The rectangular space of the Capilla Real with a semi-circular end-wall and a coffered dome above it, was built by order of Charles V from 1551–1558, and it is dedicated to the city's conqueror, Ferdinand III. His remains rest in an 18th-century silver shrine above the original tomb. On its sides one can still make out the traces of Hebraic, Arabic, Latin, and Old Spanish inscriptions, which reproduce the eulogy Alfonso X wrote to his father. It states: "The most honest, the most truthful, the most magnanimous, the most courageous, most proud, most distinguished, most devoted, most humble, most God-fearing, and most dedicated servant of God, and he conquered the city of Seville, the head of all Spain." In the central niche of the wall which is divided by eight decorated pilasters, beneath a silver baldachin, stands a richly decorated and bejeweled larch wood figure of the patron saint of Seville – the *Virgen de los Reyes* (Virgin of the Kings), whose head and arms can be moved mechanically.

Sacristía Mayor: Juan de Arfe, Silver Monstrance

The central room, which, like a full-scale church, has its own altar and presbytery, was begun by Diego de Riaño in 1528, and completed by Martín de Gaínza in 1543.

It is decorated in the Plateresque style. The decoration so impressed Phillip II that he objected to the cathedral canons that this space was more beautiful than his court chapel.

The Sacristía Mayor houses the finest pieces of the church's treasure. The most valuable ritual object is a processional silver monstrance created between 1580 and 1587. It is 12.8 feet (3.9 meters) tall and weighs 1,047 pounds (475 kilograms). It was completed by Juan de Arfe y Villafañe, a grandson of Heinrich Harfe, who emigrated from Cologne and founded a dynasty of goldsmiths in Léon. The host-container is made in the form of a small temple, which the artist himself called "a temple for the

triumphal procession of the true Christ." Above a circular base with four receding levels, representatives of both earth and heaven are depicted in figures and reliefs. Even today, this monstrance is still solemnly carried in procession through the streets of Seville.

Sacristía Mayor: Bartolomé Esteban Murillo, St. Isidor and St. Leander, 1655.
Oil on canvas, each measuring 193 x 165 cm

The artist Bartolomé Esteban Murillo was responsible for the two pictures of Saints Isidor and Leander, commissioned as matching paintings. Contemporaries of the painter sat as models for the two bishops and patron saints of the city. The cleric, Cavalán, who has close links with the cathedral chapel, had his portrait painted as St. Isidor, holding a bishop's staff and a book depicting an allusion to the saint's religious writings. The model for St. Leander is said to have been Alonso de Herrera, the founder of the cathedral choir. The parchment bearing the inscription *Credite o gothi consubstantialem patri* (Believe it, you Visigoths, he is at one with God the Father). These words, which Leander used to defend Christ's divine nature, symbolize his struggle against the Arians' heresy.

Capilla de San Andrés: Juan Martínez Montañés, Cristo de la Clemencia, 1603

The small chapel of San Andrés is located at the western end. A red baldachin houses one of the cathedral's most valuable works of art: the crucifix made by Juan Martínez Montañés in 1603. According to the contract, Christ was to be depicted "as if alive, as if talking to the people praying at his feet." The naturalistic and beautifully formed body of the dying Christ, who is shown without any traces of blood and only with the requisite signs of suffering, is considered an outstanding example of *Estofado* sculpture, which prompts viewers to focus on emotions. Juan Martínez Montañés – also called the Phidias of Seville – is the leading exponent of this school of Sevillean sculpture at the crossroads between Mannerism and the Baroque.

Sacristía de los Cálices: Francisco de Goya, Justina and Rufina, 1817
Oil on canvas, 310 x 178 cm

In one of his rare religious paintings, in 1817 Francisco de Goya completed a commission from the cathedral chapter to paint the two patron saints of the city, St. Justina and St. Rufina. Murillo had already formed the groundwork for this subject in the 17th century. The subjects of the painting are two young women potters from the Sevillean quarter of Trian. They are being thrown to the lions by the Romans because they have destroyed an idol. Goya depicts them against a background of the Guadalquivir, the cathedral, and the Giralda. As the light falls on the two women, who are looking towards heaven, it forms a halo around them. As signs of martyrdom, they are holding pottery and palm-leaves. Before them lies the shattered idol. A lion is licking St. Rufina's feet.

Patio de los Naranjos (Courtyard of the Oranges)

The mosque which the Almohades built in 1172 was among the largest Islamic places of worship then in existence. The merlon-adorned walls which used to enclose the courtyard of the Islamic church have remained standing. Even today the orange-trees still waft their scent here and beautify the courtyard. In the center is a marble fountain which dates from the Visigothic period and which the Arabs used for their ritual ablutions. The 16th century Puerta del Pardón, a Mudéjar-style portal which is ornately decorated with stucco, forms the northern entrance. The arcades along the courtyard's eastern side have been integrated into later additions. The exceptional Biblioteca Colombina contains 3,000 volumes which Fernán Colón, the son of Christopher Columbus donated to the chapter. Along with a Bible once owned by Alfonso X, there are a number of fascinating manuscripts with hand-written notes by the man who discovered the New World.

The Giralda

Today, the glories of the Great Mosque of Seville are still proclaimed far and wide by its erstwhile minaret – the 318-foot (97 meters) Giralda, which has become one of the city's landmarks. Now it serves as the cathedral's clocktower. When the mosque was demolished in the early 15th century only the minaret was spared. It is an Almohadic structure, built from 1184–1196. Around a central core with seven domed rooms built one above the other, a spiral ramp leads to a platform from which one can enjoy an impressive view of the city. Above the smooth base the side-walls are decorated with a filigree network of diamonds over the blind arcades, between which twin windows open. A blind arcade with intersecting pointed arches completes the architectural features. Originally, there was a small tower here, whose ceramic dome was crowned by four gilded spheres – but this was destroyed by an earthquake on August 24, 1355. From 1560-1568 Hernán Ruiz II built the new five-story extenstion,

which can be seen far and wide as a triumph of Christianity. This is crowned by a 13-foot (4 meters) statue of *Fides* (faith), holding a standard and a palm-branch. The tower takes its name from this statue. The standard serves as a weather-vane and makes the figure girate in the wind. In Spanish this is known as *Giradillo* (from *girar*, to girate).

Alcázares Reales

On the Plaza del Triunfo one can find the *Alcázares Reales* (Royal Palace Buildings), which is among the most historic building complexes in Seville. Several epochs have left their vestiges here but despite the architectonic complexity, a harmonious entity has been created, one whose highly ornate splendor exudes a special charm. The patios, rooms, bedchambers, and gardens in the palace complex have been the sites of important historical events as well as the meeting-places of famous personalities. Even today, some of the rooms

are still available to the royal house for their visits to the city.

The origins of the Alcázares Reales date back to the early days of Arab rule in Seville, when the representatives of the caliphate of Córdoba, and later the Abbadide rulers, used to live there. The only vestiges of this period now left are the remnants of the Jardín de Crucero from the 11th century. The palace was not extended into a large-scale, imposing royal residence until the 12th century, when the Almohades made Seville the new capital of their taifa empire. Only the exquisite Patio del Yeso gives us any idea of the magnificence which characterized this complex at that time. After the Reconquista in 1248, the Alcázar became a Christian residence and underwent extensive changes under Ferdinand III. The core of the present-day complex is the palace built by Pedro I, the Cruel (1350-1369).

Among the profane buildings, this palace stands out as one of the finest examples of Mudéjar architecture. Pedro I went to a great deal of trouble for the residence of his mistress, María de Padilla. He had remnants of Islamic buildings transported to Seville, and he summoned artisans from Toledo and Granada to erect a palace according to his own design. The result is a magnificent building in which aspects of Islamic tradition blend with Spanish Christian elements. Subsequent Catholic kings carried out further renovations and extensions to make the royal residence meet their own needs. Such renovations included converting the upper story of Pedro I's palace into a winter residence – refered to as the Upper Palace – and the addition of various gardens. Since then, apart from comprehensive restoration work in the 19th century in accordance with the current fashion of the time, the complex has undergone no further substantial renovations or changes.

Patio del Yeso

The Puerta del Léon, a gate in the Almohadic wall, forms the northwestern entrance
to this enormous complex of buildings. Its
name originates from an azulejos depicting
a crowned lion holding a cross and a scroll
on which *Ad Utrunque* (ready for anything)
is written. Across from the Patio del Léon
one enters the Sala de la Justicia, a court-

room built by Alfonso XI in the 14th century, and further on, one finds the Patio del
Yeso. This long, rectangular garden with
several beds, a canal in the center, and
brick buildings used to be part of the Almohadic fortifications. On a long wall you find
a seven-arch portico which can be admired
as a rare example of Almohadic palace-
architecture. Its facade is tripartite – the
center is taken up by a serrated arch rising

to a point, whose spandrel is covered with a network of intersecting arches. It is flanked by two sets of three lancet arches, each surmounted by perforated diamond panels. Above the doorway, formed by two horseshoe arches, windows have also been installed. The ornate stonework tracery of the windows ensured sufficient light and air in the room.

Facade of the Palacio de Don Pedro

From the Patio del Léon there is a view of the two-story facade of the Palace of Pedro I, which immediately can be recognized as a masterpiece of Mudéjar decorative art. Among the artisans who worked on the

facade were Moorish building workers. These Moorish building workers were sent to Seville by Mohammed V, ruler of Granada, in return for Pedro I's military support. There is probably a reference to this in the blue and white azulejos frieze above the windows. The saying "There is no victor except Allah" is inscribed in the Cufic script of the Nasridic rulers of Granada. At first glance the building looks entirely Islamic in construction. Then the viewer notices the decorative Gothic lettering which frames this inscription, and that it mentions the name of the architect and the date of construction (1364-1366). The same is true of the stalactite crown surmounting the side columns made of brick, and Pedro I's coat-of-arms, which depicts a combination of the lion of Léon and Castilian towers.

**Cuartos del Almirante: Alejo Fernández,
Virgen de los Navegantes (with detail),
1531–1536.**
Oil on wood

In the west wing of the Patio del Léon one finds the *Cuartos del Almirante* (Rooms of the Admiral), with which the history of the Conquista is closely connected. It was here that a great many of the undertakings which brought the name and existence of Spain to the various countries in the New World were planned. It was, for instance, in those rooms that in 1503 Isabella established the Casa de Contratación, the chamber of commerce for trade with the New World. In the Sala de Audiencias, the kings of Spain received seafarers and explorers. Christopher Columbus was one of them in 1496, after returning from his second voyage to America, as was Fernão de Magelhães (1480–1521), known as Magellan, before he sailed around the world.

The Sala de Audiencias is impressive both for its beautiful *artesonado* ceiling, with its painted and gilded geometric inlays, and for its fabric-hung walls, on which coats-of-arms of famous Spanish admirals are reproduced. Located in the chapel behind this room is the famous retable *Virgen de los*

Navegantes (The Madonna of Seafarers). The protectress of seafaring, venerated in numerous mariners' churches and also referred to as the "Madonna of Favorable Winds," is spreading her protective mantle over ordinary Spaniards and Christian explorers in the Age of Discovery. Figures supposed to be depicted here include: on the right, Christopher Columbus and his companions, the Pinzón brothers (wearing berets); and on the left – in profile – Emperor Charles V, as well as Sancho de Matienzo, the first treasurer of the Casa de Contratación, Amerigo Vespucci, and Juan de la Cosa. Depicted in the foreground are the various ships on which voyages to the New World were taken. The wing panels depict saints Jacob, Sebastian, Telmo, and John.

Alcázares Reales

One of the most impressive groupings of buildings in Seville is the royal palace complex. From the Puerta del León, a path leads to the Patio del León, on the left of which is located the Sala de la Justicia and the Patio del Yeso. Beyond this is the Patio de la Montería (Hunting Courtyard), where the king's hunting parties once gathered. On the western side one finds the Cuartos del Almirante, across from which is the entrance to the former Alcázar of Alfons X, the Wise. The cross-shaped garden is named after the mistress of Peter I., Doña María de Padilla, whereas the rooms are referred to as the Palace of Charles V, since this is where the wedding of the emperor and Isabella from Portugal took place. The front side of the Patio de la Montería is bordered by the Palace of Peter I, which opens up to the gardens.

Gardens, p. 62

Pabellón de Carlos V, p. 63

Cuartos del Almirante, p. 52

Patio del Yeso, p. 50

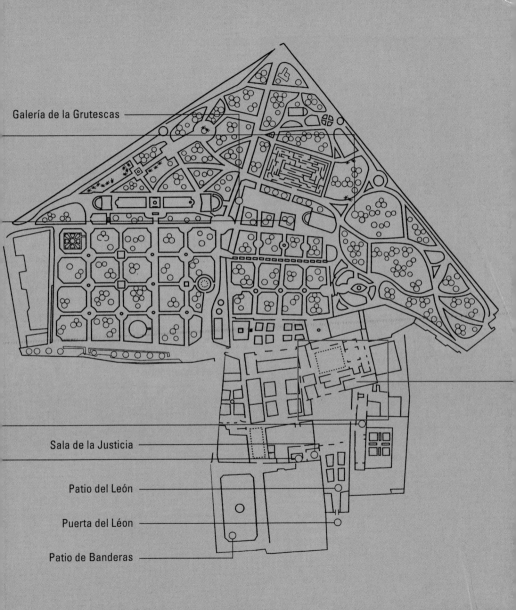

Galería de la Grutescas

Sala de la Justicia

Patio del León

Puerta del Léon

Patio de Banderas

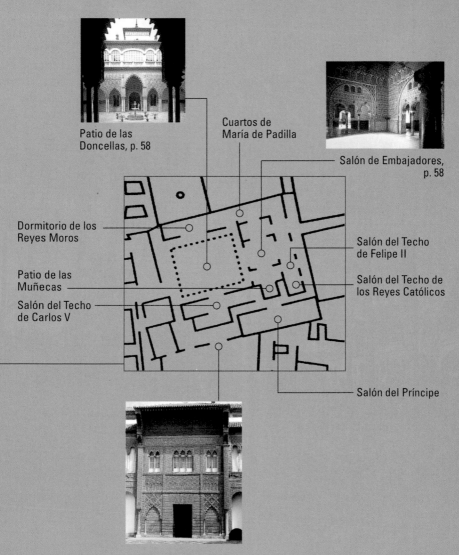

Patio de las
Doncellas, p. 58

Cuartos de
María de Padilla

Salón de Embajadores,
p. 58

Dormitorio de los
Reyes Moros

Salón del Techo
de Felipe II

Patio de las
Muñecas

Salón del Techo de
los Reyes Católicos

Salón del Techo
de Carlos V

Salón del Príncipe

Palacio de Don Pedro,
p. 51

motifs, tendrils, and Cufic signs cover the walls. Arcades that consist of triple horseshoe arches, whose columns originated in earlier Moorish palaces, open the room on three sides to the adjacent rooms. Stalactites and honeycombs lead the eye up to the elaborate ceiling made of larchwood, with which Diego Ruiz replaced the original ceiling in 1427. It is covered with an exquisite network of stars which symbolize the universe and, in the center, form a star with twelve beams. In the 16th century Phillip II had a frieze installed with the portraits of Castillian kings in the upper-wall section. He also had some balconies built which connect the *Salón de Embajadores* with the Upper Palace.

Moorish Gardens

Anyone talking about Andalusia must be shure to mention its gardens, in which, thanks to the favorable climate, several non-native plants thrive. The incredible wealth of color and intoxicating fragrance make a powerful impression on all visitors. The gardens have been created with great love and they are remarkable for their scent, water, and tranquility. Horticulture has a long tradition which dates back to the country's Moorish past. In Andalusia the Arabs found ideal conditions in which to convert their gardening style into a paradise on earth, full of lush, beautifully arranged vegetation. They came from a country which had developed horticulture to a fine art and they were experts at providing wild nature the necessary a human touch. Accordingly, they landscaped large gardens subtly and

Installing a Pond. Miniature from the Book of Babar, 1598. Delhi, Museum

elegantly. The gardens consisted of several different patios separated from one another – and, at the same time connected to each other – by wrought-iron gates. Planting the same species of trees created an overall sense of harmony. These were generally evergreens, whose leaves or needles symbolized eternal spring. The brilliant colorfulness of the flowers made the otherwise uniform green lighter and more appealing. Water wheels and cisterns ensured adequate irrigation. The water was distributed along a system of canals and tunnels, which would occasionally be interrupted by cascades, fountains or ponds. Sometimes, in areas without walls, visitors come across water-courses divided into four – an image of the heavenly garden. The four parts form a cross in whose centera circular basin is formed, and they represent the four rivers of Paradise which flow out towards the four points of the compass or, conversely, flow from those four points towards the center. Brightly colored azulejos, whose hues match their surroundings, also contrast with the gardens' greenery, and shimmer through the water or adorn a bank, a staircase or the small architectural features.

A lot has changed since the days of Moors. The Christians completely transformed almost all the gardens. Only one garden has remained the same as it was when it was first laid out, and it is among the loveliest gardens in the world. A visitor feels transported into an earthly paradise when walking through the Alhambra gardens in Granada. Benches beneath orange trees and cypresses or bowers makes the visitor wish to

linger. Blossoms from a host of different bushes such as rosemary, myrtle, thyme, and jasmine waft forth their fragrance while water splashes from numerous fountains and rivulets. Here, the descriptions of the Islamic Garden of Paradise in the Koran, which inspired Moorish horticulturalists, become reality. This is truly a place of tranquility and an oasis of comfort, whose trees offer shade and always bear fruit, and whose sources of water never run dry.

Granada, The Alhambra, Generalife

Gardens of the Alcázares Reales

Even though only a small section of the gardens adjoining the southern side of the Palace has kept its original form, it is worth your while spending some time there. Directly behind the Palace lies the strictly geometric Renaissance garden, whose austerity is broken up by terraces, grottoes, waterworks, fountains, and statues. From the arcades of the 17th-century Galería de las Grutescas on the eastern side one has a marvelous view of these gardens. On the arches of the building, which was made of volcanic rock, there are capitals from the era of the caliphs, which come from various parts of the Palace. However, originally, this building did not look as bare as it does today, but was decorated with allegorical and mythological frescoes,

telling of Seville's prodigious wealth in the 16th century. Through the portal one reaches an extensive park which was landscaped in the early 20th-century under the rule of King Alfonso XIII. At one end rises a Gothic portal from the period of the Catholic kings which used to be part of the Palace of the Dukes of Arcos in Marchena. This portal came into the private possession of Alfonso XIII as a result of an auction.

Pabellón de Carlos V

The *Pabellón de Carlos V* was built by Juan Hernández in 1543 on the occasion of the marriage of the king and the Portuguese princess, Isabella. It is a square building enclosed by a colonnade. Along with the coffered dome of cedar wood, one can admire the stucco and tile decoration, which fuse Mudéjar stucco elements with those of the Renaissance.

Iglesia del Segrario

On the west side of the Patio de los Naranjos there is a 17th-century Baroque chapel which was designed by Miguel de Zumárraga. Like the cathedral, it has a rectangular groundplan and a domed crossing with chapels located between the supporting columns. Pilasters and blind windows divide the three-story exterior.

Retable of the High Altar

The high altar (1665-1669) was brought into the chapel from the erstwhile Convento de Francisco. The works on the retable – the *Deposition*, the angels in the side niches, and the relief *The Entry into Jerusalem* are by Pedro Roldán. The gable sculptures – St. Clement and St. Veronica with Angels – are by Pedro Duque Cornejo. Along the sides of the interior space stand eight large stone figures of apostles and ecclesiastical scholars by José de Arce, which were completed in 1657.

Casa de la Lonja (Archivo General de Indias)

Until the 16th century, commodity exchange took place every day in the Patio de los Naranjos at the cathedral. In bad weather, business was transacted inside. However, after the archbishop had repeatedly denounced the merchants' noise as blasphemous and finally threatened the traders with excommunication, Phillip II (1585-1598) had the Stock Exchange built opposite the south portal. Architecturally, this two-story building on a square groundplan with a monumental inner courtyard follows the Escorial in Madrid, and the plans for it are thought to originate with the Escorial's architect, Juan de Herrera. As the Stock Exchange became less and less important, Charles III installed the Archivo General de Indias there. This archive contains all the historical documents up to the 19th century on the exploration of the New World. Among these are memoires of Hernán Cortés and Francisco Pizarro, the conqueror of Mexico and Peru, as well as of Fernão de Magalhães, the first to circumnavigate the globe. Also located there is the Contract of Tordesillas, according to which the royal houses of Spain and Portugal divided the New World between them.

Hospital de la Caridad

The sculpture in the garden in front of the Hospital of Mercy recalls the man with whom the installation of the hospital and the history of the building are closely connected – Miguel de Mañara. After a life of vice, he decided to turn to the path of virtue. Converted by a vision – during a brawl he is supposed to have seen his funeral procession pass – he joined the Fraternity of Sacred Mercy in 1662. Thanks to his great wealth he made it possible for the church to be expanded and in 1664 he founded the hospital which is still devoted to caring for people. Further, he gave the Fraternity new regulations whose message was that only love of ones neighbor could save the self from eternal damnation.

The hospital is built on the site formerly occupied by the Royal Wharf, so its earlier construction is partially built into the three large rooms. From the left of the entrance one look out on to the blue and white tile pictures on the facade of the hospital church. The two figures of saints – St. George and St. Jacob, as well as the allegories of faith, hope, and mercy – all refer to the Fraternity's program of charity work. It concerned itself with the burial of people who drowned in the Guadalquivir as well as those condemned to death.

Inner Courtyard

Through the gateway the visitor steps into an inner courtyard with Tuscan colonnades which is divided by a two-story archway. In the center on both sides there is an octagonal fountain depicting the allegorical figures of "Mercy" or "Benevolence." The walls are decorated with late 17th-century Dutch tiles, which depict scenes from the Bible. These are wrongly described in the inscription as *De tien Geboden* (The Ten Commandments). Parallel to the church stand the three large rooms of the hospital, to which in the 19th-century a fourth room, now the refectory, was added.

Interior Room of the Hospital Church:
Valdés Leal, In ictu oculi, 1671/72
Oil on canvas, 220 x 216 cm

The hall of this church contains one of the most important collections of paintings in the city – a collection which is thematically linked to Mañaras' message. The depictions of *Vanitas* by Juan Valdés Leal are among the most magnificent of these paintings. On the left-hand side of the north wall, the painting *In ictu oculi* illustrates the vanity of human beings and their greedy lust for earthly beauty. A skeleton, which has one foot planted on the globe, is carrying a coffin, and is symbolically extinguishing the flame of life. On the ground are scattered a tiara, crown, scepter, splendid garments, books, and rolls of parchment. In this picture Valdés Leal presents an uncompromising vision of how death can extinguish life at any moment and render the transistory attributes of wealth, renown, power, and learning useless.

Interior Room of the Hospital Church:
Valdés Leal, Finis gloriae mundi, 1671/72
Oil on canvas, 220 x 216 cm

On the south wall there is a second painting by Valdés Leal which also alludes to the transience of worldly renown. The corpses of a bishop and a knight of the Calatrava Order (to which Mañara himself belonged) lie in a crypt, their bodies eaten by worms and insects. In the background we glimpse the skeleton of a king and several skulls. Above it the hand of Christ is holding a pair of scales, which weigh the Seven Deadly Sins against symbols of Christian faith such as prayer, repentance, and love of one's neighbor. This symbolic depiction is meant to make it clear to the viewer that all human beings are equal in death. At the Last Judgment, their damnation or salvation will be decided according to what they did on earth.

lepers, removing ringworm from a sick man's head over a bowl of water. This realistic depiction of treating wounds fulfills Mañaras's rules. He exhorted to his brothers: "no matter how repulsive the wounds may be, do not turn aside as you minister to the sick, but steadfastly offer God this self-mortification." In the background the viewer can see a another scene, depicted, in italien style, of charitable work taking place.

Interior Room of the Hospital Church:
High Altar: Pedro Roldán, Deposition of Christ, 1670

The visual focus of the church is the high altar, on which the colored sculpture "Deposition of Christ" by Pedro Roldán stands in front of Valdés Leal's painting of an empty cross. It symbolizes the final act of loving one's neighbor – burying the dead. The sculpture offers a graphic example of the realism of Spanish art, which does not shrink from depicting pain, sorrow, and even death.

Interior Room of the Hospital Church:
Bartolomé Esteban Murillo, St. Elisabeth Ministering to Lepers, 1671-1674
Oil on canvas, 325 x 245 cm

On the side walls there are several paintings by Murillo on the subject of loving one's neighbor. One painting depicts St. Elisabeth of Thuringia surrounded by

Torre del Oro

One of the great landmarks of Seville is the *Torre del Oro* (Golden Tower). It is the 13th-century tower on the banks of the Río Guadalquivir. Of the 166 defensive towers making up the Almohadic system of fortification, this tower had particular importance. From here a chain could be thrown to another tower – now destroyed – on the other side of the river, to prevent enemy ships from entering the harbor. At one time the tower was covered in gold-glazed azulejos – something which only its name now recalls. The lower level of this dodecagonal building, which has a central sexagonal stairwell, has minimal features: a few windows and slits, as well as a frieze of blind arches. It is surmounted by pyramidal merlons. Above the platform rises a more slender tower – also dodecagonal – with an 18th-century lantern. Today, the Torre del Oro houses a small naval museum.

Palacio de San Telmo

Opposite the Jardines de Santa Cristina stands one of the loveliest palaces of the Sevillean Baroque, the Palacio de San Telmo. The *pièce de résistance* of the otherwise bare main facade is the three-story entrance structure, designed by the leading architect of Sevillean Baroque, Leonardo de Figueroa, and his son Antonio Matías de Figueroa. Ornately ornamented columns and figures, thematically relating to maritime arts and sciences, frame the entrance portal, the central balcony, and the filigree gable. In the open arcades we see a statue of the Dominican friar Pedro Telmo, who has been venerated by the sailors of Seville since the 16th century. He appeared near the masts holding a torch, and calmed the raging seas. This palace, built between 1628 and 1734, originally functioned as an academy for the art of navigation. In 1849 it came into the possession of the Count of Montpensier. Finally, in 1897, the Infanta María Luisa Fernanda, Countess of Montpensier and sister of Queen Isabella II, decreed on her deathbed that it should accommodate a priests' seminary.

North Side

On the palace's northern facade stand twelve statues of famous men from Seville, including Velázquez, Mañara, Lope, Rueda, and Murillo, fashioned by Antonio Susillo in 1895.

Seville and the Golden Age of Spanish Culture

In the 17th century Spain offered a totally different picture to the outside world from that of the previous century. In the previous century, when the world was in the midst of political and religious chaos, the Spanish empire presented an externally stable image of political and religious unity. In the 17th century, however, the region experienced the start of inexorable political, economic, and social decline. The literature of that period draws a striking picture of the country's social situation. That said, while the symptoms of crisis were unmistakable everywhere, cultural development under Philip III and Philip IV reached its zenith. During these

View of the City of Seville, 1738. Copper engraving, 350 x 510 mm. Seville, Archivo Municipal

decades Spain experienced the high-point of its *Siglo de Oro*, the Golden Age, as the heyday of Spanish culture between 1550 and 1650 is known. In this period many of Spain's most important contributions to world literature were created. From Madrid, *Don Juan* by the dramatist Tirso de Molina, *Don Quixote* by Miguel de Cervantes, the dramas of Calderón de la Barca, the theater of Lope de Vega, and the poems of Luis de Góngora conquered the whole world.

The Commissions

In 1603 an Academy of Fine Arts was established in Madrid. There were educational institutions in every important city in the country which confirmed the high regard in which painting and sculpture were held. After the capital, Madrid, the second most important art center was the capital city of Andalusia, which had grown wealthy through its trade with the new colonies. Seville, one of the largest cities in Europe with some 150,000 inhabitants, remained at the height of its economic success until the 1620s, at which point it fell victim to the economic and political crises which engulfed the country. Even so, these crises did not affect the arts until later. Here, they were able to develop freely, and there was no shortage of patronage. Seville was the trading center for European products, and Spanish settlers in the New World purchased works of art both for their churches or monasteries and for their private homes. Further, in the wake of the Counter-Reformation, numerous places of worship had been founded, and there was a great demand

Gottfried Zschoch, Portrait of Lope de Vega, Copper engraving after a contemporary portrait. 9.2 x 7 cm, Berlin, collection of the Archive for Art and History.

for works of art to decorate them. Wealth and piety fused together into a unique kind of patronage which greatly benefited sculptors' and painters' studios. They received countless commissions from wealthy citizens, parish churches, hospitals, and fraternities; as well as, a little later, from various monastic Orders, who needed a large number of works for their churches, chapels, sacristies, cloisters, and refectories. These included large-scale altarretables, comprehensive pictorial cycles, choir-stalls and *pasos* (figures from the Passion), which are still carried in procession through the city at Easter. The conditions for a flourishing of the arts were ideal.

The Subjects

For patrons, religious subjects always came first. As the second most powerful force in the country, the church had a vested interest in increasing its influence. In long-running disputes between the supporters of the Reformation and Counter-Reformation, works of art played an important role, not least because

Diego Velázquez, Las Meninas, 1656. Madrid, Museo del Prado. Detail

they were a proven means of conveying the church doctrine to ordinary people and of making them more religious. As early as 1563, the Council of Trent had issued statements recommending that works of art should emphasize their didactic role and always be clear, straightforward, and comprehensible. They should, it argued, engage viewers' religious devotion not by rational but by emotional means. This meant that in the course of time certain subjects gained priority over others where panel paintings and sculptures were concerned. For instance, the devotion of the Virgin Mary was given immense significance, insofar as the role she played in saving humanity was emphasized. This is shown by the numerous depictions of the *Dolorosa*. The Spanish Church's struggle to have Mary's Immaculate Conception accepted unleashed a whole flood of pictures of the *Immaculada*. Sculptures of St. Peter were intended to strengthen the public perception of the Pope's authority. Pictures of repentant saints symbolized the sacraments – or love of one's neighbor – by showing the saints setting an example.

On the other hand, secular subjects were also depicted in painting. As well as numerous portraits of Spanish aristocrats and church dignitaries, a great many *bodegones* were painted. These were paintings of kitchen interiors whose subject was mainly still life. There were also religious scenes depicting ordinary people at mealtime. In addition to this, for many painters other important sources of income came from work as *doradores* (gilders) or *policromadores* ("appliers of color"), who painted sculptures.

Francisco de Zurbarán, Apotheosis of
St. Thomas Aquinas, 1631. Oil on canvas,
480 x 400 cm Seville, Museo de Bellas Artes

Detail from the Apotheosis of St. Thomas Aquinas:
Self-portrait of Francisco de Zurbarán

The Artists

Seville's importance as a center of the arts was not entirely due, however, to its economic prosperity. Ever since the Renaissance, the city had been highly regarded as an intellectual center, and, as the *nueva Roma*, it had attracted many leading personalities. One of the most important exponents of the Sevillean school of painting was Francisco Pacheco (1564–1625), who had gathered a group of artists, humanists, poets, and theologians around him. Their literary works and writings on art had a decisive effect on the succeeding generation of the Golden Age, which gave rise to several significant artist personalities. Pacheco taught the painter who is probably Seville's best known artist – Diego Velázquez (1599-1660) – who became a member of the San Luca painters' guild at the age of 18, and by the age of 23 had begun his extremely successful career as Philip IV's court painter in Madrid. Francisco de Zurbarán (1598-1664), from Estremadura, who is remembered in art history as the "painter of monks" because of his cycles of paintings taken from monastic history, also finally settled in the city. By as early as the

1630s, he was involved in numerous court projects. Even though Madrid grew more and more attractive for the artists as a center of art as the 17th century advanced, there were several other artists who remained active in Seville their entire lives. One of them was Bartolomé Esteban Murillo (1618–1682), one of the greatest painters of the Spanish Baroque, known for his exquisite pictures of the Madonna and of saints. He became famous for the paintings he made for the Monastery of San Francesco in Seville, which were taken from the history of the Franciscan Order. He later developed into one of the leading painters in Seville. Indeed, in 1660 he was appointed

Bartolomé Esteban Murillo,
Self-portrait c. 1670. London, National Gallery

President of the newly founded Academy of Painters. Another well-known artist was Juan Valdés Leal (1622–1690), whose work is characterized by religious pictures with highly dramatic scenes and by uncompromising allegories.

In the decoration of sacred buildings, sculptures were considered just as important as panel paintings. Accordingly, it was only natural that, from the late 16th century onwards, this expanding city should also open its own school of sculpture. It owes its existence and renown to the leading Andalusian sculptor of the transitional phase between Mannerism and the Baroque, namely Juan Martínez Montañés (1568-1649). His work, notable mainly for his efforts to achieve harmonious beauty and an internalized expression of emotion without resorting to melodrama, had a profound influence even during his lifetime. The sculptures by his pupil and leading collaborator, Juan de Mesa (1583–1627), on the other hand, reveal stronger and more expressive features. This style had a decisive effect on the later realism of the Sevillean school.

Another important pupil was Alonso Cano (1601–1667), who was later to become the leading exponent of the Granadan school of sculpture. He is considered one of the most versatile artists of the 17th century. Trained by his father to be an architect, Cano initially worked in the studio of the painter Pacheco, subsequently becoming a pupil of Montañés. After working as a court painter in Madrid, he returned to his native city, Granada, where numerous examples of his paintings and his fine, small-scale sculptures can still be found.

Diego Velázquez, Kitchen scene showing Christ in the House of Mary and Martha, 1618.
Oil on canvas, 60 x 103.5 cm. London, National Gallery

In 1636, the arrival in Seville of the Flemish sculptor José de Arce (who died in 1667) introduced the city to European Baroque. His style, which was characterized by dynamic forms and impressive compositional drama, helped the Baroque style to finally break through in Seville.

During the course of the 17th century the overall crises in the country did not spare the rich trading city of Seville. Further, the plague epidemic of 1649 and the ensuing starvation worsened the situation. The result was that many artists moved to the capital, Madrid. The accession of Philip IV in 1621 brought a young and cultivated man to the helm. He was a monarch committed to literature and the arts. During Philip IV's reign several major architectural projects involving numerous artists were set in motion. Under the reign of his son, the sickly and weak Charles II, Spain's decline continued swiftly. The whole country was shaken by a series of serious crises – both internal and external – which left little room for anything that would foster literature or the arts. Thus the Golden Age of Spanish culture had come to an end.

Gonzalo Bilbao y Martínez, The Cigar Workers, 1915, Sevilla, Museo de Bellas Artes

Universidad
Antigua Fábrica de Tabacos

The plaza in front of the gate to the *Antigua Fábrica de Tabacos* (the Old Tobacco Factory) is wellknown as the scene where the first act of the opera *Carmen*, by George Bizet, takes place. In earlier days, this was where thousands of women rolled leaves of tobacco to form cigars. It now houses part of the university. Through the main portal, which is surmounted by a statue of *Fama* (Fame), the visitor enters the interior of the four-wing site. This used to comprise several factory wings, inner courtyards, stables for horses and mules (used to rotate the mills) as well as ten fountains. In the storage terraces, where the tobacco leaves were spread out in special ovens before the drying process began, an underground water-system ensured that the air was

always very moist. It is also interesting to note that the tobacco factory had its own prison, a military guard to prevent disturbances, and its own legal system.

sides by a moat and initially accessible only by bridge, resembles an impregnable military fortress. At that time, tobacco was one of the most sought-after and expensive stimulants available. Until the early 18th century it was fashionable to smoke tobacco in half-length pipes. At around the first decade of the 1700s, however, a kind of tobacco-roll came to Europe from America. Due to its similarity to a cicada (*cigarra* in Spanish) it was dubbed *el cigarro* and quickly caught on. The crumbs of tobacco that fell out during production were wrapped in paper by the women workers and smoked as cigarettes.

Portal to the South Side
Portal to the East Side

This huge two-story complex (820.3 x 590.6 feet or 250 x 180 meters) is the work of the Dutch military architect Sebastian van der Borcht, who built the factory on open land outside the city between 1728 and 1771. This building, with its unadorned, sober facade, surrounded on three

Parque de María Luisa
Plaza de España with the Palacio Español

The grounds which originally formed part of the Palacio de San Telmo take their name from the Infanta María Luisa Fernanda de Orléans, who presented the site to the city of Seville in 1893. Originally landscaped in the English style, the grounds were redesigned by the French landscape-architekt Le Forestier. The present-day combination of lawns and hedges, ponds and fountains, ceramic amphorae and monuments to Sevillean intellectual figures is largely his design. Long avenues, named after famous *conquistadores*, criss-cross through the grounds. To mark the Ibero-American exhibition of 1929/30, the Plaza de España and the Plaza de América were built. Both of these are integrated into the grounds. The exhibition pavilions of the twenty participating countries have survived to this day. The Sevillean architect Aníbal González won the competition to manage the *exposición*, but in 1926, after a dispute, he resigned as director. He was responsible for the most beautiful square, the enormous crescent of the Plaza de España. Along with the semi-circular Palacio Español, the Plaza de España invokes several historical styles in its overall design and is a striking illustration of Spain's importance as a world-power in the Golden Age. The design recalls the corner towers of the Giralda, displaying many Mannerist features. The central facade is Baroque, and the remainder of the building is built in the Renaissance style. As a representation of the Venetian style, a canal following the curves of the square is criss-crossed by bridges with exquisite ceramic balustrades. Along the base of the monumental palace, all the provinces of Spain are depicted on large azulejos, with a famous scene from their respective histories.

At one time books from the individual provinces were placed in small tiled shelves.

Museo Arquelógico Provincial

Plaza América, Pabellón del Renacimiento

Aníbal González designed the Plaza which took the place of honor in the exhibition, Plaza América. To the south of Plaza América is the *Pabellón del Renacimiento* (Renaissance Pavilion), which now houses the Archaeological Museum. Its collection is among the most important in Spain. It contains finds from prehistoric times to the 15th century. Special emphasis is placed on exhibits from the province of Seville.

Carambolo Hoard of Gold

The hoard of gold from Carambolo, discovered near Seville, is on exhibition in the basement. The hoard consists of sixteen sheets of gold (for belt or head decoration), two breast-clasps, two broad armbands and a chain with a pendant of heavy gold. These decorative pieces, dating from the 8th/7th century B.C., were presumably owned by a high-ranking priest. They are linked with the culture of the legendary empire of Tartessos, although there is no agreement as to their origins. There are two possibilities: either the articles were

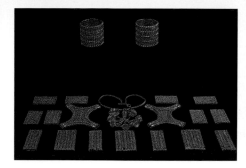

fashioned in one of the local workshops in the Phoenician settlement of Andalusia, or they were imported from the eastern Mediterranean.

Venus Itálica

The upper level of the archaelogical museum houses finds from the Roman period. The most magnificent pieces include the superb marble statue of the Venus Itálica from the reign of Hadrian (117-138), discovered on the site of the Itálica theater. Despite serious damage, it is possible to discern from her attributes – the lotus leaf and the dolphin by her side – that she was depicted as an Anadyomene, a goddess rising from the sea. The heavy, water-soaked garment wrapped around her hips serves as a backdrop before which the goddess reveals her splendid body. At one time her head would have been tilted toward the right and her arms would have been hanging down at the side to hold up her garment.

Casa de Pilatos

One of the most important city palaces in Seville is located in the Barrio de San Bartolomé. Today it is owned by the Dukes of Medicaneli. The royal governor Pedro Enríquez and his wife Catalina de Ribera started building the palace in 1492, and it was eventually completed by their son Fadrique, the first Marqués de Tarifa. From 1519-1521 Fadrique was on a pilgrimage to Jerusalem. When he came back, he discovered that his palace was the same distance from the church of Cruz del Campo, outside Seville, as Pontius Pilate's house was from Golgotha, where Christ was crucified. Accordingly, he had the fourteen stations of the Cross installed along the route to the church. The first station, where Jesus was brought before Pilate, was in his own house. This led to the erroneous conclusion that his palace was a copy of Pilate's house, something of which the name still reminds us. When, on his journey home from Jerusalem, Fadrique arrived in Italy, he was so taken with the architecture and decoration of the Italian High Renaissance that he commissioned several decorative pieces for his palace in Seville. Among these is the marble portal in the facade, fashioned in Genoa, above which runs a frieze showing the family coat-of-arms.

Patio Principal

The center of the palace complex is the inner courtyard. It is enclosed by two-story arcades in which Moorish decorative elements are marvelously fused with Renaissance forms and ancient sculptures. White marble pillars support the arcades, which are covered with stucco, and a filigree balustrade runs around the upper story. Along the base of the walls azulejo panels have been added to a height of 13 feet (4 meters). The walls are broken up only by twin-arched windows, which allow light into the rooms located behind the courtyard. In the center of the courtyard there is a fountain, also completed in Genoa, whose upper dish is borne by dolphins. The

head of Janus shows its two faces above the jets of water. There is a Roman statue at each of the four corners of the room: a copy of the famous Athena Lemnia by Phidias, another warlike Minerva, Ceres, the Goddess of Fertility, and a Muse. In wall niches, the busts of the Roman emperors Cicero and Emperor Charles V have been placed.

Iglesia de San Salvador

This three-nave Church of the Redeemer was built between 1674 and 1712 on the site of an old 9th century mosque. It has a vast crossing dome, surmounted by a lantern. Today, the only vestiges of the mosque that still remain are the base of the minaret in the clocktower and the remains of the courtyard of orange trees on the north side. Until the last century, layers of mud were deposited when the Río Guadalquivir repeatedly flooded. This has raised the floor level by some 6.5 feet (2 meters). As a result, the capitals – Roman and Visigothic spoils – are now only 1 to 2 feet (30–60 centimeters) clear of the floor. The facade was designed by Leonardo de Figueroa, who took charge of completing the architectural work on the Baroque church. In this building the visitor can see the first signs of what was to become a hallmark of Figueroa's later style: the use of bricks – within the light colored walls. In comparison to hewn natural stone, this was a less expensive material. Further more, in accordance with Andalusian tradition, Figueroa would often cover roofs and domes with polychromatic glazed tiles. In the enormous dome above the crossing there is a large 17th century retable created by Martínez Montañés.

Ayuntamiento

In earlier times, the Plaza de San Francisco was the center of Seville and the scene of festivals, tournaments, and bullfights. During the centuries of the Inquisition, this was also the place where the *Autos de fé*, public trials of faith, were held against heretics. Along its west side the visitor can see the Plateresque facade of the *Ayuntamiento* (townhall), designed by Diego de Riaño in 1527. This is decorated with a wealth of grotesques, medallions, allegorical and historical figures, as well as floral ornamentation. The Renaissance structure was built to Riaño's plans between 1527 and 1564. It is characteristic of the Spanish Plateresque style. The classical facade fronting the Plaza Nueva was added with the building's 19th-century redesign and extension. The Upper Chapter-house now contains the city archives, which include fascinating documents on the city's history since the days of the Catholic kings.

The Start of the Reign of Terror –
The Spanish Inquisition

In the summer of 1391 a raving crowd burst into the Jewish quarter of Seville. The infuriated Christians killed approximately 4,000 Jews and destroyed the synagogues. This marked the beginning of the events that, almost a century

Bernard Picart, the Banner of the Spanish Inquisition, copper engraving, 165 x 107 mm, Dresden, Staatliche Kunstsammlungen, Kupferstichkabinett

later, would lead to the Spanish Inquisition. A tax increase in 1391 had provoked the anger of the Christian population. Their fury was directed at the people whom the unpopular task of tax collection was entrusted – the Jews. The royal authorities took action against the ringleaders of this vendetta, but they did not act resolutely enough. Before that summer was out, the Jewish quarters of Córdoba, Valencia, and other cities were also attacked. Starting that year, many Jews – out of fear, desperation or sheer opportunism – had themselves baptized. But these *conversos*, Christian converts, were treated just as badly by the population. Religious fanatics felt that the Christian faith was being threatened by the *conversos*, the number of which increased throughout the 15th century. At the same time, ordinary people envied their high positions at court, to which, as baptized Christians, they now had access. Mistrust was exacerbated by the fact that many Jews only pretended to convert. These Jews did not have their children baptized, they continued to be circumsized, avoided church sacraments, and continued respecting the Sabbath. They were particularly unpopular with Dominicans and Franciscans. These saw the *conversos* as turncoats and traitors who had sold their souls for social advancement.

Francisco de Goya, Inquisitorial Tribunal, c. 1812/1814. Oil on wood, 46 x 73 cm, Madrid, Real Academia de San Fernando

The Institution of the Spanish Inquisition

As it happens, it was a Dominican who took the first concrete steps toward establishing the Spanish Inquisition. While Isabella and Ferdinand were in Seville in 1477 to restore peace and lawfulness to a city divided by two powerful aristocrats, they were approached by the Dominican prior Alonso de Hojeda. He complained to them that the majority of conversions were "pretend-converts" who often "resorted to Jewishness." By referring to a secret conspiracy, he persuaded the royal couple to take inquisatorial measures. Before the following year was out, Pope Sixtus IV gave his blessing to a Tribunal of the Holy Inquisition. At first, Isabella and Ferdinand were not much in favor of the Inquisition, especially as they counted a lot of conversos among their friends and advisers. It was probably for this reason that they charged the archbishop of Seville, Cardinal Mendoza, with the task of issuing instructions about the Christian faith for the benefit of new converts. Nonetheless, in October 1480 two Dominican monks, aided and abetted by two assistant judges, began inquisitorial activities. Without showing any mercy, they condemned everyone who showed the slightest suspicion of "uncertain" or wavering faith to be burnt at the stake. Anyone who recanted and renounced their former behavior was punished with imprisonment and torture, and all their assets were confiscated. By 1488, about 700 executions and 5,000 other punishments had been carried out in Seville alone (in the whole of Castile the totals amounted to 2,000 executions and 15,000 other punishments by 1490). The fanatical denunciations and the inquisitors' merciless procedures persuaded many people to flee the religion. Some raised objections with the Holy See, which resulted in the first Inquisitors being dismissed.

The Grand Inquisitor

In the autumn of 1483, by orders of the king, Tomás Torquemada (1420-1498), the Dominican and erstwhile father confessor to Isabella, was appointed Grand Inquisitor of all Spain. He, more than anyone else, organized and led the reign of terror that characterized the Spanish Inquisition. Under his supervision, the Suprema,

Francisco Rizzi, Autodefé on the Plaza Mayor in Madrid, 1683. Oil on wood, 277 x 438 cm, Madrid, Museo del Prado

the Inquisition's Tribunal, became an independent body with extensive powers. It was the only institution that had legal jurisdiction – and hence, power – over the twin kingdoms of Castile and Aragón. More importantly, Tomás de Torquemada was the "theoretician" of the Spanish Inquisition. His *instrucciones*, the directions for the new Inquisition, were virtually adapted as a handbook by the tribunals.

Considering the inconceivable power concentrated in the hands of the Grand Inquisitor, it is astonishing that the Catholic kings allowed this institution to operate independently, if at all. That said, it is doubtful whether the royalty would have been in any position to stop the machinery once it was put in motion. In the first place, the Inquisition provided Isabella and Ferdinand with the means to unify their country. The Inquisition's activities had brought a certain tranquility – perhaps at the price of fear – to the whole country. Further, it yielded brought financial all the confiscated assets were crown. Above all, however, the Inquisition

Pedro Berruguete, Autodefé, Santo Domingo de Guzmán, c. 1495. Tempera and oil on wood, 154 x 92 cm, Madrid, Museo del Prado

profit, since seized by the was met with popular favor, for the public Autodefés were considered an appealing, if gruesome, spectacle.

Iglesia de San Luis

In a narrow street in the densely populated Macarena quarter, one of the loveliest churches of the Sevillean Baroque period can be found. The erstwhile church of the Jesuit Novitiate was dedicated to St. Louis of France, in honor of the new King of Spain, Philip V. The architect of the central building, erected from 1699-1731 in the form of a Greek cross, was Leonardo de Figueroa, the founder of the illustrious dynasty of artists, whose numerous buildings made a striking impact on Seville's cityscape. De Figueroas virtuosity is reflected in the ornately decorated facade with its twin octagonal turrets forming a kind of monumental base for the dome, which is made of green and white bricks. Its outline recalls well-known Roman Baroque buildings, and elements from Borromini's Sant'Agnese on the Piazza Navona are adopted here.

Dome, Interior View

The groundplan, recalls the Roman prototype as well. Eight free-standing, serpentine columns, whose lower thirds are fluted, flank the domed center. Together with the galleries, the drum and the pieces of pseudo-architecture in the vast dome create a space that appears to be infinitely high. The drum, situated under the dome, is illuminated by large, light windows and adorned with statues. The paintings in the dome are by Lucas Valdéz.

and a transept. In the process, Figueroa raised the nave-walls considerably and illuminated the space by building a stylish octagonal dome. The dome's lantern is decorated on the outside with telamons reminiscent of Inca figures.

Interior View

The interior, which is ornately decorated with stucco and appliqué gilded wood, is

Iglesia de Santa María Magdalena

The present-day parish Church of Santa María Magdalena had its origins in the church in the Dominican monastery of San Pablo, which was founded by Ferdinand the Holy in 1248. Largely retaining the Gothic groundplan, Leonardo de Figueroa rebuilt it from 1691 to 1709 in the form of a three-nave structure with five chapels especially striking for its magnificent paintings, most · of them executed by Lucas Valdés and his studio. Among a wealth of different subjects, particularly worthy of mentioning are "The Entry of Ferdinand the Holy into Seville" and the "Autodefé" in the transept. In one of the side-chapels, namely the Capilla de la Hermandad de la Quinta Angustia, a lovely Mudéjar dome has survived. The chapel itself has a rectangular shape with three dome-vaulted bays. The Mudéjar dome has intersecting ribbon-like ribs which form a magnificent star shape in the center.

Capilla Sacramental: Francisco de Zurbarán, The Miraculous Entry of the True Likeness of St. Dominicus into the Monastery of Soriano, 1626/27. Oil on canvas, 190 x 230 cm

In 1626 the Dominicans commissioned Francisco de Zurbarán to paint 21 pictures to decorate the interior of the Church of San Pablo. For 4,000 *reales* the painter was to complete 14 paintings depicting scenes from the life of the founder of the Order, four paintings of the canons, as well as one each of the saints Buenaventura, Thomas, and Dominicus. Today, most of these have

disappeared or found their way to other locations. Only two can still be viewed in the Capilla Sacramental. One depicts the "Miraculous Healing of the Late Reginald of Orléans." The other takes as its subject an episode from the life of the founder of the Order which was often depicted in 17th century Spanish painting: the Madonna handing the portrait of St. Dominicus to a monk from the Dominican monastery of Soriano, in Italy. She is accompanied by St. Magdalena (on the right) and St. Catherine, who is holding the painting. What is interesting here is the stark contrast between the simple, black and white robes of the Dominican monks and the splendid, colored garments worn by the Virgin Mary and Mary Magdalene.

Museo de Bellas Artes

**Diego Velázquez,
Portrait of Don Cristóbal
Suárez de Ribera, 1620**
Oil on canvas, 207 x 148 cm

Only a handful of early paintings from the time Diego Velázquez spent in Seville is dated or even recorded. One exception is the portrait of Don Cristóbal Suárez de Ribera, which originally hung in the Ermita or the Capilla de San Hermenegildo in Seville. De Ribera was the godfather of Juana Pacheco, who was married to Diego Velázquez. When the picture was cleaned, folds in the canvas revealed the monogram DOVZ as well as the date 1620. Since the subject died in 1618, the portrait must have been painted posthumously. This would also explain the subject's kneeling position and the youthful appearance of the deceased, who died at the age of 68. The way the subject's head stands out against the dimly lit background clearly shows the influence of Caravaggio (1571-1610), whose style of painting with light and dark contrasts was explored intensively by all Baroque painters. Unlike Caravaggio, however, Velázquez fills the room with a diffuse, greenish light, which surrounds the subject like a flowing contour. At the same time this lighting emphasizes the structure of the garment.

**Diego Velázquez, Mary presenting
the Chasuble to St. Ildefenso, c. 1620**
Oil on canvas, 166 x 120 cm

The painter's early work includes not only
bodegones and portraits but also a few religious paintings, for which there was great
demand at the time in prosperous Seville

with its many churches and
monasteries. The painting
from the Convento de San
Antonio in Seville depicts
Archbishop Ildefonso of
Toledo (c. 606-667), whose
writings on the Marians
were very popular during
the Middle Ages. In this
picture Velázquez chose a
frequently depicted scene
from the saint's life – the
appearance of the Virgin
Mary handing the saint
the chasuble, the Mass
vestment worn over the alb.
The painter's wife Juana
modeled not only the
Madonna but also the other
female figures. The vertical
format limited to only a few
picture-filling figures as
well as the arrangement of
the kneeling saint shown
in profile and the Virgin
looking down on a diagonal
draws on traditional Spanish
sources. However, there is
one striking innovation
here: the way the chasuble adventurously
divides the pictorial space, separating
the saint from the complex figure-group in
the upper half of the picture. In true
chiaroscuro manner, the face of Ildefonso
and the Virgin's hand are both highlighted,
becoming focal points of the whole
composition.

A Painter among Painters

Diego Velázquez developed into the greatest painter in 17th century Spain. Kings, aristocrats, dwarves, and artists, ordinary people as well as divine figures, religious and mythologica scenes or historical events – these were all depicted with the same sensitivity. This characterizes the work of Velázquez. He was a Court Painter, Palace Chamberlain, and a Knight of the Order of Santiago. On the way from Seville to Madrid, he transformed himself from artisan to great painter and courtier. In keeping with his aristocratic roots, Diego Velázquez also changed his name – and became known as Diego de Silva y Velázquez.

In the "Golden Cage of Art"

His career began in Seville, the city where he was born. At the age of 11 he was apprenticed to Francisco Pacheco (1564-1654), an exponent of dry academic painting. The training Velázquez received there was to prove crucial for his whole life. This was because Pacheco's house not only contained a painting studio but, following the pattern of Italian Modernists, it was also a meeting-place for leading artists, humanists, poets, scholars, and theologians.

Philip IV, 1623, repainted 1628.
Oil on canvas, 198 x 101.5 cm,
Madrid, Museo del Prado

In this "golden cage of art" – as Palomino, the Spanish Vasari, described Pacheco's private academy – the young painter was able to hear discussions about philosophy, literature, art theory, and religious questions. He was also able to explore the literary works and writings on art which this circle produced. Perhaps the most important of these was *El Arte de la Pintura*, an art-historical treatise by Pacheco, in which the artist expatiated upon questions of art as well as Christian iconography. Above all, however, Pacheco wanted painting to be included among the *artes liberales* (liberal arts). Unlike in Italy, Spanish painters were still regarded as artisans and had to fulfill appropriate tasks. On March 14, 1617, scarcely 18 years of age, Velázquez sat for his mastership before Pacheco and Juan de Uceda, a well-respected painter in Seville. His mastership would entitle him to exercise the profession of painter in any part of the kingdom of Spain. However, his relationship to his teacher became even closer when, a year later, he married his daughter. "After five years of education and training, impressed by his skills, his integrity, and his outstanding qualities, as well as by his promising, prodigious, natural genius – I gave him my daughter in marriage."

The Court Painter

Pacheco's assessment proved to be correct, for only five years later Velázquez began his meteoric rise. He never returned to the *bodegones* which he had painted in his early years in Seville. Friends of Pacheco who had good connections at court with the Duke of Olivares, the Prime Minister, made it easier for Velázquez to settle in Madrid. In 1623 he was appointed Court Painter at the royal court. Thanks to a portrait of Philip IV which he completed in a single day, he gained the King's favor. As a result, for more than three decades he painted portraits of the king and members of the royal family. Within a short period of time a close, life-long friendship developed between the two men. Their friendship was of decisive importance for Diego Velázquez's career. His Majesty thought so highly of

Bacchus, 1628/29. Oil on canvas. 165.5 x 227.5 cm, Madrid, Museo del Prado

Velázquez as a human being that he trusted him more than a monarch usually trusts a vassal. Palomino reports that he discussed even difficult problems with him, especially at more intimate moments when the grandees and courtiers had withdrawn. And Pacheco writes: "One can hardly believe how much generosity and friendship such a great monarch gave Velázquez. His Majesty has a key to the studio of the court painter in the royal palace. In it, there is a chair on which he can observe the artist painting, which he does almost every day." Although his exceptional gifts as a portrait-painter won him enormous respect at court, there was a great deal of envy among other painters, who reproached him for being able to paint nothing but heads. In 1627 the King organized a painting competition between Velázquez and the three other court painters – the Italian, Vincente Carducho, and the two Spaniards, Caxés and Nardi. The subject for the competition was the expulsion of the Moors from Spain and Velázquez was the clear winner. In time, the artist became so highly regarded by the King that he would only allow Velázquez to paint his likeness. When, in early 1631, the artist came back from a two-year stay in Italy, he was greeted with Olivares's request to hurry immediately to the King to thank him "for having allowed no other painter to paint his portrait and for also waiting for him to complete a portrait of the prince."

The Courtier

Even so, life as a courtier had its problems. The higher Velázquez rose in the hierarchy at the royal court, the less time he had at his diposal left to carry out his actual profession. The fact that, despite his multifarious tasks at court, Velasquez was still able to find time to complete some of his greatest masterpieces, confirms his genius. Finally, however, when he had reached the position of Palace Chamberlain and Court Decorator, the demands his royal patron made proved too much for him, and led to his death. In 1660, after the conclusion of a Peace Treaty between Spain and France, the finale was to be a meeting between Philip IV and the French king, Louis XIV, the arrangements for which were entrusted to Velázquez. He made such magnificent and successful arrangements that "even an unsuccessful monarch would have appeared splendid and powerful." That said, the

Isabella of Bourbon, 1634/35. Oil on canvas, 304,5 x 317.5 cm, Madrid, Museo del Prado

efforts and exertions these arrangements required proved beyond the abilities of the 61 year-old painter. A month after his return from Italy, he fell sick and died in Madrid on the 6th of August of the same year. On the very next day, in a solemn ceremony, his body – draped in the mantle of the Knights of the Order of Santiago – was interred in the Church of San Juan Bautista.

The Crowning Achievement of his Art

Even though Velázquez as the Court Painter devoted himself time and again to the portrait, his far-reaching life's work is notable for its rich range of subjects. Mythological, allegorical, and religious themes interested him as much as landscapes and genre subjects. His importance lies not merely in his great originality but above all in his ability to find a new way of painting most of his subjects. It is always people who are at the center of his observations. Kings and dwarves, nobles and beggars were all subjects which he portrayed with moving humanity and realism, showing not only their greatness but also their vulnerability. His love of Titian, his encounter with Rubens, and his two Italian journeys all had a lasting influence on his style, but he blended all these stimuli into his own innovative style. He had a unique ability to give objects depth and to capture them in terms of light and shadow by a light brush-stroke.

The crowning achievement of his art could be regarded as *Las Meninas* (The Young Ladies of the Court), an appeal for painting to be recognized as one of the *artes liberales*. This

Court Dwarf Francisco Lezcano, c. 1643–1645.
Oil on canvas, 107.5 x 83.5 cm,
Madrid, Museo del Prado

demand, expounded in several 17th century writings on art theory, was bound up with the grim social plight of artists. Almost all of them had to earn their living by other means, unless they were supported by a wealthy patron. This is the reason why, throughout his life, Velázquez undertook administrative duties at court. The recognition of painting's importance had a practical as well as an ideal side: If art were a result of leisure and pleasure rather than labor, the artist was the equal of the aristocrat, allowed the same privileges and priorities, without being obliged to fufill any menial tasks. This did not become official court policy until 1677, seventeen years after Velázquez's death. Nonetheless, the artist was given a degree of social recognition before he died. Shortly before his death Philip IV dubbed him a Knight of the Order of Santiago – three years after he had painted *Las Meninas.*

Las Meninas (1656)

The painting is set in a room in the royal palace, whose walls are decorated with copies of paintings by Rubens. In the center stands the five year-old Infanta Margarita, with her ladies-in-waiting. On the left stands the painter himself, dressed as a courtier, with the Palace Chamberlain's key hanging from his belt and the red cross of the Order of Santiago on his dark doublet (added after the painter's death at the king's request). He is standing in front of a vast canvas holding paintbrush, palette, and crayon. However, the figures, who are illuminated by the window in the foreground of the sidewall, only occupy the lower half of the picture. Thus the viewer's gaze is directed to the mirror in the center of the rear wall, in which reflections of the King and Queen appear. By this means Velázquez is making it clear to anyone seeing the picture that the royal couple were present while the portrait of the Infanta was being painted. Their imaginary presence is crucial for the painting's interpretation. The monarch's visit to the artist in his studio was the strongest argument since Pliny's story about Alexander the Great and his visit to the artist Apelles for painting to be recognized as one of the liberal arts. The King's presence elevates art to a noble status. This is reinforced by the way Velázquez has depicted the painter, who is shown in a moment of inspiration, not in the actual act of painting. Even the paintings on the back wall – *Minerva punishing Ariadne* and *Apollo and Pan* should be interpreted in this context, as they illustrate the victory of divine art over handicraft and the unjustly punished artist. By presenting a complex network of viewer, painter, and model, on several different by pictorial planes, and by showing the interplay between appearance and reality – or painting and the real world – Velázquez has given us a thematic depiction of how one can raise the status of painting and his own position as a painter. The brilliance of the colors and the assured execution of this picture also speak for the creator's nobility. Like Edouard Manet, two centuries later, Velázquez considered himself a "painter among painters."

Las Meninas, 1656. Oil on canvas, 310 x 276 cm, Madrid, Museo del Prado

**Bartolomé Esteban Murillo,
St. Thomas of Villanueva,
c. 1668**
Oil on Canvas, 283 x 188 cm

Bartolomé Esteban Murillo supposedly thought this painting, which used to hang in the Capuchin church in Seville, among his finest. It depicts St. Thomas of Villanueva (1486-1555) turning aside from his theological writings to distribute alms. It may well be surprising to see this saint in the context of a Franciscan church, as he belonged to the Augustinian Order. However, he was not simply one of the most venerated Spanish saints in the second half of the 17th century. From 1544 on he was also Archbishop of Valencia, the native city of the founders of the church in whose honor the painting was commissioned. Further, Thomas of Villanueva had prescribed himself a life of charitable acts – which was also one of the Franciscans' principle goals. The main figure in the painting is emphasized by the bright light coming from the background. The distinguished figure of the saint, holding the bishops' staff, looks full of sympathy and love of one's neighbor as he hands a cripple a coin. This figure creates a striking contrast with the other people receiving alms. In the bottom corner of the picture the viewer can see a beautiful genre-group of the mother and child, who, like the other figures, stand out from one another in chiaroscuro contrasts. Through the archway on the right we glimpse a Renaissance facade. On the table in the left-center lies an open book, alluding to the saint's work as Charles V's priest. The book also implies the dogma of the Franciscan Order, that acts of charity are more important than intellectual pursuits.

Bartolomé Esteban Murillo, Immaculada, c. 1668
Oil on canvas, 436 x 292 cm

The Holy Virgin's immaculate conception, which promised the Mother of God eternal virginity and released her from the burden of original sin, had been the object of numerous discussions for centuries. In the early 17th century Christian believers in Spain pressed hard for a positive answer to this question from the Holy See in Rome, which eventually, in 1654, elevated belief in the immaculate conception a dogma. Murillo painted one version of this subject, of which he completed at least fifteen others, for the high altar of the Seville church of the Franciscan Order, which – unlike the Dominicans – had believed in this theological doctrine since the 13th century. The exceptionally large-scale format is intimately bound up with this originally specified location. Only from a good distance and from a viewpoint looking upwards at an angle, does the Holy Virgin

appear brilliantly foreshortened. All other viewpoints make the painting seem over-dimensional. What is most striking about the work are the painting's fluidity and dynamism both characteristics of Baroque art. Above the globe, accompanied by angels, the Holy Virgin appears with her mantle flowing and her hands solemnly

raised in prayer. She is characterized by nothing else except her peaceful spiritual expression.

Francisco de Zurbarán, Apotheosis of St. Thomas Aquinas, 1631
Oil on canvas, 480 x 400 cm

At one time this large-scale painting by Francisco de Zurbarán, which in the 17th century was considered the painter's *chef d'oeuvre*, adorned the erstwhile Dominican College in Seville. It depicts the founding of

the College by the Dominican Archbishop of Seville, Diego de Deza, in 1517. In the lower section, representing the temporal world, we see the donor of the College and Emperor Charles V, as well as several Dominican monks beside a table on which the founding documents are displayed. Immediately behind the Emperor the painter has depicted himself. The kneeling figures are looking upwards to the heavenly sphere, where St. Thomas Aquinas, surrounded by the four canons, is writing his *Summa theologica*. Above him on the left we see Jesus and Mary, and on the right, St. Paul and St. Dominic.

Francisco de Zurbarán, The Miracle of St. Hugo in the Refectory, c. 1645-1655
Oil on canvas, 262 x 317 cm

The sacristy of the former Carthusian Monastery in Seville used to contain three paintings illustrating the virtues of Carthusians. To illustrate "Abstinence" the monks wanted a depiction of the miracle which the founders of the Order interpreted as a sign of divine approval for their order. When St. Hugo, Arch-

bishop of Grenoble (1053-1132), appears in the refectory of a newly founded chapter house at the very moment the monks are eating meat without permission, their meal turns to ashes. The painter executed this scene, which he painted almost entirely in white and gray, on three levels. In the foreground stand St. Hugo and his servant. The center ground is filled up by the table with food on it and the hieratic line of the founders of the carthusian Order. In the background we can see a painting that depicts the Order's patron saint, the Virgin Mary and St. John the Baptist.

Isla de la Cartuja
Expo-area

In the northwestern corner of the city, on the Isla de la Cartuja, an island formed by two tributaries of the Río Guadalquivir, lie more than 531 acres (215 hectares) of the land that was set aside for the World Exhibition of 1992. The center is the 15th century Carthusian Monastery of Santa María de las Cuevas, in which Christopher Columbus met the Carthusian monk Gaspar de Gorricio, planned his second Atlantic voyage, and stored his most important personal papers. For 27 years after his death his corpse was interred here in the simple crypt of a chapel erected for the purpose. In 1841 the monastery came into the possession of a London businessman, namely Charles Pickman, who converted the buildings into a ceramic factory.

Torre Panorámica
Pabellón de España

Over the duration of 176 days, the World Exhibition attracted nearly 42,000 visitors. Opened to celebrate the 500th anniversary of the discovery of America, the island was transformed into a colorful park and garden landscape: 350,000 trees and green hedges with a total length of almost 25 miles (40 kilometers) intersect the area, which also has a man-made lake, as well as numerous canals, foun-

tains, and waterfalls. After the Exhibition, the land was put to a variety of uses. The main pavilions of the World Exhibition, the *Torre Panorámica* (Panoramic Tower), and various new buildings were combined into a theme park, which offers visitors multimedia shows and permanent exhibitions in the areas of nature, science, and culture. In the Spanish Pavilion visitors can take a multimedia journey through the history and literature of Spain. The Lago de España shows exotic islands, as well as a reconstruction of the 16th-century harbor of Seville. In the high-tech Omnimax cinema, a more than 78-foot (24 meter) diameter semi-circular screen shows films about the earth, the early explorers, and present-day space travel. To the west of the Expo-area lies the new Science and Technology Park, where several international companies have settled.

Iglesia de Santa Ana

On the far side of the Río Guadalquivir the visitor can find the old Pottery Quarter of Triana, which is among the most traditional and lively districts in Seville. Its roots date back to Roman times, which the name – supposedly derived from the Roman Emperor, Trajan – suggests. Legend has it that St. Justina and St. Rufina used to live here. In former times, Triana used to be an independent city inhabited by sailors, tradespeople, and artisans. Ceramic workshops set the character of the picturesque streets. In addition, as a former gypsy city – a royal edict had decreed that gypsies were allowed to settle here – this district is also the home of flamenco. Some people even think flamenco was born here in the cellars. The focal point of the district is the church of Santa Ana, presumably built by architects from Burgos between 1276 and 1280, and considered the oldest church in Seville. Alfonso X founded it, after he was miraculously cured of an eye infection. That said, in its present form, most of this three-nave basilica of yellow brick can be traced back to King Pedro I, who had parts of it rebuilt in the mid-14th century. Further rebuilding work was undertaken in the 15th and 16th centuries and after the severe earthquake of 1755. On the outer walls – and also on surrounding houses – the visitor can see many azulejos pictures, showing Jesus and Mary at various points in the Passion story. Of the

Capilla del Patrocino

The modern church is the headquarters of the Passion Fraternity Santísimo Cristo de la Expiración y Nuestra Señora del Patrocino and was added to the 18th century Baroque building. Inside the visitor can find one of the finest Expressionistic examples of Sevillean Baroque sculpture. This is a crucifix by Francisco Antonio Gijón from 1682, which depicts the "Dying Christ" and quite graphically shows the Redeemer's suffering.

ornate interior decoration, the most notable piece is the retable. On a total of 17 panels, scenes from the lives of the Holy Virgin, St. Joachim and St. Anna are depicted. The retable dates from 1542-1557 and is attributed to Pedro de Campaña, a Flemish artist living in Seville, as well as to several other Seville painters.

Carmona

East of Seville and on the fertile plain of the Campiña, on a 787 foot-(240 meter)high promontory, lies the picturesque little town of Carmona, whose settlement dates back to prehistoric times. In the first century B.C., Phoenicians, Carthaginians, and Romans alternately occupied this strategically well-located spot. Behind the city walls, Karmounah (as it was then known) achieved renewed importance. In fact, the Old City, with its cobblestoned alleys and small squares, still has Moorish features. When Ferdinand III conquered the city in 1247 he apparently proclaimed: "As the morning star glows in the dawn sky, so Carmona shines out in Andalusia!" At the highest point of the city, King Pedro I had the Moorish Alcázar built, which became one of his favorite residences. Numerous Renaissance and Baroque buildings bear witness to the Castilian feudal period.

Necrópolis Romana, Avenida de Jorge Bonsor, p. 122

Puerta de Sevilla, p. 118

Iglesia de Santa María, Calle de San José, p. 119

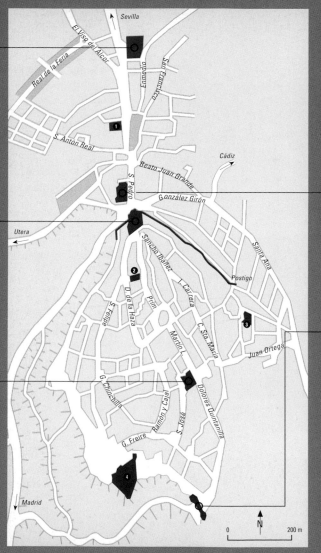

Iglesia de San Pedro,
Calle de San Pedro, p. 116

Puerta de Córdoba,
Calle Dolores Quintanilla, p. 121

Also Worth seeing:

1 Iglesia del Convento de la
  Concepción, Calle S. Pedro

2 Iglesia de San Bartolomé,
  Calle Prim

3 Iglesia de San Blas

4 Alcázar del Rey Pedro (Parador
  Nacional), Los Alcázares

lar church, dating from the 15th century. Three hundred years later it was rebuilt in the Baroque style. This phase of rebuilding included the 184 foot- (56 meter)high Baroque tower, whose bell tower was designed in the style of the Giralda in Seville. The brick building is reminiscent of a tabernacle with three sections decreasing in width, and it is punctuated by windows letting light into the stairwell.

Tabernacle

A particularly striking feature of the interior of the basilica is the Capilla Sacramental, located south of the transept. It was designed in a circular ground-plan and was decorated in 1760 by Ambrosio de Figueroa in the flamboyant decorative style of Sevillean Baroque. The chapel's focal point is formed by the altar, above which a baldachin, borne by angels, extends. The tabernacle is striking for its interplay of different columns. Within stands the statue of the Virgen de la Antigua, dating back to the mid-16th century.

Iglesia de San Pedro

Outside the gates of the Old City the visitor will find Iglesia de San Pedro. It is a three-nave basilica with a transept and rectangu-

Puerta de Seville

Where the Old City joins the new town of Carmona in the west, there stands a vast, imposing gateway from the third century B.C. It reveals the remnants of a Punic bastion and it also formed part of the Roman city wall. On both sides of a rectangular tower, 10 foot-wide (3 meter) gates open in the wall. In front of these, in Almohadic times, a third gate stood. Dating from the time of Emperor Augustus (27 B.C.-14 A.D.), the bastion-like structure had an area of worship above it. On a square almost 20 feet (6 meters) wide and enclosed by a portico, a small temple used to stand on the rear side. Today, only the external southern facade of the portico survives, divided by ashlar wall columns. In between the columns there are sections of a wall made of smaller stones.

Iglesia de Santa María

Among the many churches the three-nave Gothic portico-church of Santa María is exceptional. It was completed by 1578, but underwent several changes from the 17th to 19th centuries. Inside, one should note the Plateresque high altar, made by Nufro de Ortega and Juan Bautista Vázquez in the mid-16th century. Its reliefs depict canons, scenes from the life of Christ, the Coronation of the Holy Virgin, and the Crucifixion. In the Capilla de San José, in the southern side aisle there is a retable depicting St. Joseph attributed to Pedro de Campaña.

Patio de los Naranjos

Like so many churches in Andalusia, Santa María was built over the ruins of an Almohadic mosque destroyed in 1424. Evidence of this Moorish past comes from the Patio de los Naranjos, on the northern side of the basilica. With its horseshoe arcades, it makes the climb up through the Old City worthwhile. On one of the column shafts a Visigothic calendar was found. It is a summary of church holidays, dating from the mid-6th century. This indicates that it is an original Visigothic building.

Puerta de Córdoba

According to Caesar's description, Roman Carmo was the most important fortified city in Baetica. East of the city the Puerta de Córdoba once formed part of the Roman fortifications. Leading directly to the Puerta de Sevilla, the Roman road led through the city gate of Seville, with its octagonal turrets, towards Córdoba. We find other vestiges of the Roman road network about 3 miles (5 kilometers) further north,

where a Roman bridge, with five arches, spans the Río Corbones. After many changes (during Moorish times and under Charles II in 1668), the gate was extended into a triumphal gateway in the 18th century. Blind windows frame the entrance, which consists of a round arch flanked by double columns. From the gable superstructure there is a fine view over the surrounding plain.

Necrópolis Romana

Through the Puerta de Sevilla the road leads to the city outskirts, where, opposite the remains of an Augustinian amphitheater, the Roman necropolis extends. The graves of the necropolis date from the first to fourth centuries A.D. and were discovered in 1868. However, only about a quarter of the 1,000 plus, mostly rectangular, subterranean grave-chambers have been excavated. These were hewn into the rockface, and they contain recesses which used to contain the urns of ashes – cremation being the usual form of burial. The stuccoed limestone walls are decorated with paintings, depicting not merely geometric and floral designs, but also funereal ceremonies. The museum of the necropolis has the various finds – which include grave goods, urns, and bronze figures – on exhibition. These give the visitor an idea of how the richly furnished grave-chambers once looked.

Tumba del Elefante

Immediately left of the entrance to the Necrópolis Romana lies one of the most elaborate graves, named after an approximately 22 inch (57 centimeter)-tall sculpture of an elephant which was discovered here. The elephant was once stuccoed and painted. Its significance has led to a great deal of speculation, but as yet the riddle remains unsolved. The elephant can be interpreted as representing longevity. It has also been associated with the battle of Ilipa, in 206 B.C., in which the Carthaginians deployed elephants. Possibly also it is simply a classic Punic "heraldic animal," such as the type that was stamped on coins minted in Spain. This large-scale first century grave consisted of a nearly square "courtyard," as well as two *triclinii* (dining rooms); In addition, there were other small

Tumba de Servilia

In the western section of the necropolis the visitor finds the largest and most unusual grave. It is named after the inscription found there on the base of a marble statue of a woman. This grave area used to belong to the prosperous and influential Servilia family from Carmo and was laid out like a Roman "peristyle house," a colonnaded hall. The center is formed by a large courtyard (78.7 x 57.7 feet or 24 x 17.6 meters), which at one time was surrounded by a two-story portico as well as several main and subsidiary rooms. The grave-chambers hewn into the rockface are beautifully decorated with wall-paintings and sculptures. The best preserved wall-paintings include a seated female figure playing the harp. Behind her stands a woman servant holding a palm fan. Faux pilasters are painted *al fresco* on the walls, creating a sense of open space.

rooms, including a third triclinium, a grave-chamber, a kitchen, and a fountain. These opulent grave-furnishings confirm Roman notions of the after life – that in the realm of death, the dead should not have to forsake the luxuries of their former lives. In one of the rooms a fragmented figure of Attis, with crossed legs, was discovered. This was assumed to be a grave-guard. As for a badly damaged seated statue hewn out of the rock, and positioned near the pond, this may well be the grave statue of the builder.

Écija

The road from Seville to Córdoba leads past the small town of Écija. It is known principally for its wealth of Baroque churches and is well worth a visit. The town dates back to a Greek settlement, which the Romans used to call Astigi. Legend has it that the apostle Paul once preached here. In Moorish times Écija used to belong to the caliphate of Córdoba, and in 1240 it was seized by the Christians. Thereafter, Écija went on growing more and more important. However, the earthquake of 1755 destroyed large areas of the town, so today it is striking mainly for its Baroque architecture. Most of the high bell towers also date from this period of rebuilding. With their distinctive brick color and ornate azulejos decoration, these give the townscape its most striking feature. They have also led to Écija being called "the town of towers."

Iglesia de Santa Cruz, Plaza del Nuestra Señora del Valle, p. 130

Plaza de España, p. 126

Also Worth Visiting:

1 Convento de San Pablo y Santo Domingo

2 Palacio de los Garcilaso, Calle Carmona

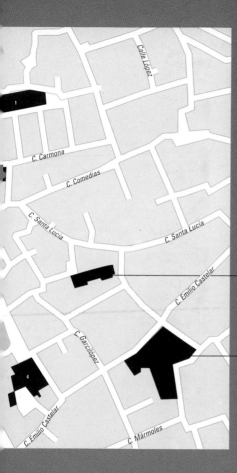

Iglesia de San Juan,
Calle Cordera, p. 128

Palacio de los Marqueses de
Peñaflor, Calle Emilio Castelar,
p. 129

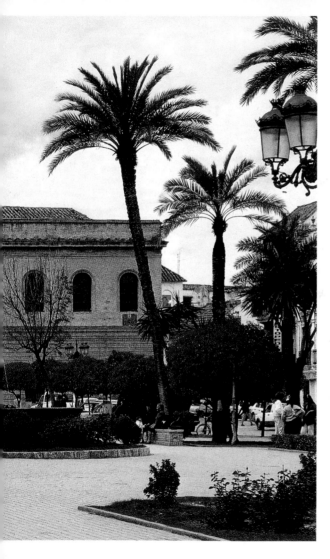

Plaza de España

In the center of the city is the extensive 18th-century square that is rich in palm trees, affectionately called *El Salón* (the Parlor) by many of locals. It is fringed by the facades of stylish houses and palaces with big balconies and galleries several stories high. In earlier times, the inhabitants could stand on their balconies and watch fiestas, equestrian games, and *corridas*. On the main side of the square stands the Ayuntamiento (townhall). It houses a small museum in which the visitor can see a Roman mosaic depicting the "punishment of Queen Dirke." Immediately behind the Ayuntamiento, on the Plaza de Santa María, there is a three-nave church of the same name which was built in the 18th century. It contains an outstanding art collection, including Sevillean School paintings from the 16th and 17th century choir stalls.

Iglesia de San Juan

Diagonally opposite the Iglesia de Santa Bárbara, whose portal is framed by Roman columns, stands a Baroque tower dating from 1745. It is one of the few towers that survived the earthquake of 1755 and forms part of the Iglesia de San Juan, built at the end of the 18th century. Among the many towers in Écija, this one stands out as the finest, and it has become a symbol of the city. Covered with ornamental decoration, the blue of its azulejos is quite a contrast against the light brick. The two little-known architects, Lucas Bazán and Antonio Corrales, both of whom were employed by the Marqués of Alcántara, ingeniously solved the problem of the transition between the two sections of the tower, which are different in size. Simply by going into the sacristy of the single-nave hall-church, it is possible to view several Baroque altar pieces, paintings of the Sevillean School, and a figure of the crucified Christ by Pedro Roldán.

Palacio de los Marquéses de Peñaflor

Northeast of the Plaza de España stands one of the most important aristocratic palaces in the city, completed by the third Marqués de Peñaflor in 1726. The Baroque facade of this palace, which the locals call "the house with long balconies," follows the curves of a winding street. The balconies run along the whole length of the upper story and are decorated with frescoes which are predominantly yellow and green. At the upper end one finds the main portal, decorated with the owner's coat-of-arms. This then leads into a complex living area complete with stables and a patio. On the left, the corner tower is completed by an arcade.

Iglesia de Santa Cruz

The Calle de Santa Cruz leads from the Plaza de España into the oldest part of the small town Écija, where the narrow streets and isolated monastery facade make it the most picturesque district. Also on the Calle de Santa Cruz is the three-nave parish church of the same name. After the earthquake of 1755, the church was rebuilt (1776–1836) inside the skeleton of the original building. It was never finished, for of the five bays, the two western ones were not vaulted over. On the north side some sections of the original church were incorporated in the new structure. A chapter house in the patio provides evidence of the Visigothic church which used to be the bishopric of St. Fulgentius. A horseshoe arch, covered with arabesques and coats-of-arms, originally came from a previous Mudéjar building. In the northeastern tower (completely rebuilt in 1869), two stone tablets, dating from the years 930

and 977, are built into the walls. They describe how fountains were constructed under the first and third caliphs of Córdoba, Abd ar-Rahman III and Hisham II. Since the Alzázar was totally destroyed after the Christian Reconquest, these are the only relics that have survived from Moorish times, when Écija was still known as *Medina Estighia* (Wealthy Town). Inside the church is an early Christian sarcophagus dating from the 5th century. Today it is used in the choir as an altar-mensa. The remains of St. Fulgentius supposedly lie in this sarcophagus. The long side is decorated with scenes from the Old Testament. In the center is the "Good Shepherd," on the left the "Sacrifice of Isaac," and on the right, "Daniel in the Lions' Den." The sarcophagus is adorned with a statue of the patron saint of the city, Nuestra Señora del Valle, dating from the late 16th century. A monstrance made by the silversmith Francisco de Alfaro in 1586 is stored in the sacristy. The side aisles are decorated with Baroque and classical retables.

Itálica

Behind the village of Santiponce lies the archaeological site of Itálica, the first town the Romans established on Iberian soil. At the end of the Second Punic War, after the battle of Ilipa (Alcalá del Río) Scipio Africanus the Elder arranged it as a settlement for veterans. The Roman historian Appian writes: "After allowing them a small army, as was compulsory in peace-time, Scipio settled the wounded in a town which, in memory of Italy, he called Itálica." Roman soldiers, who were awarded money and land after their military service, settled here, married local women and soon mingled with the resident population. As a result, the small settlement soon grew into a large town. It was not long before this town, located north of the Guadalquivir, was economically important. It became the most significant trade junction in western Andalusia. Its population reached a peak of around 10,000. It was from here that Romanization of the whole peninsula, whose official language was Latin, began. Two aristocratic families resident in Itálica produced the Roman Emperors Trajan (A.D. 98-A.D. 117) and Hadrian (A.D. 117-A.D. 138), who made the town historically important.

Itálica has these emperors to thank for a far-reaching extension of the whole town. It is because of them that in addition to numerous public buildings, a new residential district, the Nova Urbs, was built

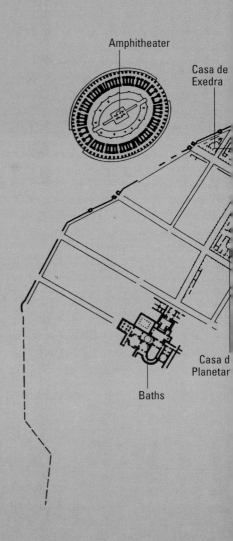

Amphitheater

Casa de Exedra

Casa d Planetar

Baths

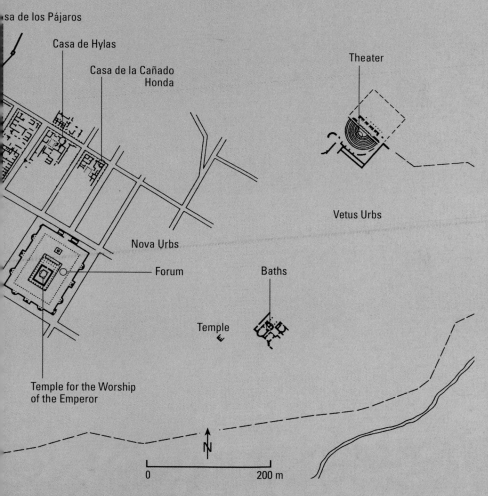

sa de los Pájaros

Casa de Hylas

Casa de la Cañado Honda

Theater

Nova Urbs

Vetus Urbs

Forum

Baths

Temple

Temple for the Worship of the Emperor

0   200 m

N

complete with a monumental city wall. The town survived into Visigothic times, and was not abandoned until the Arabs took over. From then on it served as a quarry, and was a popular site for treasure-hunters. After several severe floods of the Guadalquivir in the 17th century, the inhabitants of Santiponce moved up into the hills and used what remained of wall and marble cladding to rebuild their houses. During the Napoleonic War, Marshall Soult and the Duke of Wellington both came to Itálica in search of archaeological finds. Systematic excavation did not begin until the 20th century. All findings thereafter went to the Archaeological Museum in Seville. In the context of the World Exhibition of 1992, radical restoration was carried out, affecting, among other things, the amphitheater and the mosaics.

Itálica is one of the most important archaeological sites on Spanish soil, because it reveals a Roman town almost in its entirety. Of the original town (Vetus Urbs) only a few buildings (the theater, temple, and some houses) have been excavated. The rest are presumably beneath the village of Santiponce, where excavation work has now begun. Even so, the whole area of Nova Urbs has been exposed to view. Like most Roman towns, it is laid out in a geometric plan with intersecting streets. The *decumanus* (main road) which leads to the amphitheater used to be fringed with an arcade of pilasters. It is an incredible 50.5 feet (15.4 meters) wide, whereas in Pompeii, for instance, the

streets are only about 33 feet (10 meters) wide. Twenty-six feet (8 meters) was allocated to road traffic, with 13 feet (4 meters) on both sides reserved for pedestrians. In the *insulae* (the rectangles formed by the streets), large colonnaded houses were situated. Their luxurious decoration, featuring opulent floor-mosaics, bears witness to the Roman families' wealth. In the southern part of the city there were extensive public baths decorated with numerous statues. The monumental focal point and political center of this new area of the city was a large forum, whose outer wall opened into alternating round and rectangular recesses. In the center stood a temple, which, deemed from the inscriptions and sculptures, was probably dedicated to the worship of the Emperor.

Amphitheater

Outside the town walls, at the foot of the hill on which it is built, the vast oval of the amphitheater extends 525 feet (160 meters) in length and 449.5 feet (137 meters) in width. It was among the largest in the Roman empire and could seat 25,000 spectators. Originally, the *cavea* (spectators' grandstand), built on the sloping side, was enclosed by an external structure. Access was through a covered walkway, from which steps and exits led to the grandstands. The front rows have

names chiseled into them, which indicate that they were reserved for high-ranking personalities. From the three rows of seats then available, spectators could watch animal-baiting and gladiatorial combat, though these activities – according to a bronze tablet from Itálica currently housed in the Archaeological Museum in Madrid – was curtailed by the Roman Emperor Marcus Aurelius (A.D.161-180). The cruciform indentation with eight columns in the center of the arena once used to be covered, and functioned as a storehouse.

Casa de los Pájaros

The Casa de los Pájaros, so called because of the 32 different birds depicted on one of its mosaic floors, opened on to the *decumanus*. One of its two entrances led into a room with an oven (presumably there used to be a bakery here), and the other led visitors into the vestibule, which once used to be roofed over. From here one could reach the peristyle, the colonnaded garden courtyard, in whose center there used to be a subterranean reservoir. The living rooms which lead off the courtyard have exquisi-

te floor mosaics which have survived, including the bird-mosaic and a depiction of Bacchus. Parallel with the peristyle is the triclinium, the banquet hall with the U-shaped *clini* (lying couches), which were used for dining. On one side the banquet hall leads into two unroofed courtyards. The right-hand one has a *piscina* (swimming-pool) and the left-hand one has a small colonnade. Between the left-hand courtyard and the peristyle was the semi-circular *lararium*, in which the Roman household gods, called the *larum*, were worshipped. The area at the rear was taken up by utility rooms.

Mulva (Munigua)

Another fascinating excavation site lies near the mining township of Villanueva del Río y Minas, on the edge of the Sierra Morena, near the Río Guadalquivir. On a hillside the visitor comes across the ruins of Munigua, an Iberian settlement founded in the fourth century B.C., which was later taken over by the Romans. The Romans called it Municipium Flavium Muniguense. Judging by the buildings and the discoveries made here (now housed in the Museo Arquelógico Provincial, Seville), this site must have been important for the network of Roman administrative centers – despite its remote location. The most important complex of buildings is comprised of a large terraced shrine, which most likely dates from the second half of the first century A.D., and is built symmetrically on the rear of the hillside. Steps and ramps lead up to the man-made terraces, on the top one of which we find a temple with an exedra laid in front. Outside the shrine there is a late first century temple area, supported by high terraced walls and buttresses. South of this one finds the forum, flanked by porticoes on three sides, with a podium temple in the center, and auxiliary rooms along the sides. A letter from Emperor Titus (dated A.D. 79-A.D. 81) has been discovered in the room assumed to be a tabularium. Several dwelling houses and baths have also recently been excavated in the town, which was enclosed by a city wall in the second half of the second century. The city wall also enclosed quite a few graves, which were evidently later abandoned during the severe economic crisis of the third century.

Life under the Inquisition

"Deafening peals from the cathedral and nearby churches... The first thing your eye seized upon was the crucifix. An enormous Cross, swathed in black crepe, carried on the shoulders of Dominican monks from the Royal

Bernard Picart, The Heretic, 1723. Copper engraving, 163 x 105 mm, Dresden, Staatliche Kunstsammlungen, Kupferstichkabinett

Monastery. Only spectators who had seen the spectacle before knew what color it was. The dark green would not become visible until the moment of solemn absolution. In the shadow of the Cross, helmeted soldiers followed, bearing halberds, as well as monks and priests, wearing cowls, and singing the Lord's praises.

In two hierarchically ordered and strictly disciplined parallel processions, the civil and ecclesiastical dignitaries marched along: the *corregidor* behind the assistant judges, the dean behind the canons, who, for their part, walked behind the members of the court. The prosecutor carried the standard, a scarlet taffeta square, edged with silver fringes and tassels, on which the coat-of-arms of the Inquisition – the war-flag of faith – was emblazoned.

The penitents led the actual procession. There were about one hundred of them, wearing saffron yellow wool smocks, and carrying candles in their hands, with pointed caps on their heads. All around, a mass of ordinary people pushed and jostled.... Halfway between the rostrum and the platform, a podium enclosed by iron railings had been set up. Here, the condemned were put on show in cages. The public was therefore aware of all their responses – whether shame, pain, or repentance. On a desk, some pages placed a little box containing the verdicts, and on another, two large trays, finished in gold. A curate held out missal and crucifix towards the faithful. Then, in a loud voice, he intoned: "We, the *corregidor*, the mayor, bailiffs, and notables, inhabitants of the noble city of Toledo, obedient to Holy Mother Church, true and loyal Christians – hereby swear by the four Evangelists who lie before us, that we shall maintain and defend the holy faith of Jesus Christ. Accordingly, we shall pursue, seize hold of and capture any who are suspected of heresy or of having fallen from faith…" (A) priest moved to a desk. His eyes lingered for a

Theodor Goetz, The French Garrucha, 18th century. Drawing

moment on the condemned in their cages. Then, he drew a deep breath and declaimed: "What sinners could be worse enemies of the Lord God, who could deserve severer punishment than those who follow the commandments of Moses, the faithless ones? With them, hope would be illusory, and patience merely self-indulgent. For you, whose life has sunk into shamefulness, to whom God and man are equally hateful, – it is only fair and just that the holy court punishes you, and today defends the rights of the Lord. *Exurge Domine, judica causam tuam!* Stand up, Lord God, and speak out for your cause! … A Dominican monk (began) reading the *méritos*, a summary of all the charges that had been laid and the corresponding punishments. Soon, a second priest followed him. Then a third…. How long did it take to read out the charges? Six hours? Eight hours? By the time it was over, the sun had disappeared behind the cathedral.

(At the enclosed – in burning-area outside the city walls) no representatives of the Inquisitorial court were present – but only the "qualificators" those qualified to attend the condemned and – most important responsibility of all – to decide whether they should be granted the privilege of being strangled.

The funeral pyres, on which sticks had been piled since the previous day, towered up against the reddish glow of the evening sky. The executioners waited with impassive expressions. Those posthumously condemned were – in a macabre way – also present, for what remained of them lay in boxes painted with bitumen. It took a while for the delinquents - of whom there were only about twenty – to be seen. The crowd stood there just as densely packed as hours before, but now one sensed an uninhibited lust for punishment. The first stone flew into the air, then another. Some people cursed. It is quite

Theodor Goetz, Burning Heretics, 18th century. Copper engraving

likely that had it not been for the soldiers, the anger of the mob would have turned the sentencing into a stoning…. Two of the condemned (were) already in the flames. The first fought his death-struggle without a sound. The second bellowed, begged, and wriggled so violently that the burnt ropes gave way. He toppled off the pyre, a living torch. Immediately, the executioners leapt on him…. The next burning took place in effigy. People saw an articulated puppet, holding a coffin, on which the name was written in big letters…. Scarcely had coffin and puppet been consumed by the flames, then a woman of about sixty, tied to a massive beam,

was pushed toward the pyre. Unlike the others, she did not land in the flames at once. In his infinite mercy, and because she had confessed, the "qualificator" had shown her the kindness of first strangling her."
(taken from: Gilbert Sinoué, *The Blue Stone*)

This, or something similar may well have happened on February 6, 1481, when in Seville the first *autodafé* (from the Spanish: *auto da fé*, meaning "act of faith") of the Spanish Inquisition took place. However, the condemned person had to wait many long weeks before hearing the verdict and suffering the punishment.

The Denunciation

In accordance with the proverb: "No complaint, no redress," the proceedings could not begin unless there was a denunciation. The Inquisitorial trial started as soon as someone who was proven to have committed – or even suspected of – heresy (false faith) was denounced and arrested. The name of the denouncer, however, always remained secret. Once the tribunal believed the accusations, the accused could hardly escape the machinery of the Inquisition. For rather than the denouncer having to prove his allegations, the accused had to prove his innocence – something which was, in effect, almost impossible. Certainly he or she was entitled to any defense the tribunal suggested, but this would only help if one could track down a witness who was willing to deny the charge. Then the court had the right to determine the witness' reliability.

Jacquemin Woeirit,
Tortura del'aqua, 1541.
Woodcut from Milles de
Sauvigny's Praxis criminis
persequendi, Paris

When someone was arrested, all their worldly wealth, out of which the prisoner had to pay the costs of their imprisonment, were confiscated. This marked the beginning of a time of grinding anxiety, for prisoners were not allowed to have any contact with their family, write letters, or

have visitors. Nor were they aware of what was happening outside prison.

The Cross-examination

The Inquisitorial tribunal's main goal was to make the accused confess their own errors and recant – for this was the most striking and convincing proof of their guilt. To this end, interrogation and torture applied psychological pressure. During cross-examination Inquisitors were required to be friendly, to make it easier for the accused to confess. There were certain simple but effective "tricks" to help make this possible, as Nicolaus Eymericus described in his 16th-century handbook, *Directorium inquisitorum*. "The Inquisitor should behave in a friendly fashion, acting as if he already knows everything. He should thumb through the documents and say: "It is perfectly clear that you are not

Bernard Picart, "Procession of Judges of Heretics and Heretics Condemned to Death in Spain", 1723. Copper engraving

telling the truth." Or he should pick up a piece of paper with writing on it and exclaim, with an expression of surprise: "How can you go on denying everything when it's all here in black and white?" Then he should go on: "Feel free, confess, you can see I know everything." If the accused refused to confess, long intervals between interrogations would be imposed. The accused would spend this time in their cells – often in solitary confinement – examining their conscience, a task with which task confessors and priests were meant to help.

Torture

If the suspect persisted in denial, torture could be applied. For the duration of the cross examination, there were exact instructions. The suspect to be tortured could not be asked specific questions which he could answer with a simple "Yes" or "No." The Inquisition was well aware that, to avoid further torment, the suspect would be prepared to confess anything. The Inquisitor's task during the whole torture process was more a matter of urging the accused to tell the truth. As the church hypocritically argued that no blood must flow and the body of the suspect must not show any outward signs of mistreatment, the methods of torture were restricted. In the *garrucha*, the victim's hands were first tied behind his back.

Then, by means of a rope which was attached to his wrists, he would be hoisted up. If the suspect did not confess, the pain could be increased. To do this, either extra weights were added to the feet or the rope would be suddenly

Bernard Picart, Execution and Burning of Heretics in Spain, c. 1722. Copper engraving

tightened, then let go. Another method which left no visible signs of physical torment was the *tortura del'aqua*. In this case, the accused was tied to a ladder in such a way that his head lay lower than his body. His mouth was forcibly opened and a linen cloth was laid over it, which served as a filter. Then, water was dripped over the cloth so that the victim was in danger of choking. At certain intervals, the Inquisitors would remove the cloth to urge the torture victim to tell the truth. But no matter whether he confessed or not, judgment would be passed on him and the verdict solemnly proclaimed at the next *autodafé*....

Osuna

This small town with its charming marketplace lies off the tourist map. In Spain it is best known as a ducal town. Not surprisingly, as the Condes de Girón, to whom Philip II gave the title Dukes of Osuna in 1562, became some of the most powerful nobles in Spain in the 16th and 17th centuries. This is reflected in buildings such as the university, which was founded in 1549 and helped Osuna develop into a center of artistic and intellectual history. That said, the town's history dates back a long way. In Roman times, the erstwhile Iberian settlement of Urso fought on Pompey's side against Caesar. It was the last town to surrender to the victor. This is emblazoned on the bronze tablets proclaiming the *Lex Julia Colonialis* (a name derived from the "Julian" family, to which Caesar belonged).

These tablets are now in the National Archaeological Museum, Madrid. Moorish Oxuna became Castilian in 1239 and was given to the Calatrava Order.

Monasterio de la Encarnación

The Convent of the Barefoot Sisters of Mercy, founded as a hospital in 1549, is well worth visiting to see its two-story cloister. In the base area, the walls are clad with Baroque azulejos, which depict, among other things, the four seasons and the five senses, as well as scenes of hunting and war. In the museum there is a fine collection of sculptures of the Christ child.

Palacio de los Condes de la Gomera

The curving facade of the Palacio de los Condes de la Gomera is impressive for its yellow-painted moldings on a white base, its black window-grilles, and picturesque gargoyles in the form of canons.

Antigua Cilla del Cabildo

Osuna owes its period as an influential ducal town to its magnificent aristocratic palaces built in the course of it's expansion in the 18th century. In the Calle de San Pedro there are many splendid residences, their opulently decorated portals concealing exquisite patios. One important building is the Antigua Cilla del Cabildo, the former grainstore of the cathedral chapter house, which Alonso Ruiz Florindo, from Fuentes, built in 1773. The portal gable is adorned with an alto-rilievo depicting the Giralda and Seville's two patron saints, St. Justina and St. Rufina.

Collegiate Chruch of Santa María de la Asunción

On the hillside above the town stands the imposing church which was founded in 1530 by Don Juan Téllez-Girón, a member of the future ducal family. With its huge flying buttresses, from the outside this three-nave collegiate church looks like a fortress. The only exception to this impression is the Plateresque ornamentation of the Puerta del Sol on the west facade, which leads inside the church. The naves are of equal height, and have ribbed vaults. In the rooms of the former sacristy a museum has been installed. Along with 16th century Flemish paintings, four pictures by José de Ribera, which used to be on the high altar, are exhibited here. By way of the square Patio del Capellá, an inner courtyard which is fringed by two-storey arcades and is ornately decorated in the Plateresque style, the visitor can reach the Panteón Ducal, the sepulcher of the Dukes of Osuna.

José de Ribera, Crucifixion, 1616-1620
Oil on canvas, 336 x 230 cm

The Collegiate Church owes its importance mainly to its art treasures, among which the outstanding *Crucifixion* by Ribera is located in one of the northern side-chapels. After training in Valencia, Parma, and Rome, Ribera settled in Naples in 1616. One of the Dukes of Osuna, who was Viceroy of Naples in the early 17th century, commissioned the artist to paint ten pictures for his Andalusian homeland. From 1616-1620 Ribera completed the *Crucifixion*, which is one of the most important works of early-17th century Spanish painting. The painting is typical of Ribera's style. Heavily influenced by naturalism and Caravaggio's

chiaroscuro, this style was also capable of luminous color, combined with technical brilliance and an often acute realism characteristic of Spanish painting.

Santiponce

San Isidoro del Campo

Santiponce, which used to lie on the banks of the Guadalquivir until the great flood in the 17th century, today extends over parts of Vetus Urbs, Itálica. Here one finds the monastery of San Isidoro del Campo, which Guzmán el Bueno (the Good) founded as a Cistercian Abbey in 1300. On behalf of the Castilian King, Tarifa, he had defended Andalusia against the Moors. In 1309, his son, Juan Pérez de Guzmán, had a second, smaller church erected immediately next to the first, and the two were later connected. In 1431 the whole complex was

given to the Hieronymites, in whose hands it remained until 1836. This Order was founded in Spain in 1370. It was named after Hieronymus (St. Jerome), the Father of the Church, who was responsible for translating the Bible into Latin – essential as a means of spreading the Christian doctrine. From the outside the twin-church, complete with flying buttresses, looks like a fortified building with battlements. The whole complex includes two cloisters with 15th-century frescoes and annexes, as well as another inner courtyard, which now belongs to the adjoining factory.

High Altar

In the older Gothic church, which underwent extensive restoration as early as the 16th century, there is a carved, Baroque high altar, which is considered a masterpiece of polychromatic sculpture in Spain. This magnificent sculpture was created by Juan Martínes Montañés between 1609 and 1613. In the sunken central niche St. Jerome is depicted as a penitent. Although he is shown face on, his figure is so well sculpted on all sides that it can be removed and carried in processions. The anatomically exact depiction confirms the sculpter's supreme skill. The tensed arm, with its musculature, and the veins which protrude beneath the skin are reproduced exactly. On either side of this figure we see reliefs depicting the Adoration of the Shepherds and the Magi, flanked by the two figures of St. John the Baptist and St. John the Evangelist, as well as two angels. The name of the monastery's patron saint – St. Isidor – appears above. He is framed by reliefs depicting the Resurrection and the Ascension, as well as by two more angels. In the attic Montañés installed the Ascension of the Holy Virgin as well as four personifications of the virtues. The retable culminates in a crucifixion. On either side of the altar find one the tombs, with statues kneeling in prayer, of the founding couple – Guzmán el Bueno and his wife, María Alonso Coronel.

The Province of Huelva

The Province of Huelva

People traveling through southern Spain rarely pay a visit to the most westerly province in all Andalusia. Most people know it only as a transit-point on the way to the Algarve coast of Portugal. The region has many attractive features – not least its contrasting landscape. In the North lie the forests of the Sierra Aracena, with chestnut-oaks, cork, piñon, and chestnut trees. Also, in the Guadalquivir estuary there is the nature reserve of Coto de Doñana (an area of over 75,000 hectares) which, with its wealth of rare animals and birds, is one of the most important bird sanctuaries in Europe. Along the coastline, there are lovely sandy beaches and isolated bays. Yet, building the resort town of Matalscañas in the 1970s marked the beginning of a struggle between nature protection and tourism. In cultural and historic terms, the region also has a lot to offer. Due to the rich ore deposits in the mountains – espe-

Vista del Coto

cially copper – the Phoenicians established the first trading settlements, to be followed by Romans, Visigoths, Moors and Christians.

The province achieved historical importance during the Age of Discoveries. In 1486, in the Monastery of La Rábida, thanks to the support of the monks resident there, Columbus was given Queen Isabella's permission to set sail from the harbor of Palos de la Frontera, and on August 3, 1492 started his voyage of exploration with three caravels. In 1528 Hernán Cortés also landed here after his conquest of Mexico. "Columbus" is a subject one encounters everywhere. Huelva, the capital city, which has the same name as the province, bears the proud title of "La Orilla de las tres Carabelas" (Bank of the three Caravels), even if its old buildings were completely destroyed in the severe earthquake of 1755; it is now better known as an industrial center with oil refineries, chemical industries, and an important ore-shipping harbor. The Ruta Colombina leads to several places which are associated with Columbus and his voyages. Our starting-point is the Costa Colombina, the coast off Huelva, from which one can travel along the bank of the Río Odiel as far as the estuary of the Río Tinto. On its headland one sees the towering form of the monumental granite statue of Cristóbal Colón (Colombus), made by the American woman sculptor, Gertrude Vanderbilt Whithney. Further stops are the monastery of La Rábida on the eastern bank of the Río Tinto, as well as the two towns, Palos de la

Getrude Vanderbilt Whitney, Statue of Columbus, 1929

Frontera and Moguer, whose monastery, Santa Clara, is the most important Mudéjar building in this province.

Once a year this remote province is filled with bustle and color, when, at Whit, thousands of pilgrims head toward El Rocío. On foot, horseback, or by opulently decked-out ox-cart, they make their way to the pilgrimage site on the outskirts of the Coto de Doñana, to venerate the Santíssima Virgen del Rocío (Madonna of the Morning Dew), and, at the same time, spend four days in boisterous celebration.

Niebla

This little town lies tucked away on a hillside on the banks of the Río Tinto. Under the Romans it was known as Ilipula, and under the Visigoths, it was the bishopric of Elebla. Called Lebla, it was once the capital of a taifa empire, until it could be absorbed by Alfonso X in 1257. Despite this explanation of the name's etymological derivation, when, from a distance, one sees the town's outline emerging indistinctly from the mist that rises from the Río Tinto, the visitor is more likely to assume it is the Spanish word for mist (*niebla*) that gave the place its name.

Iglesia de Santa María de la Granada

Behind the Plaza in the town center one finds the three-nave church of Santa María de la Granada, which can look back on an eventful history. In the 10th and 11th centuries a church used to stand here that was tolerated by the Moors – a church of which two portals still survive. In the 13th century a mosque was constructed out of these, the origin of the Gothic structure.

The entrance patio, with its two rows of horseshoe arcades, used to be the orange courtyard, and the bell tower, built on a square groundplan, recalls the erstwhile minaret.

City Wall (Murallas)

The town's main attraction is its 3 km – (1.8 mile) long city wall, which has 46 towers and four gates. For nine months this wall withstood the Christians' siege. Apart from small sections, which are Roman and Visigothic in origin, it largely dates back to the Moors. The four gates confirm this. In the North lies the Puerta de Socorro, with a horseshoe arch through which a typically Moorish right-angled passageway leads into the town. In the East one comes across the Puerta de Sevilla, which dates back to Roman times. The South Gate, which leads to the river, is called the Puerta del Agua, because women supposedly went from here to fetch water from the river. With its horseshoe arch, framed by an *alfiz* and its brick blind arcades, the Puerta del Buey (Ox Gate) in the West is most reminiscent of its Moorish builders.

Palos de la Frontera

Monasterio de Santa María de la Rábida

Approximately 5 km (3 miles) south-west of Palos de la Frontera one finds the Franciscan monastery which has many associations with Columbus. Here, in 1485, when Columbus came from Lisbon to Palos, he supposedly asked for accommodation for his son, Diego. The oldest part of the monastery is the single-nave Mudéjar church from the 14th century, to which a small chapel is connected. This is where the early-14th century Virgen de los Milagros is venerated – before their voyage, Columbus and the Pinzón brothers asked for her protection. Behind the monastery church there is a two-story cloister with brick-walled arcades, from which the visitor can reach the monks' cells and the refectory. In the chapter house there is a table with armchairs. This is where Columbus and the Pinzón brothers are supposed to have planned their first exploration with the Franciscan prior.

Daniel Vázquez Díaz, 1929/30, Frescoes

In 1929/30, the painter Daniel Vázquez Díaz (1881–1969) decorated a side entrance room with murals in the Cubist style.

They record for posterity scenes showing events in the monastery and also of the later discoveries, and include scenes depicting the discussion with the monks and the disembarkation from the port of Palos.

A Magnificent Mistake – Columbus Discovers America

When, on August 3, 1492, Christopher Columbus disembarked from the port of Palos de la Frontera, a new chapter began for Spain, which was recorded in history as the Age of Discoveries. The Conquista, as the conquest of the Central and South American continent is known, created a colonial empire of enormous size, whose gold and silver were to help establish the conditions for Spain to become a world power. For the seafarer, however, a lengthy period of waiting came to an end. For almost fifteen years Columbus had tried to find enough interest in, and agreement for, his vision. He was convinced that toward the West, sailing over the open sea, one could reach India.

The Beginnings

Christopher Columbus, born in Genoa in 1451 the son of a wool weaver, had his first seafaring experiences on small merchant ships before arriving in Portugal in 1476. He settled in Lisbon, deepening his knowledge of seafaring by making trading voyages to Madeira, to the North, and to Guinea, familiarizing himself with winds and currents. During these years he became increasingly convinced that the lands of the East could easily be reached by taking the western route, across the Atlantic. India, which at that time was synonymous with Asia, had fascinated Europeans ever since Marco Polo

Ridolfo Ghirlandaio, Christopher Columbus, Genoa, Seafaring Museum

described in his legendary travel report of 1298/99 the unimaginable wealth in Cathay (China), the empire of the Great Khan, and Cipangu (the Japanese islands). In those days many of the most sought-after delicacies, such as spices, fragrances and silk – things that all European royal and noble houses demanded – came from the East.

However, from the mid-15th century onwards, the Ottoman Empire's machinations had severely affected the traditional trade route, which over the course of many centuries had been developed along the Silk Road. For this reason, European traders were very interested in finding a way to the Far East which would allow for a direct exchange of goods. All attention turned toward Portugal, in particular, after the seafarer Bartolomeu Diaz (c. 1450–1500) accidentally succeeded in sailing round the southern tip of Africa. This more or less opened up the direct sea-route to India.

The World View of an Explorer

At the time, it was believed that the earth was made up of three continents – Europe, Africa, and Asia. It therefore seemed obvious to Columbus that there must be another, very much shorter sea-route to the East, if one assumed that the earth, as had generally been thought in the Middle Ages, was not disc-shaped, but spherical. This assumption was already familiar to the ancient world. However, in post-Christian centuries this idea was drastically suppressed, especially by the Church, since only the disc shape could be reconciled with the Biblical view of Jerusalem as the center of the world.

By the time of Columbus, however, scholars had again started to believe the ancients on

Columbus expounding his plans to the Franciscan Monks of Granada. Monastery of La Rábida

this point. The French bishop, Pierre d'Ailly (1352–1420) had stressed this as early as 1410 in his work *Imago mundi* (World Picture). He also believed that land mass covered a greater portion of the earth's surface than water did, and that the largest areas of land were concentrated in the East. These reflections led to only one conclusion – that the ocean now called the Atlantic must also include a shore in the West (India). Columbus read this work as confirmation of his own theories, and sought further proof in other works of geography and astronomy.

Columbus paid special attention to writings by the Florentine doctor and humanist Paolo

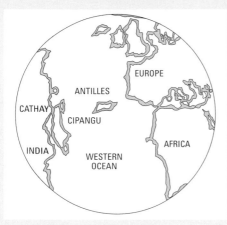

The Earth, as Columbus conceived it

Toscanelli (1397–1482), who had already spent a great deal of time reflecting on the nature of the earth's structure, and had worked out a western sea-route to India. Toscanelli's map strengthened Columbus's determination to carry out his plans. However, he also believed Toscanelli's erroneous cosmographic calculations as to how far apart Europe and Asia really were as land masses, and applied his own measurements which shortened the distance to a quarter of what it actually was: 4,000 km (2,400 miles) instead of 20,000 km (12,000 miles). Never has a great mistake led to an even greater discovery," proclaimed the German historian Leopold von Ranke in the 19th century.

A Long Time Waiting

Nevertheless, before Columbus could actually set foot on American soil several more years were to elapse. After Portugal rejected his plans as impractical, he sailed to Castile, and together with his son Diego disembarked at Palos de la Frontera in early 1485. In Juan Pérez, the prior of the Monastery of La Rábida, and the Franciscan, Antonio de Marchena, scholarly cosmograph and humanist, Columbus found allies for his plans. Their support helped Columbus gain an audience with the Spanish royal couple in 1486. They were favorably inclined toward the project, but at this period were entirely preoccupied with conquering Granada. Accordingly, it was decided to set up an expert commission of inquiry, whose verdict – after nearly five years' wait – proved negative. Seeing all his hopes dashed, Columbus reached the lowest point of his life. As he was about to leave the country in summer 1491, the Catholic kings summoned him to their fortified siege town near Granada. However, Columbus made such outrageous demands – among other things, he insisted that he and his heirs should be given the title of Viceroy of all the countries he discovered, a tenth of the treasures, as well as an eighth share in all trade transactions – that the royal couple found them unacceptable. A short time after Granada was captured, Columbus set off for home. However, a few miles beyond the town he was brought back by a royal messenger. The treasurer, Luis de Santángel, had reminded the Queen about the treasures that such an undertaking might bring in to fill their empty coffers, and convinced her to change her mind. Over and above that, the treasurer declared himself willing to meet a large part of the expenses. He also pointed out the religious advantages of this kind of venture – that it would be of enormous benefit to "God and the praise of His Church." Accordingly, on April 17, 1492, the contract was concluded, and on the third of August Columbus was able to disembark from the port of Palos with three caravels and ninety experienced seamen, including the Pinzón brothers.

The New World

The first part of the voyage took the crew to the Canary Islands, from where they disembarked on September 7 into the unexplored part of the Atlantic. Fearing that the crew might not cope psychologically with a long voyage into uncharted seas, from the very start Columbus falsified the log-book entries to make the distances covered seem smaller. After they had sailed the open sea for four weeks, the mood on board ship became more and more tense, and shouts for a return to base became ever louder. Then, on October 12, the redeeming shout of "Tierra, tierra" (Land, land) went up at long last. The ships laid anchor at a small island called Guanahani, which, in honor of the Redeemer, the crew renamed "San Salvador." In ceremonial dress, Columbus, now Viceroy of the Indian Land, strode on to the shore, where he unfurled the royal banner and officially took possession of the land in the name of the Spanish crown. The Spaniards stayed on the island for only a few days, for Columbus thought this was only one of some 7,000 islands in Marco Polo's account. Reports that in the South there was a land rich in gold persuaded them to disembark. After two weeks, the ships landed on the northern coast of Cuba, which, in honor of the Spanish King, they baptized "Fernandina." Here, neither gold nor spices were to be

Columbus's first Landfall. Copper engraving, colored by Theodore de Bry, taken from H. Benzano, Americae Retectio, 1596, Frankfurt

found, and the "Indians," as Columbus called the inhabitants of "India," kept pointing toward the East, where, they said, "gold, pearls and spices aplenty were to be found." Accordingly, he changed course and sailed East. In early December they reached an island which Columbus named "Hispaniola" (the future Haiti). The inhabitants owned a great deal of gold and reported to the crew that the gold came from Cibao in the east, which Columbus immediately identified with Marco Polo's Cipangu. However, while exploring the coastline, the flagship, the "Santa María," ran aground and had to be abandoned. Columbus built a small settlement, which he called "La Navidad," out of the wreck's planks, and promised to come back for the men the following year.

The Triumphant Homecoming

Bringing generous gifts of gold from the local population, Columbus began his voyage home on January 4, 1493. However the ships ran into a storm near the Azores, and this threatened to ruin the expedition shortly before its completion. In the end, "Nina" returned to Palos on March 15, 1493, seven and a half months after originally setting sail. Only a few hours later the second vessel, all sign of which had been lost since the Azores, sailed back into harbor. Ferdinand and Isabella received Columbus with every conceivable honor. He was granted the privilege of publicly sitting beside the King and Queen to tell of his adventures. He had brought a lot of gold coins and gold leaf with him, to give

Paolo Toscanelli, Planisphere, c. 1457, Florence, Biblioteca Nationale

them a small idea of the "wealth of these countries." "I am certain we would find colossal amounts of gold if your Majesty were to permit me to go back there." To those facing the impoverished finances of Spain, the wealth Columbus spoke of must have seemed like a gift from God, and they duly granted their permission.

The Last Years

Columbus was to undertake three more expeditions, not all of which were to yield the hoped-for amounts of gold.

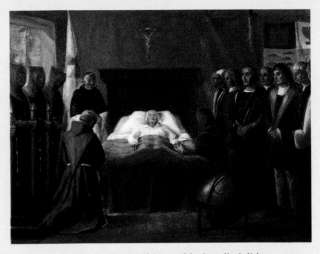

B. Rementeira, *Columbus on his Deathbed*. Valladolid, Museo Casa de Cristóbal Colón

Initially he discovered Puerto Rico and Jamaica. On his third voyage he reached Central America, without ever realizing the full significance of his discoveries. Columbus came back a sick, exhausted man from his unsuccessful fourth voyage (1502–1504), during which bad weather and storms sank all his ships off the coast of Jamaica. Not only had his most loyal friend, Queen Isabella, just died, but Portuguese and Spanish seafarers had also made important discoveries in the mean time, so that the pioneer of all great seafarers was soon forgotten. Columbus died a broken man in Villadolid in 1506. It was not until 400 years later that he found his final resting place in the Cathedral of Seville. The realization that Columbus had discovered a new continent was due to Balboa, one of the later Conquistadores. As it happened, the new continent was not named after Columbus but after his Italian countryman, Amerigo Vespucci, who, through his travel descriptions, had made Europeans familiar with the countries and people beyond the ocean.

The Province of Cádiz

The Province of Cádiz

Due to its unique geographical position, the Province of Cádiz began at a very early date to shape the history of the whole Pyrenean peninsula. Marking the boundary between the Atlantic and the Mediterranean, the triangle jutting sharply out into the sea forms the bridgehead to Africa, where Hercules is supposed to have set up his pillars – Mount Moussa on the African side and the Rock of Gibraltar on the

Seville, Palacio Español, Azulejos picture of the Province of Cádiz

European. This is where Plato speculatively placed the legendary island kingdom of Atlantis, which was perhaps also the lost kingdom of Tartessos at the mouth of the Río Guadalquivir. In about 1100 B.C., on a long spur of rock reaching out into the sea, the Phoenicians founded Gadir, Europe's oldest city, which is now Cádiz. Known as Gades under the Romans, it became the empire's

Rock of Gibraltar

premier trading port, from where silver, copper, wine, and wool were shipped to Rome. Gades held the monopoly on salt fish, and was famous for one particular export, the graceful *puellae Gaditanae* who were much sought after as dancers at Roman feasts. Centuries later, a new golden age was to dawn for the town when in 1717 it took over the monopoly on the overseas trade of the Spanish empire from Seville. Cádiz later made history as the birthplace of liberalism, for it was here that in 1812, during the Peninsular War, the first liberal constitution in Europe was proclaimed.

Tarifa saw the start of the invasion by the Moorish conquerors, who first crossed over to Spain's southernmost town – Tarif, the name of the Berber commander, – in 710. It was from Sanlúcar de Barrameda that

Columbus embarked on his third voyage of discovery in 1498, and that Magellan set out to circumnavigate the world. Since the Spanish Wars of Succession, there has been a small piece of England on Spanish soil, namely Gibraltar where in 1805 at Cape Trafalgar Lord Nelson won his great naval victory. Besides all these historic locations, the Province of Cádiz also offers attractive landscapes: the famous wine-growing region in the triangle between Jerez, Sanlúcar de Barrameda, and El Puerto de Santa María; the vast bull pastures from Medina Sidonia to Jimena de la Frontera; the natural park of Sierra de Grazalema with its rich vegetation; and the picturesque *pueblos blancos*, the white villages in the triangle formed by Cádiz, Tarifa, and Ronda, which contrast with the dark background of the mountain ranges.

Cádiz

Museo de Cádiz,
Plaza de Mina, p. 180

Oratorio de San Felipe Neri,
Calle de Santa Inés, p. 172

Alameda Marqués de Comillas

Calderón de la Barca

Plaza de Mina

Avda. de Carlos III

Enrique de las Marinas

San José

C. del

Plaza de San Antonio

Cervantes

Benjumeda

Avenida Doctor Gómez Ulla

Plaza Manuel de Falla

Sacra

Benito Pérez Galdós

Encarnación

Ro

Dr. Marañón

Moreno de Mora

C. de los Ca

Avenida Duque de Nájera

Playa de la Caleta

P. de Cer

Oratorio de la Santa Cueva,
Calle Rosario, p. 172

Puerto

Avenida del Puerto

in Francisco

Rosario

Plaza de
San Juan
de Dios

Plaza de
Candelaria

Plaza
de la
Catedral

Dacarrete

A. Acero

San Juan

adas

Campo del Sur

0   200 m

Puerta de Tierra,
Plaza de la Constitución, p. 170

Also worth seeing:

1   Iglesia del Carmen,
    Calle Alameda Apodaca

2   Iglesia de Santa Cruz
    (Catedral Vieja),
    Plaza de Santa Cruz

3   Teatro Manuel de Falla,
    Plaza de Manuel de Falla

4   Castillo de Santa Cata-
    lina, La Caleta

Catedral Nueva,
Plaza de la Catedral, p. 171

Puerta de Tierra

Since the town was completely destroyed in 1596 by troops led by the English Earl of Essex, few traces of ancient or medieval times remain in the present-day commercial city, seaport, and provincial capital. Its present character is shaped by buildings of the 17th and 18th centuries, when a new

period of prosperity began for Cádiz. The prosperity was a result of the discovery of the New World and the transfer of the Casa de la Contratación from Seville to Cádiz. Behind the Plaza de la Constitución, the Puerta de Tierra gives access to the oldest part of Cádiz. It is one of three surviving gates that formed part of the 16th and 17th-century fortifications. The marble tower above the gateway is pierced by firing-slits and has round turrets at the top corners. Its outstanding feature is the beautiful marble portal, designed in 1755 by Torcuato Cayón. The actual gateway, framed by columns, is dominated by the monumental Castilian coat-of-arms flanked by two lions. Tall columns on either side of the main facade support the city's two patron saints, St. Servandus and St. Germanus.

Catedral Nueva

This was the last of the great Andalusian cathedrals to be built, and the gleaming dome, covered with golden-yellow azulejos, is visible from afar above the roofs of the old town. Close to the old cathedral, which is now the Parish Church of Santa Cruz, the new building was begun in 1722 to designs by Vicente Acero, but lack of funds delayed its completion until 1853. This explains the mixture of Baroque and neoclassical elements, which is most apparent in the curving west facade and its two flanking towers. In the interior, monumental pillars with engaged Corinthian columns divide up the space with its nave, two side aisles and transept, side chapels between the buttresses, and ambulatory. The mahogany choir stalls in the nave, which are the work of Agustín de Perea (1697), come from the Cartuja de las Cuevas in Seville. The crypt, which is famous for its extraordinary acoustics, contains the grave of the composer Manuel de Falla, a native of Cádiz, who died in Argentina in 1946 while working on his last composition, *L'Atlántida*. The museum adjacent to the eastern end of the cathedral is worth visiting chiefly for its opulent monstrances – including the 17th-century Custodia del Millón by Antonio Suárez, which stands more than 13 feet (4 meters) tall, – and its collection of paintings.

Oratorio de San Felipe Neri

A visit to this church, built in 1679-1719 according an oval plan, is interesting particularly for historical reasons. In 1810, during the Peninsular War, the central government fleeing before the French invasion had settled at Cádiz, where it resolved to summon the *Cortes*, the medieval assembly of the estates. The Cortes met in the Oratorio in 1811/12, and on March 11, 1812 passed the first liberal constitution in Europe, though this was finally repealed by Ferdinand VII in 1823. In addition to the memorial plaque on the western side of the church, the monument (1911) on the Plaza de España commemorates the event. Inside the church one discovers, above the altar, an *Immaculada* (Immaculate Conception) by Murillo, one of his many treatments of the subject of the Virgin Mary. Right next to the church is the entrance to the Museo Municipal, which has exhibits relating to the events of 1812 and other aspects of the city's history. Of special interest is a model of Cádiz built between 1777 and 1779, which also shows the original design for the cathedral.

Oratorio de la Santa Cueva

Alongside the small Iglesia del Rosario is the Oratory, which consists of a simple chapel below ground and a small church above, built in the shape of an ellipse. It was erected in the 18th

century by Torcuato Benjumeda to plans drawn by Torcuato Cayón. Besides the jasper columns supporting the oval dome, the five frescoes in the lunettes of the dome are worthy special attention. Three of them are by Francisco de Goya, one of Spain's most famous painters, and were executed in the years 1796/97. They are held to be among the best religious paintings by the artist, who rarely worked in this genre.

In the *Last Supper*, which shows close similarities to a drawing by Poussin, he departed from traditional iconography by showing the figures reclining. This is most likely how they did in fact eat the Jewish Passover meal. The other two paintings,

the *Miracle of the Loaves and Fishes* and the *Parable of the Guest without a Wedding Garment*, are each dominated by a central group in the foreground, surrounded by a crowd of people. The latter painting represents a parable from the Gospel of St. Matthew, in which the guest without a wedding garment is bound at the hands and feet and "cast into outer darkness." The brilliance of the painting is especially striking in the figure of the king, who according to the Scripture symbolizes the kingdom of heaven.

The Knight of the Sad Countenance

Who is not familiar with that ill-assorted pair, the gaunt Don Quixote and his corpulent squire Sancho Panza, who on their three expeditions are put to the test in countless adventures? When the first part of *Don Quixote* appeared in January 1605, the reception was extraordinary: the novel was a huge success, the characters were on everyone's lips, and by the end of the year the book had gone through seven more editions. The author, Miguel de Cervantes Saavedra (1547-1616), was 57 at the time and had not published a book for almost 20 years. He had led a checkered life: after fighting as a soldier against the Turks and being seriously wounded in the naval battle of Lepanto, he had spent five years as a captive at Algiers and had finally been employed in the provisioning of the Armada and as a tax-collector. An accusation of impropriety in the handling of tax monies landed him in prison in Seville. It was here that he began the novel that was to place him among Spain's greatest writers – *The Ingenious Gentleman Don Quixote de La Mancha*.

Juan de Jauregui y Aguilar,
Portrait of the Writer Miguel de Cervantes, 1600,
Madrid, Royal Academy of Languages

Don Quixote

The plan of the book is as simple as it is well-known: "In a village in La Mancha, the name of which I do not choose to recall" lives the impoverished nobleman Alonso Quijano, his mind filled with dreams of chivalry which are nurtured by his reading of chivalric romances of his day. He finally loses his wits as a result, and comes to believe that he himself must set out as a knight errant, as a protector of the poor, of widows, and orphans, and for the glory of God and for his own lady. Equipped with a barber's bowl as a helmet and a broken-down old nag to which he gives the sonorous name of Rocinante ("formerly a hack"), he sets out on his first expedition. He calls himself Don Quixote, and as his lady to be worshipped from afar he chooses a peasant girl named Dulcinea del Toboso, whom he enthrones as mistress of his heart. In an inn which he believes to be a castle he persuades the innkeeper to dub him a knight. In the days that follow he engages several times in "knightly" combat until, having received a beating from a muleteer, he is brought home, injured. In order to free him from his delusion, his niece and housekeeper burn most of his books and brick up the entrance to his library. The hero, true to the fantasies of his chivalric tales, believes this to be the work of a malevolent magician. Two weeks later he sets out afresh with the peasant Sancho Panza. He has persuaded this good-hearted but simple fellow to become his squire, promising him a post as a governor of an island. More adventures follow, such as the combat with the windmills, which he believes to be unfriendly giants, and the putting to flight a nocturnal funeral procession, after which he acquires the nickname of "Knight of the Sad Countenance." Finally he is brought back to his village imprisoned in a cage. In 1614, while Cervantes was working on the second part of his novel, a spurious sequel written by Alonso Fernández de Avellaneda was published. Avellaneda's criticisms caused the author to make major changes to his own second volume. When the two protagonists set out for the third time, the thought of Dulcinea becomes a prominent motif, as Don Quixote wishes to obtain her blessing. Sancho extricates himself from an awkward situation by telling his master that a peasant girl who happens to come along is his lady-love, who has been altered by a spell. Eventually they arrive at the court of a duke and duchess, and here Sancho's wish for a governorship is granted. Continuing on their way, the two heroes then meet, amongst other people, characters from Avellaneda's novel, and have a legal document drawn up confirming that they themselves have nothing in common with those figures. Having returned home, Don Quixote dies peacefully, freed from his delusion and surrounded by the members of his own household.

Miguel de Cervantes, Title Page of the First Edition, Madrid (Juan de la Cuesta), 1605

In the second volume by Cervantes (the legitimate sequel) the characters have changed. Don Quixote is no longer merely the madman led astray by his delusions, but is fooled by others who deliberately deceive him. He has lucid moments in which his thoughtful comments show acuity and knowledge of a vast range of subjects. The figure of Sancho Panza, too, has grown in stature. Where before he was only the foil to the hero, a simple, practical man acting with animal cunning, he develops in the course of the story from a mere servant into a squire, a confidant, and trusted friend. He takes part in discussions, puts forward suggestions, and even, in his role as governor, makes wise judgments.

Don Quixote – A Parody and Much More

Cervantes' underlying purpose in all this is to make fun of the most popular type of fiction of his day, the chivalric romances: "I had no other wish than to make people view with disgust the lying and nonsensical stories in the romances of chivalry." But what were these chivalric romances? They formed a literary genre which had developed in the Middle Ages from the Carolingian and Breton legends and represented a continuation of the medieval heroic epic. Heroic deeds, adventures, love stories, magic and enchantment were immoderately exaggerated. One of the most famous romances, *Amadis de Gaula* (1508), had set the standard. Much loved by the populace, the chivalric romances also attracted harsh criticism, since moralists, humanists, and theologians saw them as a waste of time. Again and again Cervantes presents his hero as an avid reader of chivalric romances, and their effect on him is shown to be ridiculous: "Finally, when he had lost the last vestige of his reason, he hit upon the strangest idea that any madman in the whole world has ever conceived: it seemed to him proper and necessary, in order both to enhance his honor and to serve the community, that he should become a knight errant."

However, Cervantes' novel is more than just a parody the romance of chivalry, it is a multilayered epic novel in which the different strands are skillfully woven together. The adventures presented in the style of the chivalric romances are complemented by a critique of the literary fashions of Cervantés time. Thus the autor introduces the theme of love, which was already a major factor in the chivalric romance, or inserts discussions on literary topics. When, for instance, his housekeeper and his niece are about to burn Don Quixote's books, the priest is introduce onto the scene as a connoisseur and writer. With sure judgment he gives a critical appraisal of each individual work and saves novels like the famous *Amadis de Gaula* or the *Palmerines* from being consigned to the flames. At the end of the first book the Bishop of Toledo gives another disquisition on the positive and negative points of the books of chivalry and expresses his views on contemporary theater – a golden opportunity for Cervantes to direct some broadsides at his rival, Lope de Vega. Also included in these discussions on art is pastoral poetry, which Cervantes views with more favor than he does the chivalric romance. Even his

Honoré Daumier, Don Quixote and Sancho Panza, c. 1866. Oil on canvas, 78 x 120 cm, Berlin, Staatliche Museen Preussischer Kulturbesitz, Nationalgalerie

own pastoral novel – his first literary work, *La Galatea*, written in 1585 – is not spared criticism. In order to demonstrate his conception of the art of the novella, the author inserts twelve novellas in between the two volumes of *Don Quixote*, which several of his critics objected to. In the second part of *Don Quixote* takes the opportunity of replying to this criticism. Altogether the literary discussions take up considerably more space in the second volume. Thus Cervantes' polemic against the impostor Avellaneda starts actually in the prologue, and in addition he includes the writing of his own work in the action of the book, and thereby allows his characters to talk about the art of commentary, the problems of translation, and literary critics: "Men who are famous for their intellectual gifts, the great poets, the celebrated

177

Miguel de Cervantes, Don Quixote: "(...) urging Rocinante to a gallop, he charged at the nearest windmill and thrust his lance into it (....)"

Miguel de Cervantes, "Don Quixote on Horseback on the Seashore, awaiting the Dawn," both woodcuts after drawings by Gustave Doré, 1863

historians, are almost always envied by those who take a personal pleasure in judging the books of others without having produced any themselves .... The risk taken by anyone who publishes a book is very great, for it is utterly and absolutely impossible to write it in such a way that it pleases and satisfies all who read it."

Don Quixote – A Mirror of the Age

What is particularly fascinating about *Don Quixote* is its setting: While the adventures and love stories of the heroes in the romances of chivalry take place in the Middle Ages, Cervantes' story is set in contemporary Spain, around 1600, when after a century of unprecedented power and splendor the brilliance of the Spanish empire was in decline. England and France were elbowing Spain out of its prominent political role, and the gold and silver from the New World were pushing up inflation and upsetting the economic order. The expulsion of the Moriscos greatly weakened the manual trades and agriculture, and to this were added the effects of epidemics and failed harvests. In Cervantes' novel the reader becomes acquainted with this country and its people. He draws portraits of servant girls, peasants, priests, soldiers, court officials, and aristocrats in such a way that, as Ortega y Gasset said, "they leap out at us." He includes well-observed genre pictures, for instance when Don Quixote encounters traveling actors and puppeteers, or finds himself at a rustic wedding. But political matters are also reflected. When, at the end of the first book, Sancho Panza and the goatherd emphasize that they are of pure Christian blood, this is an allusion to the principle of *limpieza de sangre* (purity of blood) and the issue of the conversos. In addition one frequently comes across autobiographical elements. Thus the narrative of the ransomed slave of the Moors tells of a nobleman who is captured by Moors but is able, thanks to a wealthy and influential Christian woman, to buy his freedom and return to Spain. This nobleman had fought as an ensign at the naval battle of Lepanto and had received the firm promise that he would be promoted to captain, but his military career was interrupted and ruined by his long captivity. Who could fail to link this with Cervantes' own hopes of a military career, which were brought to naught by the severe wounds he received at Lepanto and his long captivity at Algiers?

Cervantes' intention was to parody the romances of chivalry and signal the end of that genre, which centered upon an outdated conception of a mythical hero. In doing this, however, he also bequeathed to the modern age an "archive" of many of those same medieval ideas at a time when the books of chivalry from the Golden Age had been in part forgotten, in part lost.

Don Quixote's Battle with the Windmills. Colored lithograph after Alfred Comcanen, cover of the sheet music of the Don Quixote March, c. 1870. London

Museo de Cádiz

On the Plaza de Mina, in a former Franciscan monastery, is the Museo de Cádiz. The museum has an archeological department containing Phoenician and Roman finds, and Andalusia's most important collection after that of Seville.

Anthropomorphic Sacrophagi, Archeology Department

Outstanding among the exhibits in the archeological section are the two anthropomorphic marble sarcophagi from the Phoenician necropolis of Punta de Vaca near Cádiz. In the Egyptian manner, the lid corresponds to the form of the human body. The face is presented in considerable detail, while the chest and arms and the feet which protrude from under the tunic are only indicated in relief. The type of the male sarcophagus, which is dated to around 400 B.C., is familiar from Sidonian necropolises: the beard is curly, in the oriental fashion, the right arm hangs down while the left hand holds a kind of pomegranate in front of the chest. The female sarcophagus, which is about 70 years older and shows archaic traits, and which was discovered in the necropolis as recently as 1980, shows a phial in the woman's left hand. Both pieces were presumably executed by Greek artists working for the Phoenicians.

**Bartolomé Esteban Murillo,
The Mystical Betrothal of
St. Catherine, 1682.**
Oil on canvas, 440 x 315 cm

After Murillo had executed the pictures for the Hospital de la Caridad in Seville, he was summoned to Cádiz, to undertake the painting for the high altar of the Capuchin Church there. It was to be his last painting, for while engaged on the work he fell from the scaffolding on April 3, 1682 and was killed. His pupil Menesos Osorio completed the picture, in which, following the conversion of St. Catherine of Alexandria, the Infant Jesus places a betrothal ring on her finger. The balanced, pyramidal composition is broken by the diagonal shaft of heavenly light which emphasizes the main figures in the painting.

**Fracisco de Zurbarán,
John the Baptist, 1638/39**
Oil on canvas, 61 x 80.8 cm

In 1638/39 Zurbarán created a series of paintings for the Carthusian monastery at Jerez de la Frontera. It was split up in 1836 during the *desamortización*, the secularisation of monastic property, and the individual pictures up in different museums. Besides the paintings illustrated, Cádiz retained *The Apotheosis of St. Bruno* and the four panels depicting the Evangelists.

The painting of John the Baptist, the patron saint of the Carthusians, on whose birthday St. Bruno and his six companions founded the first Carthusian monastery in Grenoble, was on the left wing of the high altar. This saint, who prepared the way for Christ, was held in high honor by the Carthusians because of his ascetic way of life. Zurbarán showed this in a particularly expressive way, depicting John meditating in the wilderness. His left hand rests on the lamb (of God), "that taketh away the sins of the world."

**Francisco de Zurbarán,
St. Lawrence, 1638/39**
Oil on canvas, 61 x 80.8 cm

The companion piece to John the Baptist is the representation of St. Lawrence, who is one of the most venerated martyrs and also a Spanish national saint. Lawrence was roasted alive on a grid in A.D. 258 because he refused to relinquish the wealth of the church preserved by Pope Sixtus II to the Emperor Valerian but instead distributed it to the poor. The painting depicts Lawrence turning in prayer towards the crucified Christ – the sculpture at the center of the high altar. Symbols of his martyrdom are the gridiron and the red color of his vestments. Zurbarán conveys Lawrence's piety in masterly fashion, presenting the face in profile before a light background. Also impressive is the depiction of the richly ornamented dalmatic, a late Roman over-garment of Dalmatian wool, which with its warm tones of red and gold gives the viewer a sense of the heaviness of the material.

Bolonia

Starting in 1917, French archeologists excavated the ruins of the Roman town of Belo, about 7 miles (11 kilometers) west of Tarifa, near the small fishing village of Bolonia. The town, which was geometrically laid out, was founded in the middle of the first century A.D. under the Emperor Claudius (41–54). Portions of the town wall, which was about 13 feet (4 meters) high, are well preserved. Inside the ruins one can distinguish the dwelling-houses and the *macellum*, the colonnaded food market. Further to the east is the forum with the Capital temple complex dedicated to the triad of gods, Jupiter, Juno, and Minerva, as well as a temple to Isis and a theater. Most of the objects found there are now in Paris. Only a statue of the Emperor Trajan found its way into the Archeological Museum in Cádiz.

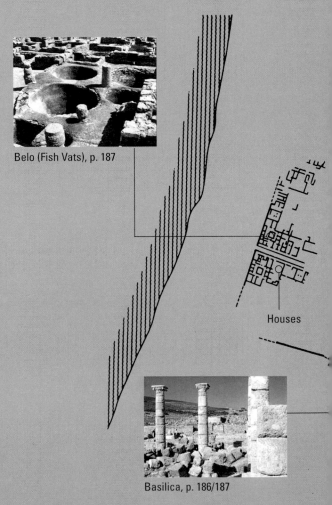

Belo (Fish Vats), p. 187

Houses

Basilica, p. 186/187

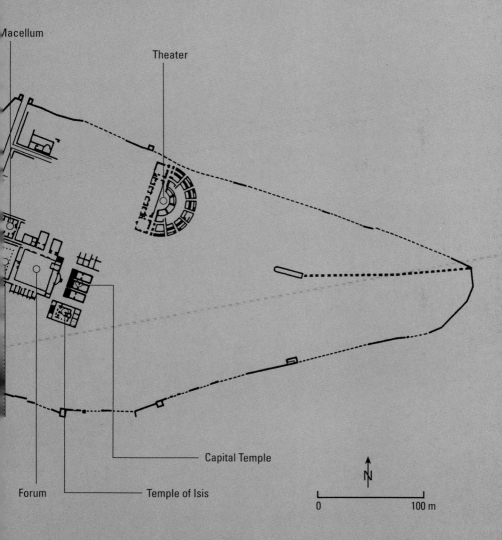

Macellum

Theater

Capital Temple

Forum

Temple of Isis

N

0   100 m

View of the Ruins
Fish Vats (Belo)

French archeologists have re-erected some of the ancient columns so that the visitor can form an impression of what the Roman settlement of Belonia Claudia used to look like.

The residential area, which reached right to the shore, probably also contained the industrial sites where fish were processed. Here a large number of square and round sunken basins have been found, which, as the remains of columns suggest, were originally under a roof. They contained 2000 year-old fish bones, some of them still preserved, which indicate the original function of the basins: they were used for salting the fish, probably in order to make *garum*, a fish sauce with which the Romans spiced their food. Fish was also a major export product of the Spanish and North African coasts.

Jerez de la Frontera

The largest town in the Province of Cádiz, Jerez de la Frontera, will mainly be associated in the visitor's mind with two things: sherry and horses. Everywhere in the town center there are *bodegas*, (wine cellars) with high, whitewashed walls. Because of their construction which is reminiscent of churches with multiple aisles, they are also called the cathedrals of wine. It was Jerez which gave its name to sherry: the English were apparently unable to pronounce the Spanish word "Jerez" and coined the softer version, "sherry." The town is also famous for horse-breeding. It is the home of the Real Escuela Andaluza del Arte Ecuestre (Royal Andalusian Riding School), and every year in May the Feria del Caballo (Horse Fair) takes place, when the best and finest-looking horses in Andalusia are put on show. Jerez enjoys great prosperity through its wine production, but its buildings, both sacral and secular, are a further attraction. The place is known to have existed from the earliest times, as the Phoenician Xera. It was at the nearby Río Guadalete that in 711 the decisive battle took place between the 90,000-strong Visigothic army of King Roderic and the 20,000 Arab invaders led by the legendary Tariq Ibn Ziad. In 1264 the Moorish city fell to Alfonso X. In the 14th century, like so many other places in the area, this border citadel of the kingdom of Granada acquired the nickname *de la Frontera*.

Alcázar

At one time Jerez was one of the main towns of Al-Andalus. An important reminder of the town's Moorish past is the Alcázar which stands on a hill to the southeast. This 12th-century Almohad fortress, which has been much restored over the centuries, is situated within the Arab defensive wall which once had 50 towers and four gates. Major parts of it – the Torre del Homenaje (Tower of Homage), the octagonal tower, the cisterns, and the Arab baths – survive from the original fortress.

The Gothic Capilla de Santa María la Real in the northeastern corner was built by Alfonso X in 1264 inside the former mosque. Despite the insertion of this Christian element, many parts of the older, brick-built Moorish place of worship have been preserved. Above the 108 foot-square (10 square meters) prayer-hall is an octagonal dome. The *mihrab* (prayer niche) is in the form of a deep square, with a dome which is repeated on a smaller scale at the corners of the *qibla wall* (the wall indicating the direction of Mecca within a mosque). On the northwestern side three horseshoe-shaped arches lead into an inner courtyard with a U-shaped walkway going around it. At the center of the courtyard is a pond, while a surviving minaret stands at the northeastern corner.

The Koran and the "Five Pillars" of Islam

The Clothing worn by Pilgrims, 19th century. Chalk lithograph, colored by J. Brandard

The revelations received by Mohammed are recorded in the holy book of Islam, the Koran (Arabic *qur'an*, "recitation"). To a Muslim, the Koran is the direct expression of the divine will, God's final word before the Day of Judgment. It became audible, through Mohammed, in the Arabic language, and for this reason the revelations are written in Arabic and may not be changed by anyone. According to Mohammed's belief, the divine revelations – like the Jewish Torah, the Psalms of David, and the Christian gospels – derive from a tablet preserved in Heaven. However, the revelations were not received by the Prophet all at once; they were revealed to him in the course of many visions during his life. Because of this, the Koran was not complete at the time of Mohammed's death in the year 632, but was compiled by his successors out of many separate pieces of text. After all the writing had been completed, copies were then made and taken to Medina, Mecca, Kufa, Basra, and Baghdad. Since then the most talented calligraphers of every century have taken pains to preserve the Word of God for posterity and to praise God through their artistry.

The Koran is divided into 114 *surahs* (chapters), which apart from the first one, *Al-fatiha* (Opening), are arranged according to length. This first chapter is the most frequently uttered Islamic prayer, and runs:

"Praise be to God, the Lord of the Universe, the Compassionate, the Merciful,
who has dominion over the Day of Judgment.
We serve you and pray to you for help.
Lead us by the straight path,

the way of those whom you have blessed, who do not incur your anger and do not go astray."

The surahs present the central concerns of Islam. They refer to the oneness of God and the duty of the believer to thank and to obey Him, they bear witness to the role played by God in history from creation to the end of the world and speak of the Judgement and of the life after death. Here the believer finds everything he needs in order to lead a life that is wellordered and pleasing to God. If the believer follows the right path, the path ordained by God, he will attain Paradise. If he turns away from it, then on the Day of Judgement he will receive the just punishment for his actions. Since the Koran accompanies the believer throughout his life, it is still the basis of a Muslim education. All pupils should learn as much as possible of the Koran by heart in Arabic, even if they have a different mother tongue. "For Muslims the Koran is not only the source of the texts of prayers, the means of prophesy, food for the spirit, the song of praise for the soul. It is also the basic law, the treasury of all branches of learning, the mirror of the ages. It is a comfort in the present, and man's hope for the future."

Overall view of the Grand Mosque with the Kabah, after an Arab faience wall in the palace of Kurshid Pasha in Cairo, 16th century

191

The Five Pillars of Islam

Islam, which regulates every aspect of the lives of its followers, imposes on the Muslim five religious duties, the so-called Five Pillars:

1. Profession of the Islamic faith (*shahada*): "There is no God but God, and Mohammed is the prophet of God."
2. Prescribed prayer: five times a day, when the muezzin gives the call to prayer from the minaret, the believer must turn his face towards Mecca and praise God.

Caravan en route to Mecca,
Baghdad, 1237. Arabic manuscript,
Paris, Bibliothèque Nationale

3. Giving alms: "Fulfill your duty of prayer and give alms!" (Koran, 58:13). Muslims are obliged to pay a precisely determined tax (*zakat*), which is used to support the poor and needy.
4. Fasting: during the ninth month of the Islamic year, Ramadan, adult Muslims must refrain from consuming food or drink and from smoking, and abstain from sexual intercourse, between daybreak and sunset. Through fasting, the spirit triumphs over the body and the will is strengthened by discipline, so that in this way the believer comes closer to God.
5. The pilgrimage to Mecca: every Muslim whose health and financial situation permit it must make the pilgrimage to Mecca at least once in his lifetime, in order to visit the holy shrine, the Kabah.

The Pilgrimage to Mecca

The high point in the life of any Muslim and the reward for his many years of striving for the right path is the pilgrimage to the holy city of Mecca – the Fifth Pillar of Islam. It takes place from the seventh to the 13th day of the last month of the Islamic year. Before arriving in Mecca, all the pilgrims put on white clothing to symbolize a departure from ordinary life and also the equality of all before God. They begin the pilgrimage by ceremoniously walking seven times around the Kabah, the foundation of which was laid, according to tradition, by Adam and which was restored by Abraham. Hundreds of prophets lie buried around the shrine. Then, in commemoration of the desperate search for water by Abraham's wife Hagar,

Pilgrims in front of the Kabah, c. 1860. Colored lithograph

the pilgrim covers the distance between two small hills, Safa and Marwah, seven times. On the third day the pilgrim sets out at dawn for the plain of Arafat and remains there praying until the evening, when he looks for 49 small stones for the next stage of the pilgrimage. This is the walk via Muzdalifah to Mina, where the stones that have been collected are thrown at three columns. These mark the place where Satan was stoned by Ishmael when he tempted him to no longer obey Abraham. On the return to Mecca, sacrificial animals are slaughtered in memory of Abraham's sacrifice when God commanded him to sacrifice his son, but then substituted a ram. Finally, the pilgrim shaves, puts his everyday clothes on again and walks around the Kabah seven more times. This concludes the pilgrimage, for which each year about two million Muslims from all over the world gather in Mecca.

Jerez de la Frontera

Colegiata de San Salvador,
Plaza de la Encarnación, p. 196

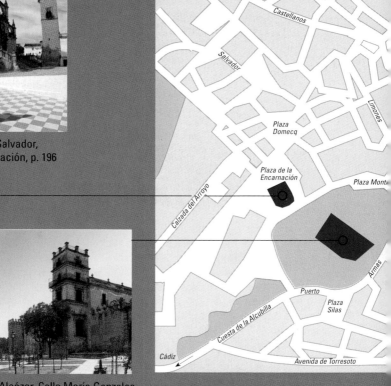

Alcázar, Calle María Gonzales,
p. 188

Casa del Cabildo Viejo,
Plaza de la Asunción, p. 197

Iglesia de San Miguel,
Plaza de San Miguel, p. 196

Also worth seeing:

1   Monasterio de Santo
    Domingo, Calle Bizcocheros

13th century on the foundations of the former mosque. A free-standing bell tower in the manner of an Italian campanile recalls the original minaret of the Moorish place of worship. The new building was begun in 1695 to designs by Diego Moreno Meléndez, and completed in late Baroque style by Torcuato Cayón de la Vega, the architect who succeeded Vicente Acero at Cádiz Cathedral. A flight of steps with balustrades leads to the west portal of the monastery church with its nave and four aisles. The main art treasures inside are the *Cristo de la Viga*, an early 17th-century crucifix, and the *Virgen Niña Dormida* (The Virgin as a sleeping child) by Zurbarán.

Colegiata de San Salvador

As one descends the steps of the Alcázar, one's eye falls on the massive dome of the monastery church, with its lantern pierced by round windows and tiled with blue-and-white azulejos. On this site, the most important sacral building in Jerez, there previously stood a church built in the

Iglesia de San Miguel

An interesting mixture of styles can be seen in the church of San Miguel, which has a nave and two aisles and was built in the Isabelline Gothic style between 1430 and the mid-16th century. This period is reflected in the beautiful south portal (1482). Diego Moreno Meléndez, the

School in the Golden Age. In the central section the *Battle of the Angels*, the *Transfiguration*, and the *Ascension* appear, while at the two sides there are depictions of the *Annunciation*, the *Birth of Christ*, and the *Adoration of the Three Kings*.

Casa del Cabildo Viejo

On the large square next to the Church of San Dionisio, built in honor of the patron saint of Jerez, is the old Town Hall. Andrés Ribera, Martín de Oliva, and Bartolomé Sánchez completed this building, probably the city's finest Renaissance palace, in 1575. It formerly housed the city library and the archeological museum. A balustrade links and unifies two very different buildings, a loggia in the Italian style and a plateresque portal facade articulated by Corinthian columns bearing statues of the heroes Hercules and Caesar.

architect of the monastery church, was responsible for the Baroque, three-storied facade of the tower with its grooved, angular, and embossed decoration (1672-1701). The top of the tower, graceful and covered with blue-and-white azulejos, rises above its surroundings and can be seen from afar. It is worth viewing the interior, not only because of the richly ornamented net vaulting but also for the retable in the Capilla Mayor, executed in the 17th century by Juan Martínez Montañés and José de Arce and considered to be among the finest Baroque works produced by the Seville

La Cartuja de Santa María de la Defensión

About three miles (5 kilometers) to the southeast of Jerez, on the road to Medina Sidonia, is the Carthusian monastery. The monastery was founded in 1463 by Alvaro Obertos de Valero y Morla, a nobleman of Genoese origin, and was once famous for its rich art treasures and its horse-breeding. The monastery church was also the nobleman's last resting place. Of the late Gothic buildings, the single-naved church with stellar vaulting above the apse, the refectory, and the two cloisters are still preserved.

The monumental doorway of 1571 was created by the architect Andrés de Ribera; a third cloister was added in 1620 by Juan Martínez Montañés. The high altar of the church, in the form of a triptych, which is regarded as one of the most beautiful creations of Spain's Golden Age, was completely dismantled in the 19th century in the course of the secularization of church property. As a result, the paintings from the series by Francisco Zurbarán ended up in various different museums, including Cádiz museum, but some of the sculptures by José de Arce remained in the Cartuja and can still be seen in the refectory.

The Facade of the Church

Entering the monastery precincts, one is first struck by the magnificent Baroque facade of the church, dating from 1667. Its structure is like a Baroque version of a Gothic retable: the eye-catching central feature is the large rose window, set in a square, in the middle section above the portal. The portal is flanked by niches, each framed by double columns, and containing statues of Carthusian monks. At the top, in a rounded niche, is the founder of the order, St. Bruno. This harmonious composition is complemented by finely-worked ornamentation and rich decoration with surmounting urns and pinnacles, which give the facade an appearance of great richness.

The Province of Málaga

The Province of Málaga

View of Málaga with the port and the bull ring

The Andalusian province which receives the largest number of visitors is probably Málaga. It owes this rather dubious distinction to the beaches of the Costa del Sol, which are shielded from wind and rain by the mountain ranges in the hinterland. The year-round mild climate makes it possible for a sub-tropical vegetation to grow, with plants such as palms, cypresses, agave and citrus trees . Already at the turn of the last century – but increasingly so since the 1950's – masses of tourists have been lured to Malaga's climate. As a result, the strip of coastline resembles a white concrete jungle expanding beyond the city's boundaries without needing geographical obstacles, and where only street signs indicate where one village ends and the next begins. When the visitor leaves the coast, he will discover the more attractive side of the province: the bizarre rock formations of El Torcal, the Dolmen graves near Anteguerra, the cave paintings of Cueva de la Pileta or the two small towns, both of art-historical interest, of Ronda and Antequera. The axial and pivotal point of this densely populated province is the capital, Málaga, the second largest city in the region after Seville, with an international airport and numerous places of interest reflecting its long history. From ancient times Malaca, as the original Phoenician foundation was called, was a port of major significance. In the late second century B.C. it fell under Roman rule, and as Malacitanum it became the most important port for trade with Northern Africa. After a brief Byzantine interlude (552-570), the Romans were finally ousted by the Visigoths in the second half of the sixth century. Under the Moors Málaga retained its importance as a trading center, but played only a subsidiary role in the caliphate. The town attained its highest prosperity when in 1237 it was incorporated into the Nasrid kingdom of Granada. Up to the Christian Reconquest in 1487 it was the chief port on the south coast of Spain and, hence, the

El Torcal de Antequera

most important link with Morocco. It was from here that all goods were conveyed along the coast to the Alhambra in Granada. Because of the trade with America the town also played a vital role in the Andalusian economy in the 16th and 17th centuries. After a recession in the 18th century, there was a renewed upturn in the early 19th century due to industrialization and to settlement by mercantile families from Castile and abroad. Today, too, Málaga is an important economic center in southern Spain.

"A las cinco de la tarde" – The Corrida Begins

Courtyard with Horses at the Plaza de Toros in Madrid just before a Bullfight, 1855. Casón del Buen Retiro

Long before the official opening of the corrida, the bullfight, the *aficionados* or devotees of the bullfight have taken their seats. Depending on their financial means, they are either sitting in the cheap seats in the sun on the side from which the bull bursts into the arena, or they have bought expensive seats on the shady side where the matadors fight. They have already seen the bulls being brought to the arena, and the toreros drawing lots for them, and then dressing and praying to the Mother of God or to some other protective saint. A mood of solemnity has descended on the scene. The corrida can commence. In addition to the corrida there is the *novillada*, in which bulls less than four or five years old are fought by beginners, *novilleros*, who are not yet entitled to bear the more prestigious title *matador de toros* (killer of bulls).

El Paseo
(The Procession)

The spectacle begins with the entry of the three matadors, each of whom will kill two bulls, accompanied their entourage consisting of two *banderilleros* and two *picadores*, the lancemen mounted on armored horses. All of them wear the *capa*, a cloak, the end of which is wound around the left arm. The procession of the *toreros*, as all the bullfighters are called, is led by two mounted constables in historical costume. They stop in the middle of the shady side in front of the box occupied by the president and his advisers. The president is in charge of the proceedings, oversees the length of the individual phases of the fight and will decide what honor is to be accorded to the matador. When he hangs a white handkerchief over the front of the box, the trumpeters give the signal to start the fight.

The Prelude

One matador and his banderilleros stay in the arena, the two others withdraw with their helpers into the *callejita*, the small alleyway behind the *barrera*, the wooden partition, in order to be able to go to the aid of the fighters, if necessary. Then the bull comes charging out of its dark box through the *toril*, the gateway in the middle of the sunny side, into the bright, noisy arena, where its life, which it has been able to spend in freedom for five years, will end in a mere twenty minutes. The matador retires behind the *burladero*, a gap in the partition, for it is one of the banderilleros who goes into action first. He has to arouse the bull's interest in the capa, which he holds in one hand and drags along behind him. While the bull follows the curving and zigzag movements of the capa, the matador watches closely since he is the first person to step out in front of the bull with the capa spread out, and so his life depends on his correct assessment of the animal and its individual personality. He performs a series of *verónicas* – passes which are so called because the matador holds the cape in front of his body just as the Spanish statues of St. Veronica hold the cloth bearing the image of the face of Christ. When the bull charges, the matador moves the cloth to one side, the bull thrusts its head into the cloth and the matador turns on his own axis. This prelude must not last longer than twenty minutes, if the matador does not want to risk his life, because by that time the bull will have realized that its horns are only making contact with the soft cloth and he will then start going directly for the matador.

Tercio de Vacas

Now a trumpet signal opens the first third of the fight. Accompanied by all three matadors, the picadors ride into the arena. It is their job to plunge the *pica* (lance) with its over one inch (three centimeter)-long steel point into a certain place on the bull's neck so that it lowers its head. This is necessary if, at the end of the fight, the matador is to make his deadly stab over the

Bullfight, chromolithograph, c. 1900

Francisco de Goya, Banderillas with Fireworks, 1815. Etching and aquatint, 24.5 x 35 cm

top of the bull's head. The picador must not attack, but rather he must wait until the three matadors, by means of the cape, lead the bull to him and – after a successful thrust of the lance – distract the bull, so that the furious animal does not lift him from the saddle. Such *quites* (distracting manuvers) can be the high points of a corrida, when the matadors vie with each other in the gracefulness and boldness of their movements.

Tercio de Banderillas

Now the second third begins. The two banderilleros run into the arena. It is their task to plunge the two banderillas – 26 inch (65 centimeters)-long wooden sticks with colored paper wound round them and with a steel barb – simultaneously into the back of the bull's neck. Usually they take turns and insert three pairs of banderillas. Their performance is dangerous, for so far the bull has only attacked the capa or the horse. But now for the first time a human body is exposed to its attack. For safety, therefore, two toreros with capas stay in the arena so that they can distract the animal from the banderilleros using their *guitar* (cape) if necessary. When the banderillero has succeeded in placing his banderillas, he must take advantage of the bull's moment of shock and move his own body out of the reach of the animal's horns.

However this procedure is not always successful: sometimes the bull refuses to respond and remains passive. Then there is a vehement reaction from the spectators, who cry out *Otro toro!*, demanding a different bull. An even the wors disgrace for a breeder occures when the president then raises his green handkerchief and oxen are let in to lead the bull from the arena. In that case this tercio, which has failed to heighten the excitement, has been won by the bull.

Francisco de Goya, The Manly Courage of the Famous Pajuleva in the Arena at Zaragoza, 1815. Etching and aquatint, 25 x 35 cm

Tercio de Muerte

Usually after being stabbed by the banderillas, the bull is roused to a state of extreme fury, so that the trumpets are able to signal the final third, the true climax of the fight. This phase belongs solely to the matador and the bull. The matador now no longer wears the capa but carries the *muleta*, a much smaller red cloth made of flannel or serge. With the help of a wooden sword he spreads this out and performs with the bull a series of artistic figures in which he can demonstrate his courage, his superiority, and his formally perfect demeanor. Whereas hitherto the toreros had reacted to the bull's attacks and were allowed, if danger threatened, to seek safety, now the matador must take the initiative. He must determine where the horns will thrust; the bull must now merely react. When the matador thinks that he has received enough applause from the spectators, and when the bull is exhausted, the *astocada*, the last and most dangerous phase of the fight, begins. The matador exchanges his wooden sword for the *estoque*, a steel sword, which he must sink powerfully up to its hilt into the neck of the bull, between the horns, in order to deliver the *coup de grâce*. There is only a single spot through which the sword will pierce the heart and lung, and he must hit it. This is the most dangerous moment of the fight, the "moment of truth" for the matador. If he misses the spot, he may lose the spectators' favor in a mere few moments. If, however, the thrust is fatal, he is certain of acclaim. The spectators break out into unending cries of *Olé*! and wave their handkerchiefs. The matador is urged to

Francisco de Goya, Pepe Romero Kills a Bull which is Standing Still, 1815.
Etching and aquatint, 24.5 x 35.5 cm

make a lap of honor around the arena, and while doing so, he is applauded and showered with flowers and gifts. The president pronounces his judgement. Depending on how elegant and masterly the conduct of the fight has been, the matador is granted one or both of the bull's ears and a piece of the tail, and on very rare occasions part of a hoof. This is the torero's reward for having risked his life.

But as Antonio Ordoñez, one of the 20th century's great matadors, said, "I have received thirty-one wounds, my body is covered in scars. But the horn-thrusts are to us toreros what punches are to boxers and falls to racing cyclists .... Of course I know fear. When the bull is facing you or charging towards you and touching you, you are always afraid. But the fear does not influence me. Dying .... *Hombre!* Dying is something you accept as natural."

Málaga

Iglesia del Sagrario, Calle Molina Larios, p. 221

Catedral Nuestra Señora de la Encarnación, Calle Molina Larios, p. 211

Also worth seeing:

1   Iglesia de Santiago, Calle de Granada

2   Teatro Romano, Calle Alcazabilla

3   Palacio Villacázar, Calle Cister

4   Palacio Episcopal (Museo Diocesano), Plaza Obispo

5   Iglesia de San Juan, Calle San Juan

6   Iglesia de Cristo de la Salud, Calle Compañía

7   Iglesia de los Mártires, Plaza de los Mártires

8   Casa Natal de Picasso, Plaza de la Merced

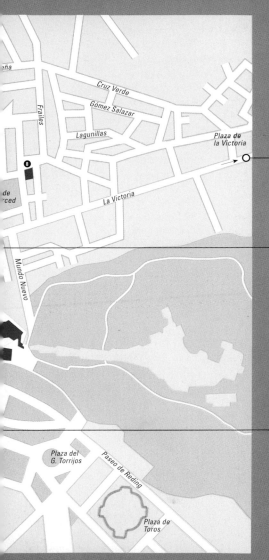

Cruz Verde

Gómez Salazar

Lagunillas

Plaza de
la Victoria

Fraíles

eña

La Victoria

8

de
rced

Mundo Nuevo

Plaza del
G. Torrijos

Paseo de Reding

Plaza de
Toros

Santuario de Nuestra
Señora de la Victoria,
Calle de la Victoria, p. 220

Palacio de los Condes de
Buenavista, Museo Provincial
de las Bellas Artes,
Calle San Augustín, p. 218

Alcazaba, Castillo de Gibralfaro,
Calle Alcazabilla, p. 210

Alcazaba
Castillo de Gibralfaro

The towering walls of the Alcazaba have a defiant and forbidding aspect. Together with the Castillo de Gibralfaro, which stands on the highest point of the same hill, they once formed the mightiest fortification system in Islamic Spain. Ascending the path to the Moorish fortress, the visitor sees just below it the semicircular rows of seats of a Roman theater; many recognizable pieces of this theater were incorporated into the fortress. This fortress was built

in the 11th century by a Berber king on top of the remains of an older Arab fortress, and was extended under the Nasrids as a fortified royal city in the style of the Alhambra. A triple ring of walls protects the complex; snake-like paths wound their

way up to it from the town. The Puerta de las Columnas leads into the area between the first two walls, and the Arco del Cristo into the first part of the fortress with the Plaza de Armas (drill ground). This was named after the artillery that was deployed here after the Reconquest of Málaga. Passing through the Arcos de Granada gateway (with an archeological museum in its upper rooms), one enters the second part, at the center of which are the Cuartos de Granada, the former palace rooms dating from the 13th and 14th centuries. To the east are the servants' quarters and a bathhouse. At the highest point on the eastern side one finds the Alcazaba's defensive tower, the square 14th-century Torre del Homenaje.

Above the Alcazaba, 427 feet (130 meters) above sea level and linked to it by walls, the Nasrid ruler Yusuf I built yet another fortress, which is now largely ruined, on the site of an earlier building dating from the 10th century. The name of this fortress derives from a Greek or Phoenician lighthouse (pharos) which originally stood here (*Gibralfaro*, the mountain with the lighthouse).

As a result of the rising ground on which it was built, the fortress is of a irregular shape. It was enclosed by two walls of varying height with buttressing towers and battlements, and had six fortified towers and four gates. Inside the fortress were living quarters and storage rooms, wells, cisterns, baths, as well as a mosque.

Catedral Nuestra Señora de la Encarnación

West facade

Towering above the houses in the old town of Málaga is one of the last great European cathedrals and one which presents a mixture of styles. Although the building work was begun in 1528, frequent interruptions prolonged the process until 1783. After the Reconquest of Málaga, the Christian rulers wanted to place an imposing building on the site of the old mosque. The plans were drawn up by Diego de Siloë, who was assisted by other distinguished architects (Enrique de Egas, Hernán Ruiz II, and Pedro López are named in the records) but they did not see eye to eye, and the group eventually disintegrated. Then, around the middle of the 16th century, Diego de Vergara took charge of the building operations, and as a result, the eastern section with the chancel was dedicated in 1588. The choir stalls, located in the nave, were completed in the following century (1592-1662). But it was not until 1719 that the cathedral chapter resolved to continue the building and commissioned José de Bada to build the nave, starting with the west facade. After his death in 1755, Antonio Ramos took over the supervision of the work. He is responsible for the relief representing the Annunciation above the center portal of the splendidly colored west facade, framed by the city's patron saints,

St. Cyriacus and St. Paul, above the two side portals. But the cathedral remained *La Manquita* (the one-armed woman), since lack of money led to a final cessation of work in 1783. The southern tower of the facade was never completed.

Catedral Nuestra Señora de la Encarnación

Because of the centuries of conflict associated with the Reconquest, the first great cathedrals in Andalusia were built at a time when in central Europe the era of monumental Gothic buildings was already drawing to a close. But the ground-plan of Málaga cathedral still follows the basilica design similar to the churches built for the French kings. This design, which had been used five centuries earlier in Granada, was adopted again here, but on a reduced scale. Between the main body of the church consisting of a nave, two aisles, and side chapels, as well as a choir which ends in a polygonal apse with an ambulatory and chapels, a transept has been inserted which does not project beyond the outer walls of the nave.

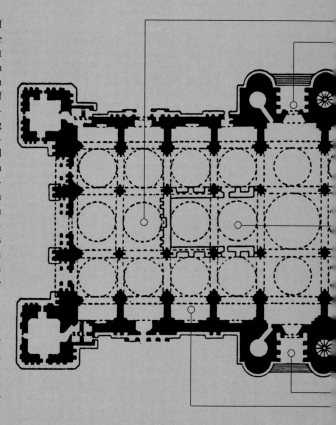

ta de las Cadenas

Sacristía Mayor

Interior view, p. 214

Capilla Mayor

Coro, p. 216

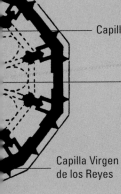

Capilla Virgen
de los Reyes

uerta del Sol

Capilla de la Virgen Rosario, p. 216

Interior view

The monumental interior makes a powerful impression through its vast size – it is 384 feet (117 meters) in length and 236 feet (72 meters) in width – and the tremendous height, 157.5 feet (48 meters), of both the nave and the aisles. Despite the Gothic groundplan, the interior is not dominated, like the French buildings of the High Gothic, by steeply soaring pointed arches, nor is it sparsely lit by stained-glass windows. Instead, early Renaissance features appear, for instance the classical orders of columns, and the whole interior is flooded with daylight. Since the later builders continued to adhere to the Renaissance style, the interior of the cathedral has a unified appearance. Thus in the nave, which was built relatively late, Corinthian clustered piers support the ceiling domes, which are richly ornamented with floral and figured motifs. The dominant motif articulating the walls is that of the continually repeated round-arched triple window surmounted by a further, smaller round-arched open-ing in between two bull's eye windows. The wealth of architectural details is complemented by an abundance of paintings and sculptures. Works of historical interest include, in the Capilla de la Virgen de los Reyes, a 15th-century statue of the Virgin Mary which the Catholic Monarchs are said to have carried around with them during the Reconquest.

Capilla de la Virgen Rosario

Among the 15 chapels, the Capilla de la Virgen Rosario in the south aisle (third chapel from the west) is of special interest. It contains a painting by Alonso Cano (1601–1667), the teacher of Pedro de Menas, a depiction of the Virgin of the Rosary inspired by Venetian models. It is not known who commissioned the painting.

Choir Stalls

The most exquisite feature of the cathedral decoration is the choir stalls, executed in the 17th century in cedar, larch, and walnut and situated in the choir beneath the organ loft. Above the two rows of seats, ornamented with richly-carved reliefs, are over three-foot (one meter)-tall figures of saints on the walls behind them, surmounted by a cornice with busts of saints. Several artists contributed to this work. The designs were by Luis Ortiz de Vargas, who had previously worked in Lima cathedral (Peru) and in Seville, and had won the competition held by the cathedral chapter in 1632. To him are attributed, among other things, the representation of the Virgin carved on the episcopal throne, which is on the end directly opposite the entrance, and the apostles Peter and Paul on the seats on either side of it. Working alongside him was José Micael Alfaro, who carved the other ten apostle figures, the small busts of saints on the cornice and decorative reliefs. It was not until nine years after Alfaro's death that the sculptor Pedro de Mena of Granada was commissioned to complete the work. Between then and 1662, he executed 42 choir stalls bearing representations of saints, of which St. Luke and St. John, who carries a sick man on his back, are considered to be among the finest. They reveal the virtuosity and the religious feeling of the artist, who concentrated all the expressiveness of his figures in their hands and faces.

as two juvenile works by Picasso. The house where he was born is located in Málaga (Plaza de la Merced). The museum also contains a library on Pablo Picasso; the first works for it were donated by his friend Jaime Sabartés.

Picasso, Man with Blanket, 1895
Watercolor on paper, 10 x 14 cm
Picasso, The Old Couple, 1894
Oil on wood, 35 x 19 cm

Palacio de los Condes de Buenavista, Museo Provincial de las Bellas Artes

This palace, built around 1520 in the Mudéjar style, today houses the Museum of Fine Arts, which holds as major paintings by Spanish and foreign artists as well

These two paintings – of only secondary rank within the artist's oeuvre – are among the early works of Pablo Picasso (1881-1973). He dedicated them to his first teacher, Antonio Muñoz Degrain (1841-1924). Degrain taught Picasso as a child, until 1891 when Picasso had to move with his family from Málaga to La Coruña. Picasso's father was a teacher of drawing at the School of Arts and Crafts, and curator of the Municipal Museum. Because his salary was inadequate to support his large family, he also sold paintings of his own. These depicted partridges, rabbits, and especially doves, which were extremely popular at the time, so that he became well known in Málaga as *El Palomero*, the painter of doves. His son Pablo, who learned to handle a pencil and paintbrush at an early age, was charged with finishing the painting of the feathers. He later claimed that as a child he had been able to draw like Raphael, but that it had taken him his whole life to learn to draw in a childlike way.

There is no other artist whose early life is so well documented, and almost none whose artistic development can be traced so accurately. For this reason Picasso's early pictures, which are outstanding for both their richness and their quality, are highly significant. These two pictures are, after all, the work of a boy only 13 or 14 years of age. They already show his interest in the human figure and in giving psychological expression to the faces.

Santuario de Nuestra Señora de la Victoria

During the siege, the Moors had defended the city so vigorously that they had almost forced the Catholic Monarchs to retreat. To give thanks for their victory, Isabella and Ferdinand had a small chapel built in 1487 on the spot where their tents had been pitched, in honor of the Virgin of the Victory. They are supposed to have had with them, at the time of the conquest of Málaga, the statue of the Virgin previously given to them by the Emperor Maximilian I. A few years later the monks of the Minim order obtained permission to make this the site of their order's first monastery in Spain. Their church, with its nave and two aisles, built on the plan of a Latin cross, was consecrated in 1518. In the late 17th century the building was remodeled in the Baroque style at the expense of the Count of Buenavista,

who had his own tomb built in the crypt. The crypt is part of the Camarín Tower at the eastern end, which merits particular attention. A spiral staircase leads from the crypt via the sacristy to the Camarín, an octagonal central room behind the high altar. Its walls are covered with luxuriant late-Baroque ornamentation in white stucco. This decoration is attributed to Francisco Hurtado Izquierdo, whose work gave the impetus for the founding of a school for stucco artists. It is in this room that the Virgen de la Victoria is displayed on a stucco pedestal, and the clothes and jewelry with which the statue is adorned according to the solemnity of the occasion are also kept here. On the altar is a Mater Dolorosa by Pedro de Mena.

Iglesia del Sagrario

Next to the Cathedral is a richly ornamented Gothic recessed portal, the Portada Gótica. It was built in 1498 by the first bishop of Málaga as the main entrance to the mosque which at that time served as a Christian church. Today it forms the entrance to the small parish church, with only a nave and no side aisles, which was completely remodeled early in the 18th century. In the niches between the pillars, under canopies of tracery crowned with pinnacles, one sees statues of Mary and the angel of the Annunciation, the Evangelists, as well as the Church Fathers. Above the

portal is Christ enthroned, with the coat-of-arms of the first bishop, César Rosario, on each side. The upper register shows, on the left, a praying cardinal believed to be Fray Hernando de Talavera, Isabella's father confessor, with an angel, and o the right Cardinal Pedro de Mendoza accompanied by a cleric.

Antequera

The small country town of Antequera lies on the fertile plain of the Río Guadalhorce at the foot of the Sierra El Torcal. This range of mountains, with an average height of 3281 feet (1,000 meters), is like a gigantic "stone museum," because the porous limestone has been shaped by sun, wind, and water into bizarre and fantastic formations, some of which have been given names like "Lizard" or "She-wolf." Settlement in this area goes back to the Neolithic Period, as is evidenced by a large number of megalithic monuments in the area around Antequera, such as the Cueva de Menga, the Cueva de Viera, or the Cueva del Romeral. Antequera was fortified by the Romans, who called it Anticaria. They were succeeded by the Moors, who built a massive and conspicuous Alcazaba on the hill of Antaqira. Today the only remains are two towers and a section of wall linking them. After Ferdinand, at the time still Infante of Castile, had reconquered the town in 1410 (earning him the nickname *El de Antequera*), it became an important base for the Reconquest. In the following centuries Antequera experienced a rapid rise in prosperity, developing between the 16th and 18th centuries into a major center of trade. Many of its monasteries, churches, and palaces date from that period, when powerful aristocratic families and religious orders settled here.

Antequera

Iglesia de San Sebastián,
Plaza de San Sebastián, p. 227

Also worth seeing:

1   Convento de la Encarnación,
    Calle Obispo Muñoz Herrera

2   Iglesia Nuestra Señora del
    Carmen, Plaza del Carmen

3   Arco de los Gigantes,
    Santa María Mayor

4   Alcazaba, Plaza Santa María

5   Iglesia San Juan, Plaza Santa
    María

6   Iglesia Santa María de Jesús,
    Plaza del Portichuelo

7   Palacio de la Marquesa de las
    Escalonias, Calle Rodrigo de
    Narváez

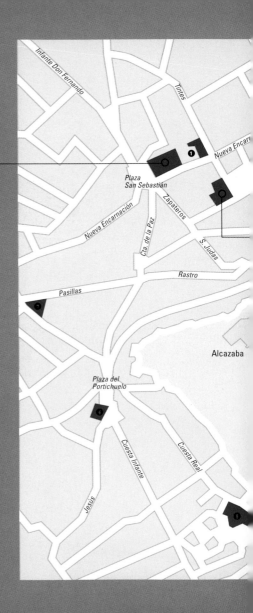

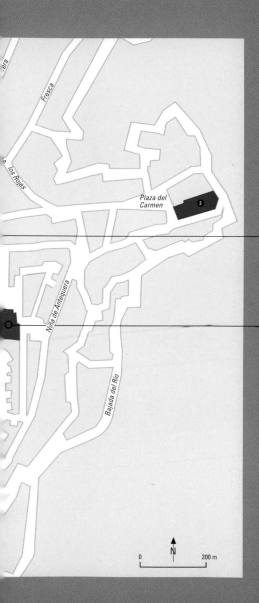

Plaza del
Carmen

2

Museo Municipal,
Plaza del Coto Viejo, p. 228

Real Colegiata de Santa María
Mayor, Plaza de Santa María,
p. 226

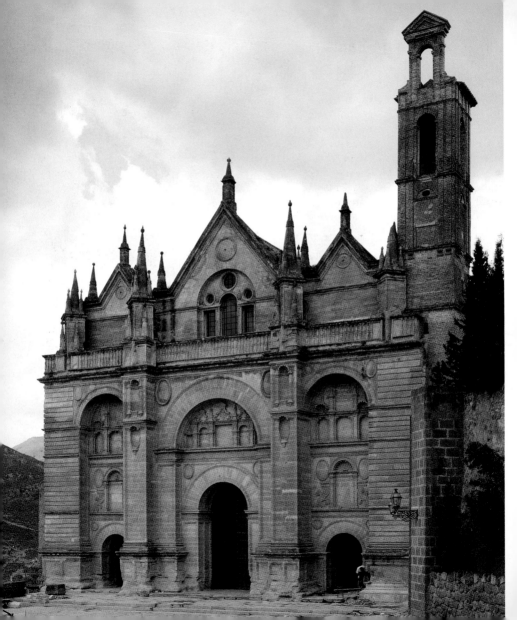

Real Colegiata de Santa María Mayor

As one climbs the hill that is dominated by the remains of the Alcazaba, one must first pass through the Arco de los Gigantes, a gateway built to replace an earlier Moorish one in 1585. Roman finds from the surrounding area, formerly embedded in the walls of the gateway, are now in the Museo Municipal. Opposite the square beyond the gateway is the monastery church. Its plateresque facade, (built between 1515 and 1550), is one of the most outstanding Renaissance facades in Andalusia. The groundplan with its nave and two aisles, is reflected externally in the design of the façade, which is divided into three by buttresses. At the upper level, round arches form niches containing blind arcades. The facade is crowned by a triple pediment surmounted by tall, triangular pointed turrets. The interior of the basilica, articulated by Ionic columns, has a superb Mudéjar artesonado ceiling. The building is renowned for its acoustics, which are especially favourable to soprano singers.

Iglesia de San Sebastián

Among the town's many church towers the most prominent is the Baroque-Mudéjar tower of the Iglesia de San Sebastián (1699-1706, pyramidal roof 1928). Diego de Vergara began to build the church, which has a nave and two aisles, in 1540. The plateresque portal, whith its statues of apostles in the niches and allegories of night and dawn on its upper part, bears the coat-of-arms of Emperor Charles V.

Museo Municipal

The Ephebe of Antequera

On the Plaza del Costo Viejo, opposite the Convento de la Encarnación, is the Palacio de Nájera. This 18th-century palace houses the municipal museum, which contains many art treasures but is especially proud of the paintings of the local artist Cristóbal Toral (b. 1940).

However, one of the museum's outstanding items, which is known far beyond the town itself, is the five-foot-(1.54 meter)tall statue of a naked youth which was found in the 1960s at Las Piletas. It is known as the Ephebe of Antequera. In ancient Greece, Ephebes were young men ranging in age from 18 to 20 who where equired to undergo a two-year course of military training in order to become full citizens. Some of the benefits of this training, which was wholly financed and organized by the state, were the supervision of their conduct, the strengthening of their religious beliefs, and the further development

of their physical prowess. The training of the Ephebes also encompassed philosophy, rhetoric, literature, and politics, in order to turn the young men into responsible citizens and good soldiers.

They were depicted in art as young athletes wearing the victor's fillet in their hair. A Greek statue of an ephebe must have been the model for the bronze figure in Antequera, which dates only from the first century A.D. and had a purely decorative function. Probably – just like a similar example at Pompeii – it once adorned the dining-room of a Roman villa and served as a lamp-holder. The lamps were placed on the garland which the ephebe originally held in his hands. Instead of the victor's fillet, he has an ivy wreath in his hair, which adds a Dionysian touch. This may have had a particular relevance to his original location.

Pedro de Mena, St. Francis

A room on the upper floor with a superb artesonado ceiling contains one of the most important works in the museum, the wooden carving of St. Francis by Pedro de Mena y Medrano, who lived in Málaga from 1658 onwards. It is a slightly built figure immersed in contemplation. The rapt facial expression of the saint conveys much of the profound emotionality which is a distinctive feature of this artist's work.

The New Tolerance

Once the Berber leader Tariq had crossed to Gibraltar for the first time in 711, it was to be only three years before the greater part of Spain would be under Islamic rule. The parlous state of the Visigothic kingdom, riddled with intrigue and internally fragmented, contributed to the incredibly rapid success of the nomadic conquerors. They could never have gained a foothold so quickly however, if they had not received massive support from the population. Hardly anyone was prepared to fight for the Visigothic rulers; on the contrary, people seemed to welcome the Muslim invaders. This was because the large majority of the indigenous population was being oppressed by a minority, the Visigothic nobility. The Jews, for their part, suffered under the pressure of the Church, the channel through which the Visigoths exerted their power. Both groups helped the Berbers in their conquest of the peninsula. And, unlike the Visigoths, the Berbers sought to live in harmony with the various population groups and showed a high degree of tolerance. Both Christians and Jews were allowed, once they had submitted to Islamic rule, to practice their own religions, retaining their churches and synagogues. In addition the basic tax that was compulsory for all, they had to pay a poll tax which exempted them from military service. The communities had their own courts of law, and their leaders represented them vis-à-vis the Muslim government. This tolerance, unique in the Christian West at that time, created a society in which Muslims (Christians who had converted to Islam), Mozarabs (Christians who had retained their faith but had adopted Islamic ways and customs), and Jews lived peacefully together. Muslims who had come to the country without wives were permitted to marry Christian women and establish families with the daughters of those they had defeated; both, Jews and Christians were given a role in government. The conquerors themselves were an ethnically mixed group, consisting of Arabs, Syrians, Egyptians, and North Africans, and they achieved the incomparable feat of creating, in Andalusia, a completely new form of social coexistence.

The Basis of the New Tolerance: Islam

The fact that the three religious communities were able to coexist side by side in one kingdom was due to the fundamental acceptance of Judaism and Christianity by Islam. Like Islam, the other two religions are based on the fundamental monotheistic doctrine of Abraham, which proclaims the belief in only one God, but according to Islam Judaism and Christianity have in part forgotten or distorted the messages

In the Land of the Poets, Arabic manuscript, Rome, Biblioteca Apostolica Vaticana

فلمـا فرغ يناصرـ(؟) من سعيه وقال لـه رباض الله حسيبـ(؟) بين غرور بـجير
في انصفـه مع انكارك الوصـل ووجـود لبسبيـل قال يا صاحي أهل الـوفا قليل
نحـن قال لـك الشعـر يا صاحـبك أنت شـاعر مفلـق واحـد يا أرب ونحـن نقـول يـا
روبتـاء وخـبطـك وسمعتـك من حـجـفـطـاء(؟) أنت نقـول من ربـع نفسـك قالـت الله
يـعمـده وقالـط اغـرورور(؟) تلغـشـائـد بالخـيـر والشـرور فـجـن الكـتـب اعبـور البـلـم ومعينـين

received from God. Islam accuses the Jews of having slandered the Holy Virgin and Christ, God's emissary, and the Christians of having succumbed to the error of the doctrine of the Trinity. But so long as they pose no threat to the Islamic community and accept the rule of Islam, Jews and Christians are permitted under Islamic law to continue practicing their own religion.

Moorish Culture

This unusual tolerance was to pave the way for a new culture, strongly Moorish in character, which influenced all aspects of life in medieval Europe. Not only did the Arabs cultivate the soil and alter the landscape by employing new irri-

Arab astrolabe, 1029. Brass, from Toledo, Berlin, Staatliche Museen, Preussischer Kulturbesitz, Staatsbibliothek

gation techniques, they also introduced new fruits and plants into agriculture. In addition, they raised particular trades such as leather work, silk and cloth weaving, and the production of ceramics and glazed tiles to the highest level of craftsmanship. They built mosques and palaces in a style which blended classical tradition with Middle Eastern techniques and types of ornamentation. In the towns the roads were surfaced and illuminated by torches, there were public sewer systems, public schools and baths, hospitals, and libraries, while everywhere else in Europe the crude conditions of the Middle Ages still prevailed.

With the Arabic conquerors a new and refined way of life came to Andalusia: different clothes were worn for different occasions, the table was festively decked, and poems were sung to a musical accompaniment. In the Moorish south the sciences and scholarship flourished, and the resulting new knowledge gained had a lasting influence on all the universities in Europe. Without the Moorish physicians and pharmacists there could have been no progress in the field of medicine. They investigated the effectiveness of plant-based remedies, performed surgical operations, and increased their knowledge of anatomy at an early date through the dissection of corpses. The writings of Moorish physicians were translated into Latin and Hebrew; Andalusia even had Europe's first pharmacies. Moorish philosophers, such as Ibn Rusd (also known as Averroës) who rediscovered Aristotle's writings and commentaries on them, were to suggest new lines of thought to the Western intellectual world, while Arabic poetry influenced the troubadour lyric of southern France.

Arabic became the language of educated people, the language in which all authors, whether philosophers, theologians, poets, or scholars, wrote their works. And while the Christians preserved their Latin liturgy, they nevertheless embraced Arab culture to an extent which prompted this criticism from a bishop named Álvaro: "My fellow Christians enjoy the poems and romances of the Arabs; they study the works of Mohammedan theologians and philosophers, not so as to refute them but in order to acquire a correct and elegant style in the Arabic language. Where is there, nowadays, a layman who can read the Latin commentaries on Holy Scripture? Alas! The young Christians, who have such obvious talents, know no other literature than Arabic literature; they read and study Arabic books; at enormous expense they amass whole libraries and everywhere sing the praises of Arab ways."

How the Catholic Church continued to detest this cultural assimilation is shown by the burning of 80,000 Arabic books as late as 1499 by Cardinal Cisneros, who called Arabic the "language of a heretical and contemptible mass." Yet, a large number of Arabic words were to enter everyday speech and remain there even to this day. Such Arabisms are a

The Story of Bayad and Riyad, 13th century. Arabic manuscript, Rome, Biblioteca Apostolica Vaticana

legacy of those centuries, in which the unique tolerance of the conquerors made possible the peaceful coexistence of different religious communities and allowed an incomparable civilization of surpassing richness to develop. In its creative diversity it represents a symbiosis of Eastern and Western cultures and ways of life.

Ronda

"The entire town and as far as you can see in any direction is romantic background," is how Ernest Hemingway summed up his impression of Ronda. With its unique location and numerous places of artistic interest, the town ranks as one of the most beautiful of the "white towns" of Andalusia. Rilke had earlier described, fascinated, that "incomparable phenomenon of a town piled up on two masses of rock." The gorge of the Río Guadalevín (called the *Tajo)*, is 525 feet (160 meters) deep and up to 295.3 feet (90 meters) wide. It divides the town into the older Moorish district in the south (the Ciudad) and the later district of El Mercadillo, laid out by Christians, in the north. On both sides of the gorge, houses perch on the very edges of the sheer cliffs and are known as *casas colgadas* (hanging houses).

Thanks to its situation, which made the town almost impregnable, Ronda can look

View of Ronda

back on a long history. It is thought, originally, to have been a Celtic settlement called Arunda, which was later taken over by the Romans. Two settlements in Roman times are known, Arunda and Acinipo (Ronda la Vieja, about 12 miles or 20 kilometers to the northwest). In the eighth century the town, on its 2560 foot-(780 meters)high plateau, was taken by the Moors, who called it Izna Rand Onda and built the massive Alcázar. From then on Ronda rose to become one of the most important towns of the Moorish kingdom, even though it underwent changing fortunes in the course of its history. Under the Umayyads the town became the capital of the Berber province of Takaruna and then in the 11th century the capital of a taifa kingdom, which in 1059 fell to al-Mutamid, the ruler of Seville. From the 13th century onwards Ronda belonged to the Nasrid kingdom of Granada and was for a time actually the property of the king of Morocco. This Moorish past, in which Ronda experienced its "Golden Age," left many traces behind and set its stamp on the whole appearance of the Ciudad. But the Christians were also prepared to attack this town, and so it was involved in the battles of the Reconquest from the beginning of the 15th century. Several unsuccessful sieges took place before Ferdinand III was finally able to capture the town in 1485. The Moors were allowed to depart unharmed on condition that they handed over all Christian prisoners. The chains of these prisoners were taken to Toledo,

Ronda, Casa del Rey Moro

where Isabella had them fixed to the outer walls of the chancel of San Juan de los Reyes, where they can still be seen. Ronda became the sovereign territory of crown prince Juan, the only son of the Catholic Monarchs, and his wife, Margarete of Austria. The centuries which followed brought peace and prosperity to the town, giving rise, especially in the 18th century, to new buildings in the Baroque style.

Ronda

Plaza de Toros,
Calle Virgen de la Paz, p. 238

Puente Nuevo,
Calle Armiñán, p. 246

Palacio de Mondragón
(Palacio del Marqués de
Villasierra), Calle M. Monte-
ro, p. 247

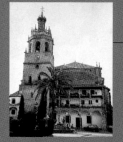

Santa María la Mayor,
Plaza de la Duquesa de
Parcent, p. 250

Plaza de
la Merced

Alameda
del Tajo

M. Souvirón

Molino

Virgen de la Paz

Plaza del
Socorro

Carre

P. Romero

Rios

Nueva

Jardines de
Blas Infante

Villanueva

Plaza de
España

Río Guadalevín

Tenorio

Pl.
Dio
de

Pl. María
Auxiliadora

M

0   200 m

N

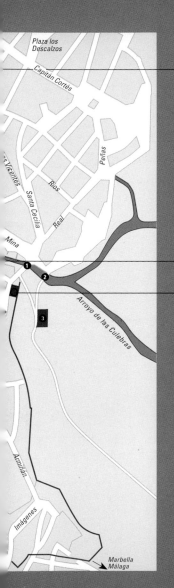

Templete de la Virgen de los Dolores, Calle Virgen de los Dolores, p. 238

Casa del Rey Moro, Calle M. de Salvatierra, p. 248

Palacio del Marqués de Salvatierra, Calle M. de Salvatierra, p. 248

Also worth seeing:

1   Puente Viejo

2   Puente Romano

3   Baños Árabes, Barrio Bajo

4   Minaret, Calle M. de Salvatierra

necks and could therefore be supposed to represent people who had been hanged. Another interpretation, however, sees the bird-like figures as being reminiscent of pre-Columbian representations.

Plaza de Toros

Probably Ronda's most famous building is the impressive bullring, which has a diameter of 216.5 feet (66 meters) and is one of the oldest and most historic in Spain. The stands, which can accommodate 5,000 spectators, have two tiers of arcades supported by Tuscan columns. When this arena was built in 1783-1785, stone was used for the first time in place of the earlier wooden beams. It belongs, to this day, to the Royal Chivalric Order of Ronda founded by Philip II, the coat-of-arms of which adorns the gable of the Baroque gateway. Ronda can boast of being the birthplace of the strictly enforced rules governing the art of bullfighting, which were established in this arena by the legendary Pedro Romero (1754-1839), grandson of the famous Francisco who founded the Romero bullfighting dynasty. His statue stands in the nearby municipal park.

Templete de la Virgen de los Dolores

Crossing either the Puente San Miguel or the Puente Viejo, the visitor reaches the district of El Mercadillo, which came into being after the Christian conquest. In Moorish times traders had settled here, outside the town walls, in order to avoid the taxes levied within the town. It is said that the site where this modest votive chapel with its three arches was built in 1734 was formerly a place where condemned criminals were put to death. The four figures which combine to form a column have ropes fastened around their

The National Spectacle: "Death"

"A las cinco de la tarde" –every Sunday in the late afternoon from Easter until the end of October, "si el tiempo lo permite" (weather permitting), the same ritual begins in Andalusia: crowds of spectators, both Spaniards and foreigners, flock to the Plaza de Toros to watch the fight between man and bull. In no other region of Spain does bullfighting enjoy greater popularity than in Andalusia, which is also the home of the most famous toreros and the most noble bulls in Spain. Nowhere else do the emotions of the *aficionados*, the lovers of the bullfight, and the opponents of this unequal contest of strength run as high as they do in southern Spain.

The Bull – A Symbol of Fertility

The origin and early history of the cult of bulls and of bullfighting can be traced to mythological times. Zeus, the father of the Greek gods, changed himself into a white bull to abduct Europa, with whom he engendered Minos, king of the Cretans. Minos in turn was so captivated by the beauty of a white bull that he refused to sacrifice it to the sea god, Poseidon, and instead sent it to join his own herd of cattle. As punishment, the gods caused his wife Pasiphae to develop a passion for the animal. The enamored Pasiphae ordered the brilliant inventor Daedalus to build her a wooden cow, in which

Acrobats Engaging in Bull Games, fresco, restored, 16th century B.C. Height 86 cm, found at palace of Knossos, Heraklion, Archeological Museum

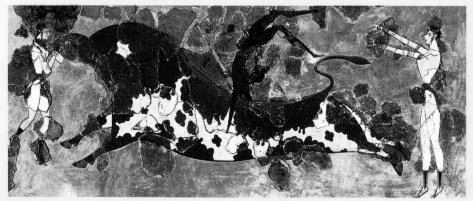

she hid and allowed the bull to mate with her. The offspring of this union was the monstrous Minotaur, half man, half bull, for whom Daedalus, at the wish of the king of Crete, built the famous Labyrinth beneath the palace at Knossos. Every year the Athenians, whom Minos had defeated, had to send twelve youths and maidens here to be devoured by the Minotaur, until the monster was slain by the Attic hero Theseus. Hercules (Heracles), the most famous hero of Greek mythology, had to travel to the end of the world – where he set up his two pillars between earth and the sky at the strait of Gibraltar – in order to steal the cattle of the three-headed giant Geryon and drive them across Spain, Gaul, and Italy to Greece.

Europa Borne on the Back of the Bull, picture in center of a plate, 4th century B.C. Vienna, Kunsthistorisches Museum

Throughout history human beings have been fascinated by bulls. In the very earliest epic in world literature, the Sumerian *Gilgamesh*, the two heroes fight the bull of heaven. The first pictorial representations of bulls appear in Spanish cave paintings from the Early Stone Age and on Cretan drinking vessels and wall paintings. The earliest known games involving bulls are depicted in a fresco at the palace of Knossos, which shows a young girl avoiding a bull's charge by leaping over its horns. Centuries later there were to be similar games in Spain, but their form seems to have been inspired by ancient wedding rituals: since the bull was venerated as a fertility symbol, the bridegroom was obliged, on the evening before the wedding, to approach close enough to a selected bull to touch it, so that – according to popular belief – its procreative power communicated itself to him, while he also proved his manhood. From an upper window the bride aimed small spears at the bull, in order to give him a bleeding wound. Elements of these rituals still form part of present day bullfighting.

Early Forms of the Bullfight

Already in ancient times fights with bulls enjoyed high esteem. Thus, for instance, the Persian god of light, Mithras, the bull-killer *par excellence*, was venerated throughout the Roman Empire. Bull-baiting on horseback took place in the arenas of Rome. This tradition was then continued by both Christians and Moors in the Iberian peninsula. The fight between mounted man and animal rose to become an aristocratic pastime and was regarded as training for warfare. Although the Castilian king Alfonso X (Alfonso the Wise, 1252-1284) attempted in his famous *Partidas*, to establish firm rules for bullfighting, it continued to be a baiting with lances, stakes, swords, daggers, and hunting-knives right up to the 18th century. Even the Inquisition could not curb the bloody spectacle. In 1567

Philip II rejected a Papal Bull issued by the Roman church, thus ordering the abolition of bullfights: "The Bull is wholly ineffective because the *corridas de toros* (running of the bulls) is a habit which Spaniards seem to have in their blood." In 1596 he obtained an amendment making the prohibition apply only to clerics. Armed noblemen continually went out to face bulls in this way on the squares of Spanish towns until the Bourbons ascended the Spanish throne in 1701. Only then was this type of fight prohibited by decree.

The Birth of the Modern Bullfight

After the nobility had had to drop bullfighting from their range of pastimes, it was adopted more and more by the ordinary people, who sought fame and fortune in playing the heroic game with death. Once, when in the course of a fight a bull had tossed a horse and its rider down on to the sand and pinned them under its horns, a new kind of corrida was born. In order to help the rider, a *chulo* (bullfighter's assistant) called Francisco Romero, a carpenter from Ronda, used his broad-brimmed hat to lure it away from its victims. As a result Ronda – which has Spain's oldest bullring, originally built of wood in 1755 – is regarded as the birthplace

Theseus Slaying the Minotaur, 540-530 B.C. Detail from a Greek amphora, height 42 cm, Paris, Musée du Louvre

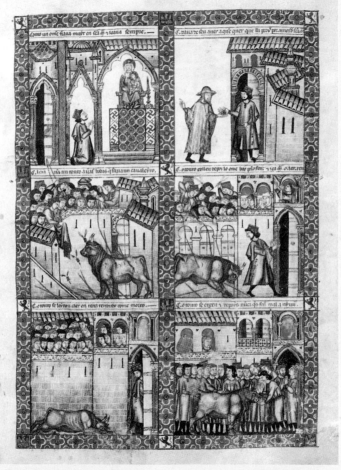

Bull Used in Marriage Ritual, Cantigas Santa María, by Alfonso the Wise, Madrid, El Escorial, Library

Francisco de Goya, Tauromaquia, 1815

of the modern bullfight. Here Francisco Romero, with his son Juan and his grandson Pedro, founded a legendary bullfighting dynasty, which set up the rules for the bullfight that are still in force today. He was the first matador to step into the arena on foot, armed only with a red cloth, the *muleta*. In addition, he only killed *recibiendo*, in other words, while waiting for the bull to attack. His celebrated grandson Pedro Romero (1754–1839), who could say with pride that he had killed more than 5,000 bulls and who was still in the arena at 80, made famous the plain, classical style of the Ronda School. Its rival is

the great Andalusian School of Seville, which prefers a more playful and showy fight. The toreros of that school are less concerned to prove their courage, but know how to present themselves dramatically and attach importance to creating particular effects.

From the time of the Romeros onwards, Andalusia has been regarded as the home of the bullfight. The region has produced many famous toreros, and the finest fighting bulls are bred on its fertile soil. Associated with Andalusia are famous names like those of Joselito (1895–1920), who died in the arena aged 25, Juan Belmonte

(1892–1962), Manolete (1917–1947), or El Cordobés (1936–1970), who came from a poor background and did not achieve his breakthrough until he was 24 – to name but a few. To become a successful torero remains to this day the poor man's dream, while the affluent compete with one another in breeding the best bulls. For, in Andalusia, to be named on the posters together with the toreros brings more fame than to be, for instance, a successful entrepreneur. Both receive the same admiration, but while the torero risks his life in the fight, the breeder can at worst suffer the disgrace of having produced a lethargic bull. There is no equality of opportunity in bullfighting, either between torero and breeder – as far as fame is concerned – or between man and animal. This latter fact is the reason for the vociferous protests of the opponents of bullfighting, who condemn the highly traditional ritual as barbaric slaughter. But in the eyes of the aficionados, the supporters and enthusiasts, the bullfight is a complex phenomenon combining spectacle, ritual, and ceremony. It is to be judged by aesthetic criteria. A bullfight is carried out according to strict rules; the costumes, the ceremonial succession of the stages of the fight, and the torero's posture have all been the same for over 200 years. For this reason, only someone who knows the ground rules, and who is familiar with the tradition, can really understand and appreciate what takes place in the arena on Sundays *a las cinco de la tarde*. Bullfighting is an aspect of Spanish culture that not only arouses passionate excitement in the people at large but has also fascinated and inspired great artists like Francisco de Goya (1746–1828) or Pablo Picasso (1881–1973). The playwright Federico García Lorca (1898–1936) described the whole spectacle as he saw it: "In every country death brings the end. As death appears on the scene, the curtain falls. Not so in Spain. This is the only country whose national drama is death: at the beginning of every spring it sounds the trumpets."

Seville, Bullring

Puente Nuevo

Ronda's most noted landmark is the third bridge, a masterpiece of 18th-century engineering resting on its massive pillars almost 329 feet (100 meters) above the gorge of the Guadalevín. As the Mercadillo continued to expand, it was decided in 1735 that an additional bridge, e Puente Nuevo, should be built across e gorge. After a first attempt which collapsed, the Aragonese architect José Martín de Aldehuela (1719–1802) succeeded in completing the aqueduct-like structure, with a lower arch and three upper ones, in 1793. To carry out this daring enterprise, he used specialized machinery devised for the purpose. The barrel-vaulted room above the tall central arch was designed to be used as an escape-proof prison.

Palacio de Mondragón

Very little now remains of the Arab palace, the residence of the last Moorish rulers. During the capture of the town, however, it served as accommodation for the Catholic Monarchs. The subterranean passages which linked the garden with the old Alcazaba are an interesting feature. The present building dates back to a new palace built in the 16th century, but it has undergone many alterations in the intervening centuries. The gable of the portal, which is

flanked by columns, bears the coat-of-arms of the original owner, Captain Melchor de Mondragón. In the 17th century the palace passed into the possession of the family of the Marqués de Villasierra, after whom it is also called the Palacio del Marqués de Villasierra.

Casa del Rey Moro

On this site, it is said, stood the house of a Moorish taifa king who was notorious throughout the land for his megalomania and cruelty. His memory is preserved to this day in the portrait in tiles above the portal. The house is particularly worth visiting because of its gardens, which overhang the gorge. A partly covered stairway cut into the rock leads down 365 steps to the river and to the spring, La Mina, which gushes out of the rock. In Moorish times this spring provided the town with water. During the battles against the Christians, it is said that Christian prisoners had to carry the water laboriously up the steps in skins and containers. "God preserve me from the water jugs of Ronda!" is a proverbial saying in Spanish.

Palacio del Marqués de Salvatierra

The facade of this 18th-century aristocratic palace displays an unusual detail: supporting the triangular gable above the portal are two pairs of naked Aztec or Inca figures standing on tiny pedastools, one of which is covering its pubic area while the other is sticking its tongue out. The reason for this decoration is explained by the family title which derives from the Mexican town of Salvatierra.

Santa María la Mayor

Beyond the southern gateway of the Moorish town wall, the Puerta de Almocábar, lies the former Moorish town. Some streets further on there stands, upon the remains of the former main mosque, the monastery church, with a nave and two aisles, which had been built as early as the end of the 15th century, but had to be rebuilt because of damage caused by the earthquake of 1580. Externally, the building is dominated by the massive square bell tower with an octagonal upper section with round-arched windows. It is reminiscent of the original Moorish minaret. The pointed turret above the octagonal balustrade dates from the 18th century. An unusual and surprising feature of the facade is a multistory loggia added to the front of the building, making it possible to step out of the church at a number of levels. It served as a grandstand from which clerical and secular dignitaries could watch games and competitions taking place on the square in front.

Mihrab

Close to the entrance one finds some surviving vaulting with a geometrical striped design and a horseshoe arch. These were part of the mihrab of the old mosque dating from the late 13th century, when Ronda belonged to the kingdom of Morocco.

Ronda la Vieja

Approximately 12 miles (20 kilometers) to the northwest of Ronda the Romans founded the town of Acinipo, which Pliny considered among the most important towns in Baetica. In 429 it was completely destroyed by the Vandals, so that today one can visit only the ruins of the theater, dating from the first century B.C. The scenic facade, built of rectangular stone blocks, with the usual three doorways, is well preserved. Originally the facade was probably subdivided by aedicules containing statues. Below the stage extends the orchestra, around which is the semicircle of rows of seats hewn out of the rock. On each side of the stage, narrow gangways lead to the seats reserved for persons of high social rank.

San Pedro de Alcántara

The Visigothic Basilica of Vega del Mar

Approximately 32 miles (55 kilometers) southeast of Ronda, in a eucalyptus grove directly on the beach, one finds the remains of the Visigothic basilica of Vega del Mar, dating from the late fifth century. The walls are sufficiently well preserved for the original layout to be clearly recognizable. This was once a church with a nave and two aisles, which had two apses and side rooms. One of these has a cruciform piscina for adult baptism and a small basin for baptizing children. Relics of sacral architecture of that era are rare in Spain, as they were either built upon or destroyed by the Moors. This basilica, like the one at Alcaracejos (Province of Córdoba), is of great interest in the context of architectural history, as it reflects the transition from the Roman basilica strucutre with two apses to the cruciform design, with only one apse, as is see in later church building. The land around the basilica was later used by the Visigoths as a necropolis; this area, to the west of the church, is thought to have been the location of the Municipium Silniana, the Roman settlement which was destroyed by a tidal wave in A.D. 365 during the reign of the Emperor Valens and his brother, Valentinian I. The residential area of Río Verde contains the ruins of a Roman villa, with not only the remains of columns but also mosaics of high quality with geometrical and figurative designs. Of particular significance is the black and white mosaic depicting Roman kitchen utensils, which has no comparison in Spain. It is among the earliest figurative mosaics in the country, dating from around 100 A.D.

The Province of Almería

The Province of Almería

For many centuries the province of Almería, with its barren landscape of desert-like sierras and rocky plains in the interior, was called *el culo de España*, Spain's backside. Only since the 1960s has this image begun to change, thanks to increasing tourism and the development of intensive fruit and vegetable growing. Many holiday resorts have sprung up, and whole stretches of land near the coast still continue to disappear under plastic sheeting to speed up the ripening of fruit for the European market. The provincial capital, is no more than a place to pass through. But first impressions are deceptive, for Almería is one of the oldest towns in Europe an illustrious history. Long before the Phoenicians, Carthaginians, Greeks, and Romans exploited the Portus Magnus, the Gulf of Almería, as a natural harbor, there were prehistoric civilizations here which lent their names to whole epochs. Thus the bell beaker culture is associated with the settlement, more than 4,000 years old, at Los Millares. The rich deposits of ores in the mines of Almería gave rise to the Bronze Age settlement at El Argar on the banks of the Antas. Almería enjoyed its heyday in the 10th century under the caliphate of Córdoba. Originally it was a small village, clustered around a watchtower, called al-Mariya. It was of little significance, no more than a satellite of Bayyana (the modern Pechina), which in the 9th century was a flourishing and substantially independent trading port. However, Abd ar-Rahman III made the town, which means "mirror of the sea," into the capital of the district. After the collapse of the Umayyad caliphate, Almería rose in the course of the 11th century to become the seat of one of the most powerful taifa kingdoms in Andalusia. Córdoba, Murcia, Jaén, and parts of Granada once also belonged to this kingdom; and Almería was, for a brief period, one of the wealthiest trading centers in Spain. From the mid-13th century Almería was a part of the Nasrid kingdom of Granada, until in 1489 it surrendered without a fight to the Catholic Monarchs. The town was thereby spared the ravages of war, but on September 22, 1522 it was struck by a powerful earthquake which reduced large areas to rubble and ashes. Further earthquakes in the 16th and 17th centuries repeatedly brought devastation and decimated the population, so that for centuries after this the people of Almería were reduced to an impoverished peasant existence. Only after the construction of a new harbor in 1847 did economic recovery gradually set in. As a result, modern buildings predominate in the present-day city. Only the twisting streets of the old quarter, are a reminder of its glorious Moorish past.

View of a deserted village, seen from the Alcazaba

Almería

Alcazaba, p. 260

Iglesia de San Juan, Calle de
San Juan, p. 261

Estación, Avenida de la
Estación, p. 270

Plaza Vieja/Plaza de la
Constitución, p. 271

Also worth seeing:

1   Catedral Nuestra Señora de
    la Encarnación, Plaza de la
    Catedral

Alcazaba

A striking reminder of the period of the caliphate is the Alcazaba, which rises almost 328 feet (100 meters) above the city. With a total area of 375,500 square feet (35,000 square meters), sufficient to accommodate 20,000 people, it is one of the largest fortresses in Andalusia. The fortifications were started in the mid-10th century by Abd ar-Rahman III, and extended and strengthened in the 11th century. Originally they consisted of two surrounding walls with defensive towers. The first walled area, now containing extensive gardens, served in earlier times as a military camp and a place of safety for the civilian population. There were cisterns and draw-wells to ensure an adequate supply of water in the event of a lengthy siege, while the Torre del Espejo, which is still standing, had a system of mirrors for sending signals to the ships in the harbor. In the compound within the second circle of wall is the Torre de la Vela, containing the bell that was rung to sound the alarm at times of danger. It also rang to tell the peasants when to

irrigate the fields. In the inner area the foundations are all that remains of the splendid palace complex, which was highly praised by contemporaries. When an earthquake completely destroyed the Alcazaba in 1487, the Catholic Monarchs had a new fortress built on the highest point of the old one. This was protected by a third encircling wall with round towers, and was so massively built that it was still used for military purposes in the early 20th century. On the portal of the rectangular Torre del Homenaje the Monarchs' coat-of-arms can be seen. From the Alcazaba there is a good view of the remains of the Moorish city wall which once linked it with the Castillo de San Cristóbal, an 11th-century fortress with five defensive towers.

Iglesia de San Juan, Mihrab Facade

There would be nothing about this early 17th-century church to attract one's attention, had traces not been discovered here a few years ago of the Moorish principal mosque which stood on this spot prior to the earthquake of 1522. Of the three-aisled late 10th-century building, which was twice enlarged under the Almohads in the 11th century, vestiges of the qiblah and mihrab still exist on the south side of the interior. The stucco ornamentation on the blind arcade above the horseshoe arch is especially significant in terms of art history, since its plant motifs exactly reproduce motifs from the Great Mosque in Córdoba. Evidently the capital city set the artistic tone, and the decorative forms employed there served as models for architects in other towns and cities.

Islam – "Submission" to God

For over 700 years Islam played a decisive part in shaping the history of Andalusia, until Christianity eventually succeeded in gaining the upper hand. At an early date Spanish Christians had mounted a crusade in their own land, though the fight on behalf of the "true faith" was in fact primarily a struggle for political power. By the 16th century practically all Muslims (adherents of Islam) had been arraigned before the court of the Holy Inquisition or expelled from Spain. Hostility towards Islam persisted in many European countries into the 19th century. Nowadays that mixture of fear and prejudice has given way to a generally sympathetic attitude which seeks to gain an understanding of this religious community's beliefs and aspirations. With its estimated 860 million adherents, Islam is, after all, the second most widespread religion in the world, after Christianity.

What exactly are the differences between the two religions? Muslims also share the belief of Christians and Jews in the one God – called Allah in Islam – as creator of the universe. Moreover, they revere the Jewish Torah, the Psalms of David, and the Christian gospels as revelations of God's word. For them it is, however, the Koran, their sacred book, that is the definitive, unalterable word of God, revealed to mankind through the last of the prophets, Mohammed. He brought to fruition the endeavor of his Jewish predecessors, Abraham, Moses, and Christ, to lead humanity to believe in the one

and only God. Unlike the Christian faith, Islam rejects the doctrine of the Trinity. To Muslims, although Christ is the prophet born of the Virgin, he is not the Son of God.

The Early History of Islam

Islam has its origin in the early seventh century A.D. in Arabia, that expanse of hot and largely desert country wedged between Africa and Asia and overshadowed at that time by two great empires, the Christian Byzantine Empire, and the Persian Sasanian Empire. In those days the region was mainly inhabited by nomadic Bedouin tribes who were constantly at war with each other over watering places, grazing, and control of the long-distance trading routes. In their tribal shrines the Bedouin worshipped natural phenomena such as trees, grottoes and rocks, as well as numerous deities. Their most important shrine was in the trading city of Mecca: this was the *Ka'bah*, a cube-shaped structure in which was set a black stone (probably a meteorite). The Ka'bah was the goal of the annual pilgrimages during the four holy months in the late summer and autumn, during which a general cessation of hostilities was observed. The Bedouin came together in this place to fulfill their religious obligations, to establish business contacts, settle feuds, and regulate relationships between the tribes.

With the intensification of conflicts between different social groups and of internal power struggles, the country found itself in an acute crisis. An additional aggravating factor was that polytheism, the belief in a multiplicity of deities, was in decline. The situation changed with the appearance of Mohammed, a trader from Mecca, who was to transform not only religion but great parts of the known world through the divine revelations which he received. He called the faith Islam, which signifies "submission to the will of Allah." His companions later brought together and wrote down all the divine revelations in the Koran, which forms the basis of Islam and regulates all aspects of human life, from eating conventions and dress to education and commerce.

Universal History by Rashid ad-Din: the Archangel Gabriel imparts a message to Mohammed, 14th-century. Arabic manuscript, Edinburgh, University Library

جبرائيل رسول الله حضرتنه كلدى ايدى ياحبيبى يامحمد الله تعا
سكا سلام قلور روسنك قدر كى عز تكى قربكى بير اهلنه وكو
اهلنه بلد وردى دى دى اندن صكره رسول عليه السلام ايتد
يا اخ جبرائيل الله تعالى نوم قدر مى منزلى قربى بو مخلوقاته

The Annunciation to Mohammed by the Archangel Gabriel, miniature from the Turkish manuscript "Sijer i-Nebi" (The Life of the Prophet), 16th century. Istanbul, Topkapi Museum

Mohammed

Mohammed Ibn Abd Allah was born around 570 A.D. in the Arabian city of Mecca. When he was six years old his parents died, and the responsibility for his upbringing was assumed by an uncle of his who, as head of the Koreish tribe, was the custodian of the Ka'bah in Mecca. As a result from an early age Mohammed became familiar with the ideas and customs of his own people, but also acquired knowledge of the religion and traditions of Jewish and Christian settlers in Arabia. It is said that Mohammed could neither read nor write, nor did he receive any other kind of formal education. To earn his living, he worked as a leader of trading caravans for the rich widow Khadijah, whom he married when he was 25 years old and who bore him several children.

Mohammed became a successful and prosperous merchant, but as the years went by he was filled with an inner disquiet. For this reason he is said often to have retreated to a cave on Mount Hira, where, it is recorded, at the age of about forty he received his first revelation. One night there appeared to him the radiant form of the angel Gabriel, who said, "Read." In answer to the question, what should he read, the angel replied: "Read in the name of thy Lord, who has created man from an embryo. Read. Thy Lord is boundless in his magnanimity, he has taught man to use the pen, he has taught him what hitherto he did not know." When Mohammed emerged from the cave he heard a voice calling from Heaven: "Mohammed, thou art the emissary of Allah, and I am Gabriel." That was the first of a series of messages which Mohammed received from God. Following this call, he felt it to be his duty from this time onwards to lead his people to the worship of the one true God, rejecting any other gods. This sense of mission was accompanied by his vision of a new kind of community, in which there would no longer be a place for tribal distinctions, and where the conflicts between rich and poor would be reduced.

Because of this, his earliest followers came from the socially deprived classes, while most of the more affluent citizens of Mecca were hostile to his revelations because they feared for their own privileged status. In 622, therefore, he took up an invitation to move to the oasis town of Yathrib, later called Medina. This was the decisive turning-point in Mohammed's divine mission, and in later years the date of the *hijrah* (emigration), was adopted as the starting-point of the Muslim calendar. Shortly after he emigrated Mohammed acquired the status of a ruler, becoming a political, military, and religious authority. Whereas in Mecca his revelations had still been of a religious nature, at Medina he was increasingly preoccupied with the political and juridical questions which inevitably accompanied the transformation of a religious community into an Islamic state. In just a few years he succeeded not only in converting nomads and town-dwellers alike to the worship of a single God, but also, through armed force and the skillful use of political alliances, in gaining control of large parts of Arabia. Thus, after he had conquered Mecca in 630 and declared the Ka'bah to be the central shrine of the new religion, ambassadors came from every corner of the Arabian peninsula to announce the accession of their peoples to Islam. In June 32 Mohammed died without having nominated a successor. In accordance with ancient tribal custom, which was retained, the new leader had to be elected.

Mohammed with his Faithful Companions on the Road to Mecca, miniature from the Turkish manuscript "Sijer i-Nebi" (The Life of the Prophet), 16th century. Istanbul, Topkapi Museum

Sunni and Shi'ite Muslims

Under the prophet's successors, military expansion continued. Within a few decades they spread out from the Arabian peninsula to conquer Byzantium and the Sasanian Empire, and

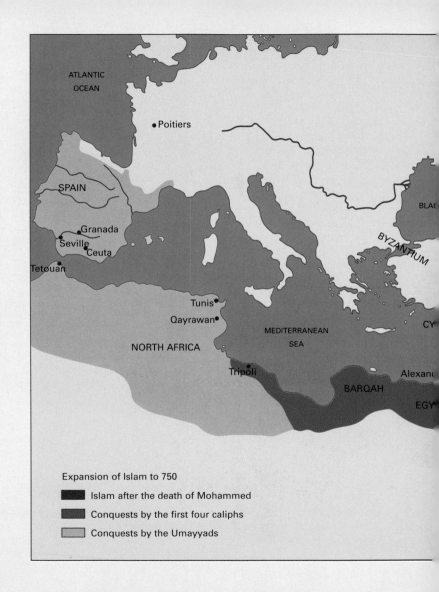

Expansion of Islam to 750

■ Islam after the death of Mohammed

■ Conquests by the first four caliphs

■ Conquests by the Umayyads

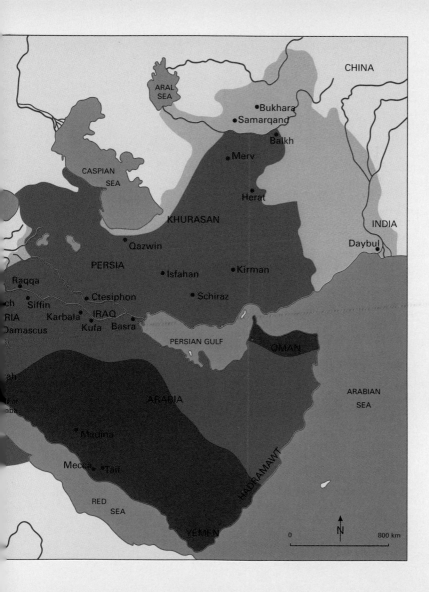

founded a vast Arab-Islamic Empire. However, within Arabia itself, disputes over the true succession to Mohammed led to bloody battles which have been recorded in Islamic historiography as the "first civil war." They gave rise to what are still the two principal sects in the Muslim world: the Sunni and the Shi'ite Muslims. Although the two groups share their adherence to the Koran and to certain traditions, they differ in their interpretation of the scriptures and of history. The Sunni Muslims, who call themselves the "people of community and tradition" and form the largest Muslim sect (about 90% of all Muslims), assert the legitimacy of the elected successor of the Prophet, the caliph. The Shi'ites, on the other hand, acknowledge only the Prophet's descendants as legitimate *imams* (heads) of the whole community of Islam. This schism began with Moham-

The Assumption into Heaven of the Prophet Mohammed, colored miniature from a manuscript of the poetic work Khamseh by Nizami, 1539-43. London, British Museum

med's cousin and son-in-law Ali, who had already gathered a political grouping around himself during the lifetime of his predecessors. His followers, known as the Shi'at Ali, claimed that only members of Mohammed's own family had the right to be religious and political leaders. When in 656, after a series of murky events, Ali was installed as the fourth caliph, violent struggles for power and influence broke out in the Islamic state. His opponent was Mu'awiya, a member of the house of Umayya and governor of Damascus, who accused Ali of having seized the caliphate illegally. Ali initially agreed to have the legitimacy of his claim tested by a tribunal. The verdict came out against him, and in 660 Mu'awiya took over power. A year later, when Ali was assassinated by a renegade from the sect called the *Khariji* ("those who leave" the camp), Mu'awiya made his residence Damascus the seat of the caliphate and declared the office of caliph hereditary. Ali's supporters, under the leadership of his sons Hasan and Huseyn, continued to assert the leadership claim of the fourth caliph, but in 680 suffered a crushing defeat. Huseyn, who refused to surrender, was executed and his severed head was taken to Damascus. It was his death, still annually commemorated as a martyrdom, which finally brought about the root-and-branch separation of the Shi'ites from the rest of Islam.

Jean Léon Gérome, Islamic Pilgrims at the Grave of the Imam Huseyn, 19th century. Oil on canvas, London, Royal Miles Gallery

Plaza Vieja

At the foot of the Alcazaba lies the picturesque district of *La Chanca* (meaning
"a place of storage for tuna fishing
equipment"), which with its colorful cube-
shaped houses and cave-dwellings evokes
the Moorish past. In the heart of the old
town, on the site of the principal mosque,
the cathedral was built between 1524 and
1542 to plans by Diego de Siloë. It has a
nave and two aisles. Its massive walls and

buttresses give it the look of a fortress, and
it did in fact serve in earlier times as a refuge
from attacks by Turkish and Moorish
pirates. From here it is only a short distance
to the arcaded Plaza Vieja with the historic
Ayuntamiento (townhall) dating from the
late 19th century. In the 16th century this
square bore the name Plaza de los Moros,
because this is where the Moorish market
was held up to the time of the Christian
Reconquest. In the western part of the city
stands the fine *Estación* (railway station),
constructed in the neo-Mudéjar style.

The Province of Granada

The Province of Granada

"If you haven't seen Granada yet, you haven't seen anything." This Spanish adage says it all. Like none other in Andalusia, the province of Granada is dominated by its capital city of the same name, which boasts the Alhambra – probably the single most visited monument in the world. But the surrounding countryside also has its charm. Large areas of the Sierra Nevada mountain range have been designated as national parks. Their snow-covered peaks provide an ideal place for wonderful excursions. The southern foothills of the Sierras merge into the fertile Alpujarra hills, which became a final refuge for the Moors when they were driven out of Granada. The Costa Tropical, the eastern strip of coastline on the Costa del Sol where exotic fruits like papayas and avocados grow, has retained some of its Moorish legacy. Here, too, tourism has taken its toll, but unlike the concrete-covered western end of the Costa del Sol, the visitor can still find a few quieter niches where the natives spend their vacations. Another great excursion is a visit to Guadix, a small town situated on the Roman Via Augusta where about a fifth of the inhabitants live in white-washed houses. Granada has often been praised for its beauty and grace. However, the road leading into Granada can be very sobering: it leads visitors past a dismal strip of sky-scrapers which makes the first impression somewhat disappointing. Granada is loud, the air is bad, and the streets are over-crowded. It takes the visitor a while to comprehend the most vivid descriptions of the city: "If you see a blind beggar in the streets of Granada, give him twice as much, for it is suffering enough to not be able to see this beauty." On the edge of the fertile Río Genil plain, whose tributary, the Darro, separates the two hills Sacromonte and Albaicín from the Alhambra, Granada does not reveal itself all at once. Visitors will discover the many wonders of this city slowly, but their efforts will be generously rewarded. Each unique part of town has a view of the hills and mountains of the Sierra Nevadas – which changes according to season and time of day – in the background.

Today, Granada is not just a tourist attraction but also a modern university town and the intellectual center of Andalusia. The university, founded by Charles V in 1531 and located in the center of the city, is the third largest in the country.

Granada is mainly marked by its Moorish past. Unlike most other Andalusian cities, Iberians, Romans, and Visigoths played only a subordinate role here. When the Berbers arrived on the banks of the Río Darro in 711, they encountered a Jewish community called Garnatha Alyehud, from which the city's name was derived. How-

Granda, Carrera del Darro

ever, it may also be that the name came from the fact that the houses of the settlement were built so close together that they looked like the seeds of a pomegranate. It was not until the 11th century that this little settlement became a city of any importance. After the fall of the caliphate, the Berber dynasty of the Zirids founded an independent taifa kingdom. The first fortress was built on the highest hill of the city. In the following one-and-a-half centuries, Granada was caught up in warring disputes between the Almoravides and the Almohades. In 1227, Granada experienced a decisive expansion as the Moorish refugees, who were exiled after Baeza was conquered by Ferdinand III, settled on Albaicín Hill. The year 1238 marked a turning point in the history of the city. While the Christians slowly conquered Andalusia, which was at that time broken up into smaller taifa kingdoms, the Nasrid Mohammed I was rebelling against the Christian forces. In 1237 he marched into Granada and one year later was able to add Almería and Málaga to his new empire, whose capital would become Granada.

This Nasrid had political finesse: not only did he maintain good relations with the Berber princes in North Africa, he also acknowledged the sovereignty of Castile, dutifully paying his tributes and demonstrating allegiance to their army. As a reward for this, he was promised a tract of land that roughly corresponds to today's provinces of Granada, Almería, and Málaga. He even fought on the side of the Christians against his own fellow Muslims and had to participate with his troops in the conquest of Seville. After the fall of Seville, he returned home victorious and was welcomed with cheers and rejoicing, but his only response to this was, "There is no other conqueror but Allah." From that point on, this became the motto of the Nasridian dynasty.

During the 250 years of Nasrid rule, Granada experienced a period of economic prosperity as well as the last and perhaps greatest flourishing of Islamic art and culture on Spanish soil. An intricate irrigation system helped agriculture to thrive, mines brought forth gold, silver, and copper, the silk industry began to grow, the trades prospered, and Christian and Muslim merchants experienced great business success. The city became a refuge for the Moors who had been driven out of other areas, increasing the population rapidly to 400,000. Schools, hospitals, a mint, and a university enriched the city, and on the highest mountain, near the Alcazaba, one of the most elaborate royal palaces of the Western world was built. Over the course of the 15th century, however, good relations with the Christian Sovereigns came to an end. Through the union of Castile and Aragón in the year 1469 a new Christian alliance was formed. When Muley Abu Hassan (the father of

Granada, Capilla Real, Tombstone of the Catholic Sovereigns

Boabdil, the last Muslim ruler) refused to pay new tributes in 1478 and attacked the border town of Zahara in 1481, the more than ten year-conquest of the last Moorish bastion began. In one military campaign after another, the Christians claimed the cities and towns of the Nasrid empire. This lasted until January 2, 1492, when Boabdil was forced to surrender the besieged Granada without resistance. In the peace agreement, the Muslims were assured religious freedom as well as the right to have their own language and justice system.

Ferdinand and Isabella had now attained their goal: Spain was united politically. Granada, the site of their greatest triumph, was decorated with grand memorials and became a symbol of the Reconquest. However the royal couple did not keep their promises to the Muslims for very long. Islamic laws and customs were soon condemned and the Moorish population was forced to choose between baptism or exile. This led to numerous rebellions by the Moriscos (the name that was given to Moors who had – for the most part perfunctorily – converted to Christianity). To put an end to the rebellions, Philipp II issued a final decree in 1609 that had all Moriscos banished from the country. This sent agriculture, the trades, and commerce into a tailspin and retarded Granada's development significantly. It was not until Washington Irving published his *Tales of the Alhambra* in 1832 and the painters of the romantic period discovered the oriental motifs of the Red Fortress that the

Felipe Bigarny, Forced Baptism, wood relief, detail of the high altar, 16th century. Granada, Capilla Real

Alhambra begin to once again attract public interest.

The Alhambra

The Alhambra rises high over a fertile plain on a foothill of the Sierra Nevadas. With a length of 2,362 feet (720 meters) and a width of more than 721 feet (220 meters), it is "like a giant ship that dropped anchor between the mountains and the plains" (L. Torres Balbás). Walls with 23 towers and four gates once encircled the palace city. The oldest part of the complex, the *Alcazaba* (citadel), is followed by the Nasridian Royal Palace to the east that is divided into a series of building complexes, each with their own courtyard, dating back to the 13th and 14th centuries. A large settlement with apartments, baths, administrative buildings, workshops, barracks, stables, prisons, and the royal were organized lay around this, while the gardens of the Generalife extend to the north.

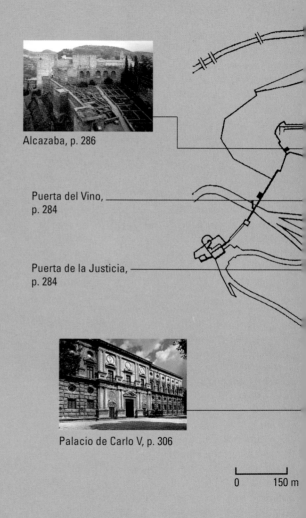

Alcazaba, p. 286

Puerta del Vino, p. 284

Puerta de la Justicia, p. 284

Palacio de Carlo V, p. 306

0   150 m

The Alhambra

"The Sabikah is Granada's crown, and the Alhambra (may Allah protect her) is the ruby at the top of this crown."
(Ibn Zamrak)

More famous than any other monument on earth, Granada's Alhambra appears from afar like an austere fortress. Although it stands out quite prominently against the grand background of the Sierra Nevadas, no one would ever begin to imagine the overwhelming splendor that is contained within its walls which attracts millions of tourists each year. Its name is derived from the Arabic word *Qalat al-Hamra* which means "red fortress." This most likely referred to the red-colored local soil that was used to build the fortress.

While in the 11th century the Zirids were still residing on the neighboring Albaicín hill, their Jewish vizier Yusuf Ibn Nagralah was the first to build a fortified palace on the far-reaching hill that the Moors named al-Sabikah. The strategic location of the highest hill in the city – unapproachable from the north and the west, and in the east it is separated from the neighboring mountains by a narrow ravine – made it an ideal headquarters especially in warring times. Thus, this fortified palace city that we now know as the Alhambra came existence being during the 250 year – reign of the Nasrid rulers.

The first Nasrid king Mohammed I (1238–1273) had the Alcazaba on the west side of the hill rebuilt, and had a wide, protective wall built around the complex. With cisterns and aqueducts, he established the requirements for a sufficient supply of water. His successors would continue to expand and improve on these facilities, adding an extensive garden referred to as the Generalife.

Today, only a small section of the original palace city remains. Included in this is the real gem, the old Royal Palace, that is mainly attributed to Yusuf I (1333–1354) and Mohammed V (1354–1359 and 1362–1391). Even to the Christian conquerors, this masterpiece of Moorish royal architecture seemed so fantastic that they did not destroy it. Except for the San Francisco convent and the Santa María chapel laid in place of the mosque, and the palace that Charles V had built next to the Moorish structure as a political manifestation of the new ruler, the complex remained intact and would inspire awe and amazement for centuries to come.

"Halls and courtyards decay, pictures and mosaics fade; but the Alhambra, despite its decaying surroundings, is still today a testimony to past magnificence and splendor and strikes a hidden cord in the heart of its visitor." (Washington Irving, 1783–1859, *Tales of the Alhambra*).

visitors in four right-angled turns through five different rooms with high, vaulted ceilings. The decorations carved into the gate's walls still today remain a mystery. On the keystone of the first arch, a hand has been chiseled whose five fingers probably represent the Five Pillars of Islam. Above the second, inner archway, a key with a band can be seen. In the capitals of the columns is the Islamic creed, "There is no god but the one God, and Mohammed is his prophet."

Puerta del Vino

On the way to the palaces visitors will go through the *Puerta del Vino* (Wine Gate) which was built by Mohammed V. It was once part of a wall that separated the northern palace area from the village in the south. The square groundplan and the room above the gateway with the open windows suggest that the gate did not serve any defensive or protective purpose. It was more likely a kind of arch of triumph erected for the victories of Mohammed V, as the inscription quotes the first verse of the Koran's victory sura: "Behold, we have granted you a clear victory so that Allah will forgive you your past and future sins and have mercy on you. Allah will lead you down the right path and support you with His might."

Puerta de la Justicia

The largest of the four main arched gates of the Alhambra is the *Puerta de la Justicia* (Justice Gate) which, according to the inscription on it, was erected by Yusuf I in 1348. As was common for most Moorish city gates, the path leading through the wide horseshoe arch to the Alhambra changes its direction many times and leads

Alcazaba

Continuing on through the Puerta del Vino, the path leads across the *Plaza de los Aljibes* (Square of the Cisterns) to the east wall of the Alcazaba with its three towers. The west side is dominated by the massive *Torre de la Vela* (Watch Tower) above which Ferdinand and Isabella hoisted their flag in 1492. From its upper platform, the entire plain of Granada could be surveyed. Today, tourists will find it a good vantage point to view the interior of the citadel since the foundations of the barracks and ammunition depots are exposed. Visitors will exit the Alcazaba through the *Torre de las Armas* (Weapons Gate) famed for its vaulted ceiling, and continue on between the walls of the Patio del Machuca and the palace of the Christian rulers on the way to Mechuar.

Mechuar

This is the first of the three palaces that make up the ancient *Casa Real* (Royal Palace). The entrance used to lead through two courtyards, whose origin and function are unknown, into an audience chamber. This long room evidently opened towards the west to the courtyard. The audience chamber, which probably served as the courtroom for the *mashwar* (emirs), seems to date back to the 13th century, but was changed considerably by the reconstruction in Christian times. In the front of the room, four marble columns support an entablature covered in thick stucco and a low wood ceiling. The gallery located behind this was added on in the 16th century. Mudéjar tiles with geometric patterns adorn the lower walls.

Connected to the chamber is a small prayer room whose magnificent mihrab is framed by a horseshoe arch. A door in the east wall leads visitors through a small courtyard towards the Cuarto Dorado.

Cuarto Dorado

The south wall of the *Cuarto Dorado* (Golden Room), built during the reign of Mohammed V, is one of the most impressive examples of Nasridian architecture. Other than the door frames and the azulejos decoration at the base, this three-story wall is completely covered in patterns of gold filigree. A mixture of floral patterns, geometric forms, and epigraphs, the motifs are framed by the clear, geometric forms of the panels, borders, spandrels, and friezes.

Wood ceiling beams and eaves project from the uppermost frieze. Five windows accentuate the wall, as well as two doors, the right one leading back to the forecourt and the left one opening to a winding hallway that leads to the Patio de los Arrayanes. The inscriptions above the door hint at the fact that this is the monumental entrance to the actual palace. They speak of a gate "at which the paths split," and quote the famous throne verse of the Koran, "His Throne doth extend over the heavens and the earth, and he feeleth no fatigue in guarding and preserving them for He is the Most High, the Supreme (in glory)."

This facade illustrates one of the unique characteristics of Alhambra architecture: visitors standing here will notice no sign, no obvious clue, that they have reached one of the most important points within the entire pathway system, the one that leads into the royal palace proper. All areas of the complex have been constructed according to this principle. Unlike the typical European palace, there is no spectacular facade, no main axis around which the various rooms are organized, no succession of rooms leading up to the inner core. Instead, visitors are constantly led down various hallways that lead to inner courtyards surrounded by more chambers. From the outside, no one would ever imagine the splendor that awaits them behind these austere walls.

Patio de los Arrayanes

In the center of the palace section that was built during the reign of Yusuf, the visitor will find the *Patio de los Arrayanes* (Court of the Myrtles). This rectangular courtyard was named for the short, trimmed myrtle bushes that rim the long, narrow reflection pond in the middle of it. The plain, longer sides with simple windows and arches emphasize the effect of the magnificent narrow sides that are adorned with a series of white marble arches and columns.

Their surfaces are further embellished by latticed diamond and *sebka* forms that are reflected like lace curtains in the water of the pond. A wood ceiling with impressive marquetry and luxuriously decorated alcoves enhance the overall impression. Towering above the northern, narrow side is the 147.7-foot-(45 meters)high, tin-crowned tower, *Torre de Comares*. The types of structures that were once located at the south end of the Patio de los Arrayanes are unknown. They were destroyed in the expansion and construction of Charles V's palace.

commissioner, while others repeat stylized phrases in endless succession such as, "There is no other conqueror but Allah." Though they may seem somewhat meaningless today, these inscriptions were once a sign of the Islamic faith and a constant reminder of the belief in the one God from whom all things come. There are also poetic inscriptions that seem to have been written especially for certain rooms of the Alhambra and are mostly attributed to the great poet, Ibn Zamrak.

Detail of the North Side

The various inscriptions, located for the most part above the tile panels and framed by ornamental borders, are an unusual feature of the Alhambra's rooms. In Islamic art, these inscriptions replace pictorial figures typical of other cultures and express the function or significance that is attributed to each room. There are various types of inscriptions. Some provide information about construction dates and the identity of the architect or

The Art of the "Little Stones"

Cuerda Seca Tile, Seville, 16th century.
Granada, Museo Hispano-Musulman

Whether in palaces, villas, or just plain houses, visitors to Andalusia will continually be met with gloriously colorful tiles that are most often incorporated into grand wall mosaics. Like a brightly colored dress strewn with a wealth of varying patterns, *azulejos* clothe the facades of buildings and the walls of patios and rooms. Pleasantly cool in the summer, long-lasting and full of variety, these glazed ceramic tiles continue to be one of the typical forms of decoration in southern Spain and are used in everything from billboards and store signs to modern commercial buildings.

The Origin of the Azulejos

Azulejos have their origin in Islamic art. The Arabs learned how to produce glazed ceramic from Chinese artisans who had traveled along the silk road all the way to art centers in Iran, Mesopotamia, and Syria in the 12th century. The Arabs called these clay squares *al-zulaich*, which means "small, shiny stone." Initially this term referred to the Roman-Byzantine mosaics of the Near East and North Africa that were then imitated with glazes on ceramic. By the end of the 13th century, this decorative art form had spread through North Africa up into the Nasridian court of Granada, and from there it spread across the entire Iberian peninsula. Here, the technical methods used in the Orient were adopted, but aesthetic aspects relating to the interplay of architecture and tile decoration were modified significantly.

In the beginning, these tile mosaics were just used for floors. Later on they also functioned as wall decorations. Monochromatic tiles cut in different geometric forms called *alicatados* were combined with other multicolored ones to make colorful patterns. This required craftspeople who were skilled in the techniques of glazing – with oxides of cobalt (blue), manganese (purple and black), iron (green), copper (red-green), tin (white), and lead or antimony (yellow) – as well as the techniques of cutting the pieces to form patterns. Over the course of many years the geometric patterns became more and more complicated, so that the single-color ceramic plates had to be cut into hundreds of multicolored forms — rectangles, squares, triangles and stars with four, six, eight or twelve points or even irregular forms. The individual shapes would then be fitted together like a puzzle on a blank background with the colored side facing down. Then they were framed in wood and mortar was poured over them. When the mortar hardened, the mosaic could be taken out of the wood frame and attached to the wall.

Alicatados and Azulejos

Colorful mosaics quickly became one of the most popular forms of Mudéjar art. All across the country, ceramic manufacturers started springing up, two of the most famous being the tile makers of Málaga and those in the Triana district of Seville. Since the production of these *alicatados* was very difficult and expensive, it gradually began to be replaced in the 14th century by the tiles that were referred to as azulejos. These were squares with sides of 4.7 to 5.7 inches (12 to 14.5 centimeters) and their entire surface was covered with a multicolored pattern. Earlier exemplars reproduced the geometric patterns of the alicatados on one single tile or a combination of four tiles. However, this procedure proved to be problematic since the glazes could run and blend into each other during the melting process. For this reason, special technical processes were developed that would preserve the contours of the designs.

Techniques

In the *cuerda seca* technique, the lines of the design would be drawn into the still wet clay and the furrows filled with a greasy material.

Bust of Fernando el Católico, Cuerda Seca Plate, Seville, 1500, Madrid, Institut Valencia Don Juan

This material would burn in the firing process and create a black line after which the technique was named (*cuerda* means "cord" or "string"). This line kept the different colors from running into each other and at the same time created a relief effect. The *cuenca* technique separated the surfaces to be glazed by sharp edges, borders or grooves that were made by pressing a wooden mold with the negative of the pattern into the soft clay. The coloring then appears to be more fluid and iridescent and makes the tile designs look like oriental rugs.

The Jester Dances with a Lady, Cuerda Seca Tile, Seville, 16th century, Madrid, Institut Valencia Don Juan

The *cuenca* technique did not only make the production process much easier, it also made a greater variety of patterns possible and was considerably much more cost-efficient.

Andalusia's Trademark

Azulejos with their luminous, iridescent colors and exotic, geometric patterns became the trademark of Andalusia. Southern Spain, which became the leading Spanish ceramic center in the 15th and 16th centuries, would hold on to this tradition of ceramic production for a long time. In Italy, however, the majolica technique was already being put to use as early as the 16th century. This technique, which works with solvents containing tin, made new decorative designs and pictorial representations possible which corresponded to the then contemporary fashion of figurative narratives. Italian majolica artist Francesco Niculoso of Pisa had already introduced this new technique in Seville around 1500. One of the most magnificent examples of his tile art is the altar of the house chapel of the Catholic Sovereigns in the Alcázares Reales, which he signed with the words, Niculoso Francesco italiano me fecit. However, the Sevillian ceramic artists only adopted the new motifs of the Italian Renaissance and not the technique. Ornamental designs of leaves, grotesques, masks, ox heads, and flowers appeared on the azulejos in place of the earlier geometric patterns. More than a half a century went by before the majolica technique (also) caught on in Andalusia. This occured when, in the second half of the 16th century, one of the leading azulejo manufacturers, Roque Hernanda, hired a certain Francisco Andrea "flamenco" to teach him the Italian art of painting *azulejos*. This is how the new technique – azulejos with a smooth surface "in the colors of Pisa," (hence their name, *pisanos*) – finally took root in Seville. However, the city could not retain its position as the center for tile production and had to abdicate to Talvera in the late 16th century. Along with the industrial revolution came the mass-production of azulejos in ceramic factories. One of the most famous was the factory built by Charles Pickman in 1841 near the Sevillian convent of Santa Maria de las Cuevas. It was shut down in 1980 during the restoration of the area for the 1992 World Expo.

Sala de los Embajadores

Continuing through the Sala de la Barca with its boat-shaped wooden ceiling, one enters the *Sala de los Embajadores* (Hall of the Ambassadors), a reception room in the largest outer tower of the Alhambra. Three alcoves on each inner wall and three windows on the outer wall offering a spectacular view of the valley below subdivide the room. Above the lower border of azulejos, a stucco latticework of arabesques, *sebka* patterns, and inscriptions covers the walls. The inscriptions are unusually abundant. Among them, the poem on the inside of the luxuriously decorated middle alcove on the north wall is especially significant. Its verses prove that the throne once stood on this spot: "From me you are welcomed morning and evening by the tongues of blessing, prosperity, happiness, and friendship. That is the elevated dome, and we (the alcoves) are her daughters; yet I possess excellence and dignity above all those of my race. Surely we are all parts of the same body; but I am like the heart in the midst of the rest; and from the heart springs all energy of soul and life. True, my fellows here may be compared to the signs of the Zodiac in the heaven of that dome: but I can boast what they are lacking, the honor of a Sun – since my lord, the victorious Yusuf, has decorated me with the robes of his glory and excellence without disguise, and has made me the throne of his empire: may its eminence be upheld by the Master of Divine Glory and the Celestial Throne!"

The Wood Ceiling

The domed ceiling in the Hall of Ambassadors, which set a precedence for the decor of palatial rooms for centuries to come, is a true masterpiece of marquetry composed of 8,017 cedar panels in varying colors. The brilliantly inlaid pieces of wood have been fitted together in an extremely complicated, seven-leveled pattern consisting of eight- and sixteen-point stars. In its entirety the ceiling is supposed to represent the "seven heavens" of Islam and depict the stars of paradise, while its diagonals symbolize the "four trees of life." Beneath this extraordinary ceiling was once the throne of the earthly ruler.

Patio de los Leones

The palace complex of Mohammed V is considered to be the pinnacle of Nasridian architecture. It is made up of separate units that served as the private living quarters for the royal family. The heart of the complex is a rectangular courtyard framed by galleries of columns that seem to be interwoven with the surrounding rooms. In the middle of this courtyard is a fountain supported on the backs of twelve lions that are evidently much older than the courtyard itself and are believed to come from the palace of Yusuf Ibn Nagrallah, the Jewish vizier of the Zirids. An extraordinary forest of columns joined by fine, imaginative latticework surrounds the patio like an elegant veil. In Nasridian times, the *Patio de los Leones* (Court of the Lions) was a *hortus conclusus* – a walled-in garden that represents the heavenly garden of Islam. To symbolize the four rivers of paradise, four narrow channels flowed into the fountain. The northern and southern ones flowed from pools in the upper rooms and the eastern and western ones emerged from the baldachin-like pavilions of the gallery. These, too, are part of the representation of paradise as they are similar to the high baldachins or canopies described in the Koran.

The Fountain of the Lions

Since the Reconquest, the courtyard has been named after the fountain with twelve water-spouting lions in its center. Supporting the fountain's basin on their backs, the lions form a solid ring from which all else seems to radiate. Each lion is a symbol of the sun, the source of all life, and as a group they represent the twelve suns of the zodiac and the twelve months, that all exist simultaneously in eternity. The rim of the twelve-cornered basin is laced with verses written by the great poet Ibn Zamrak that extol the beauty of the garden and compare its greatness to that of Allah and the kings: "Blessed is He who has bequeathed this palace to the Iman Mohammed (Mohammed V). In its perfection it is distinguished from all others, for its chambers hold miracles that are incomparable in beauty in accordance with God's will."

Sala de los Reyes

The Court of the Lions is surrounded by four rooms that seem to be woven together by their filigreed, stucco lattice-work. Consisting of three square rooms that open to the east, the *Sala de los Reyes* (Hall of the Kings) is a wonderful place to observe an artistic play of light and shadow. The individual, richly decorated room segments are joined by stalactite arches and shimmering *muqarnas* cupolas. Three small alcoves, that probably served as the royal bedchambers, open off the back wall. Their three multi-colored ceiling designs, that were painted on leather and then mounted on cedar panels and nailed to the ceiling, are what gave the hall its name. Surprisingly enough, one finds that the paintings depict narrative, figurative scenes, despite the fact that this was strictly forbidden in Islamic art. The middle alcove's ceiling design illustrates ten Islamic dignitaries whose gesturing hands suggest that they are engaged in a heated discussion. This probably portrays a fictitious assembly of the ten Nasridian kings from Mohammed I to Mohammed V, the king who had the palace rooms built. On the other hand, the ceiling designs of the side alcoves depict hunting scenes and scenes of courtly life. Although the meaning of these 14th-century paintings is still disputed, there is no question that French and Italian masters had an definite influence on the art of the Nasridian court.

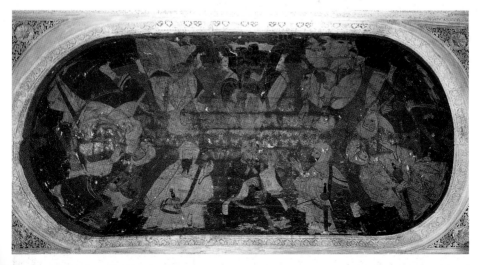

Sala de las Dos Hermanas

On the north side of the courtyard lies the most impressive part of the entire complex. It was named for two lovesick sisters who are said to have died of longing here. The legend says that the siters could look down from their quarters onto the amorous scenes in the garden below, but were not allowed to take part in them. The hall is crowned by a massive, *muqarnas* dome whose surface is broken up into a seemingly endless number of interwoven facets representing the vaults of heaven. Rays of ever-changing sun- and moonlight that shine through the window onto the base of the cupola and wander over the numerous facets almost make the dome seem to revolve. This dome is considered one of the most impressive examples of Islamic art. The square hall is bordered on three sides by long, rectangular rooms. The northern room one leads to a small, beautifully decorated pavilion *(Mirador de Daraxa)* from which the Garden of Daraxa can be seen.

Sala de los Abencerrajes

The south gallery of the Patio de los Leones leads the visitor to a sumptuously decorated, square hall, which is connected to two, long rectangular rooms. Its name – perhaps familiar to readers through Chateaubriand's novel of the same name – refers to a noble family whose members were murdered in this room near the end of Muslim rule. This hall, too, boasts a marvelous *muqarnas* dome that is supported by a

drum in the shape of an eight-pointed star. Sixteen windows, which are incorporated into the base of the dome, light up the room.

Sala de las Camas

The rooms grouped around the Garden of Daraxa were completely renovated in the course of the 16th century. These were probably at one time the living quarters of the palace, complete with the famous harem that inspired many an author's fantastical tales. The only structure remaining from the time of Yusuf I are the (restored) baths with a two-storied main room and several cold and hot pools whose ceiling vaults exhibit characteristic, star-shaped openings.

Partal
Torre de las Damas

To the east of the Daraxa wing lie extensive gardens that lead to a colonnade (arabicized to *partal*) with five arches that mark the entrance to the Torre de las Damas behind them. To the side of this, a few small livingrooms with unusual, but unfortunately poorly preserved murals dating back to the late 13th or early 14th century have been discovered. They depict activities of courtly and everyday life in several, overlapping friezes.

Generalife
Patio de la Acequia

Stretching across the upper slope of the Alhambra is the Generalife whose name was derived from the Arabic words *Jinnah al'Arif* which means "Garden of the Illustrious Ones" or "the noblest of all gardens." Despite the garden's, for the most part, modern facilities and the considerable changes, and restoration work done to its buildings, the ideals of an Islamic garden are still quite evident. The central area is dominated by the *Patio de al Acequia* (Patio of the Canal). Its elongated pool lined with plants and flowers is a remnant of the original four canals. Loggias flank both sides of the pool. A residence (Mirador) used to lie on the south side, while the complex to the north served representative purposes. Beyond this there are additional gardens and irrigation systems, including the famous staircase with water running through channels cut into its stone banisters, which has been an attraction for travelers since the 16th century.

Palacio de Carlo V – Museo Nacional de Arte Hispano-Musulmán

Like the Mezquita of Córdoba, the Alhambra is also marked by a monumental sign of the victory of Christianity. South of the Patio de los Arrayanes, a colossal Renaissance palace, commissioned by Charles V during a visit to Granada, was erected in 1526. The construction was financed by a special tax that Muslims had to pay to "buy back" their religious freedom. Although it is often criticized as a "Christian appendage," this building created by architect Pedro Machuca (who studied under Michelangelo) is considered to be one of the most beautiful Renaissance creations outside of Italy.

tains primarily treasures from the Alhambra. Its extensive ceramic exhibit contains lusterware from the heyday of the Spanish-Moorish faience period that lasted from the early 14th century to the expulsion of the Granadian Empire and whose centers were in Granada and Málaga. The museum also boasts one of the most famous vases from the Alhambra, the *Jarrón de las Gacellas* (Gazelle Vase). This 4.3-foot-(1.32 meters)high, glazed, white vase is decorated with gazelles in gold and cobalt blue and has two, characteristic, wing-like handles.

After Machuca's death in 1550, his son Luis took over. The two-story, outer facades in the style of the Tuscanian early Renaissance with rustic ashlars at the bottom and pilasters at the top. The bronze rings held by lion and eagle heads set into the walls were once used to tie horses to. The doors are framed by pairs of Doric columns whose bases are decorated with reliefs by Juan de Ora that depict various scenes from the Battle of Padua.

Jarrón de las Gacellas

Today, the palace houses two museums. The Museo Provincial de Bellas Artes, built in 1836, exhibits art work that came from the Convent of Granada which had broken up shortly before, and the Museo Nacional de Arte-Hispano-Musulmán, which con-

Granada

Albaicín, p. 347

Bañuelo, Carrera del Darro,
p. 346

Monasterio de la Cartuja,
Paseo de la Cartuja, p. 352

Catedral; Capilla Real,
Gran Vía de Colón, p. 312

Monasterio de San Jerónimo,
Calle Rector López Argueta, p. 344

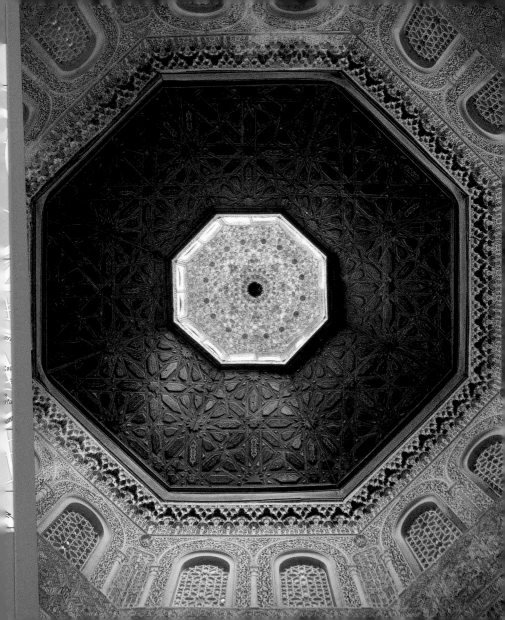

Cathedral

The events of 1492 caused Granada to become a symbol of the Reconquest. After conquering the last Moorish enclave, the Catholic Sovereigns and their successor, Charles V, began elaborate construction projects whose new, marked style of architecture was meant to be a manifest expression of a new era. In 1523, after the mosque of the Alhambra, later the San Francisco Convent and even, upon Queen Isabella's request, the former main mosque had all served as a Christian cathedral, the ground work was laid for an immense house of worship. The location chosen was right in the heart of the Muslim quarter, where the main mosque stood, which was consequently torn down. Architect Enrique Ergas conceived the original design and began construction in the Gothic style. However, only five years later, the cathedral board decided to make a change in plans and hired Diego de Siloë as head architect.

Through his travels, de Siloë was well acquainted with the styles of the Italian Renaissance, and thus, his construction plans gave rise to the first Spanish cathedral in the Renaissance style. Emperor Charles V's visit to Granada in 1526, when he commissioned a palace to be built in the Alhambra in this new style of modern Europe, probably played a decisive role as well. After de Siloë's death in 1563, a series of famous architects took over until the cathedral was eventually finished in 1704. One of them was painter, sculptor, and architect Alonso Cano, who was also one of the most versatile artists of the Golden Age. He designed the monumental main facade completed in 1667 which, instead of mirroring the five divisions on the inside, is laid out like a three-part, roman arch of triumph with high, curving round arches. By reverting to these antique architectural forms, the outside of the cathedral presents an ostentatious sign of Christianity's victory over Islam. One unusual detail of the two-story facade are the medallions in relief that Cano put in place of the more typical pilaster capitals – this idiosyncrasy of the artist was adopted by many of his students. Other statues and reliefs were not added until later in the 18th century.

Cathedral

Enrique Ergas' original Gothic design can still be seen in the groundplan of the cathedral. Diego de Siloë had to adapt his new designs to the outer walls, the bases of the columns and the measurements that had already been established by Ergas. Thus, this cathedral with its five-aisle nave, single-aisle transept and ambulatory lined with chapels shows many similarities with the Cathedral of Toledo. The Capilla Real located on the north side of the cathedral also remained unaltered by de Siloë's construction plans. Its main portal was incorporated into the construction of the new cathedral. The mausoleum of the Catholic Sovereigns was built in the form of the cross with four side chapels and a trapezoidal apse. The final addition to the complex was the 18th century Iglesia del Sagrario with a nave and two side aisles on the south side of the cathedral.

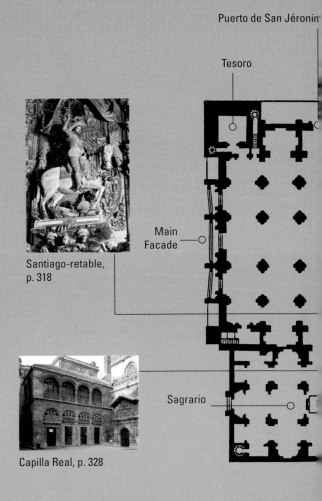

Puerto de San Jéronim

Tesoro

Main Facade

Santiago-retable, p. 318

Capilla Real, p. 328

Sagrario

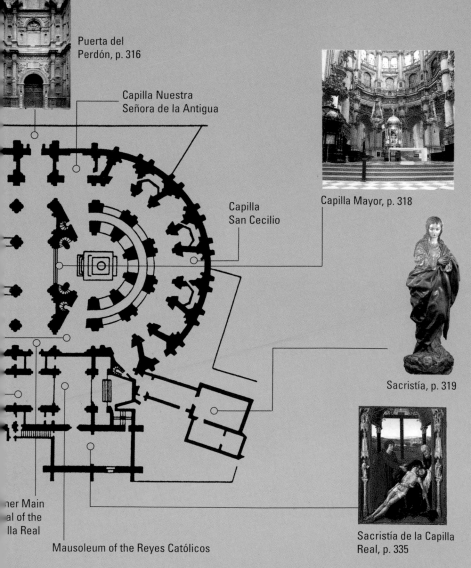

Puerta del
Perdón, p. 316

Capilla Nuestra
Señora de la Antigua

Capilla
San Cecilio

Capilla Mayor, p. 318

Sacristía, p. 319

…er Main
…al of the
…lla Real

Mausoleum of the Reyes Católicos

Sacristía de la Capilla
Real, p. 335

The North Facade
Puerta del Perdón

One of Diego de Siloë's most exceptional works of art is the plateresque penitential archway on the north facade. The spandrels of the two arches symbolizing faith and justice contain a cartouche with an inscription praising Isabella and Ferdinand for these two exact virtues "after 700 years of Moorish rule." The coat-of-arms of both the Catholic Sovereigns and Charles V on the side buttresses reflect these same praises. The Puerta San Jerónimo was also designed by Siloë.

The Interior

Flooded with light from the high, stained glass windows, the interior of the church is a juxtaposition of the Gothic groundplan and Renaissance decor. Mighty clustered columns on high pedestals with sculptures of warriors form a contrast to the high vaults with late Gothic ribbing.

The Capilla Mayor

Another masterpiece attributed almost solely to Diego de Siloë is the Capilla Mayor, which Charles V had intended to be the royal mausoleum. For this reason, Diego de Siloë designed the room as a central construction in the form of a domed round temple connected to the ambulatory and nave by coffered, semicir-

cular arches. The surrounding sculptures also correspond to this theme: saintly figures of the Catholic Sovereigns (1675–1677) sculpted by Pedro de Mena stand above the balconies on the pillars at the entrance. Alonso Cano's polychromatic busts of Adam and Eve adorn the semicircular alcoves below. Crowning the columns of the lower level are the twelve apostles, the foundation of the church of Christ.

Paintings done by Alonso Cano depicting scenes of the Life of the Virgin Mary on the upper level provide a transition to the scenes from the Passion of Christ depicted in the Flemish stained glass windows that date back to the middle of the 16th century.

The Santiago Retable

In the south chapel that lies between the choir and the nave there is a richly decorated, carved wood altar with the equestrian statue of St. Jacob (1640). Revered as Santiago or *Matamoros* (the Moor-killer) in Spain, he was the first saint with his own shrine, the Santiago de Compostela, a place of pilgrimage located on the northwest side of the peninsula that has been famous since the Middle Ages.

Sculpted by Alonso Cano, this statue was originally planned for the pulpit in the choir. The contrast between the Virgin's melancholy facial expression and folded hands and the exceedingly luxurious folds of her garment is beautifully underscored by a simple color scheme in shades of blue and green.

Alonso de Mena portrayed the saint on horseback, in his armor with a wide-rimmed hat and raised sword. Under the hoofs of his horse lies a vanquished Moor.

Sacristía

In the sacristía (sacristy), that is connected to the ambulatory, the visitor will find an almost 20 inch-(50 centimeter)high statue of the *Inmaculada* positioned under a life-sized crucifix by Martínez Montañés.

Isabella – A Queen Leads the Way

She is described as being of average height with a robust but attractive figure, a round face, blue-green eyes and reddish-blond, shimmering hair – this Queen of Castile who led Spain (which at the time of her accession to the throne did not even exist as a geographical concept) to European supremacy with clever, far-sighted, and courageous policies. At the age of 18 she resolved to marry her 11 month-younger cousin Ferdinand, the heir to the throne of Aragón. With this decision, she made the union of two of the greatest kingdoms on the Iberian peninsula possible, which would pave the way for the *Siglo de Oro*, Spain's Golden Age.

Isabella was a woman who did not conform at all to the contemporary view of feminity. She was intelligent, self-confident, and resolute. She knew what she wanted and what she had to do to get it. She possessed political leadership qualities as well as personal strength of character. Her position as her husband's equal was unusual in those days, but she had always been superior to him in strength and courage. However, Ferdinand was by no means incompetent. He knew how to form alliances and make war. He was versed in diplomatic relations with powerful noble families and could convince various interest groups to support his causes. Moreover, he distinguished himself through personal bravery. Macchiavelli had good reason to

Madrazo, Portrait of Isabella I, the Catholic, Queen of Castile and León, 19th century

deem him the ideal ruler but also appraised him as an unscrupulous politician whose diplomatic efforts were always aimed at gaining and maintaining power Ferdinand made a definite contribution, just like Isabella, to the royal couple's political, military, and economic success. Without this complementary partnership, their achievements would have been almost unthinkable. However, Isabella was always the driving force, steering the business of state. She surpassed her husband's bravery with her farsightedness and intelligence and was in every respect the stronger personality, so much so that Castilian nobles ridiculed the King with the nickname *Rey jupon* (King Petticoat). These sentiments are mirrored in the couple's tombstone in the Capilla Real of Granada: the Queen's head sinks deeper into the pillow of their deathbed, symbolizing the "weightiness" of her person.

Her First Decision

No one, least of all herself, would have believed that Isabella would one day be Queen of Castile. In 1454, when Isabella was only three, her father King John II died a premature death, leaving the Castilian throne to the son of his first marriage, Henry IV. Isabella grew up outside the royal court in Arévalo castle where she lived with her mother, Isabella of Portugal, and her younger brother Alfonso. Shielded from the outside world by castle walls, she only had one friend, Beatriz de Bobadilla, the daughter of the commander of the castle, who would remain her friend for the rest of her life. Together they were taught rhetoric, history, philosophy, poetry, and music by clergymen

from the nearby town of Ávila. When she was 11 years old, her half-brother King Henry IV summoned her and Prince Alfonso to the court of Madrid so that they could receive a "proper

Marcuello, Symbols of the Catholic Sovereigns, c. 1482. Chantilly, Musée Condé

education." In view of the fact that courtly life was notoriously lascivious, this reasoning seemed more than ironic. Few Spanish monarchs were as criticized by chroniclers of their time as Henry IV. He was considered to be a terrible monarch and a wicked person. He was

reproached for being lenient, indecisive, unassertive, and a poor judge of character, and above all for his reputed homosexual tendencies. When his second wife bore a daughter named Johanna and Henry proclaimed her to be his heir to the throne even though her real father was obviously one of his court favorites, Beltrán de la Cueva (after whom Johanna was mockingly referred to as *La Beltraneja*), the nobility revolted. Thus, Henry subsequently proclaimed Prince Alfonso XII as king, but the prince died soon after, and the position was then offered to Isabella. During the five years she had spent at the court, Isabella had always opposed its intrigues and corruption, which seemed to have further strengthened her strong moral principles. Now she stood before the first serious political decision of her life, and had nobody to whom she could turn

Isabella Prays to the Virgin with Child, Illustration from the Queen's Book of Hours, Madrid, Biblioteca del Palacio Real

to for advice. But the 17 year-old reacted with extraordinary level-headedness. She refused the crown, and urged the nobility to accept Henry as rightful king and her as mere heir apparent in order to preserve the peace. Henry and the insurgent nobility agreed to her proposition and peace was restored.

The Forbidden Marriage

In the agreements, Isabella had promised to not marry without the King's permission, while he in turn promised to not force her to marry anyone against her will. However, both would end up breaking their promise. Isabella soon found herself surrounded by a throng of suitors asking for her hand in marriage. Among them were the Duke of Berry, the brother of the French King Louis XI; Ferdinand, the only son of King John II of Aragón; and the much older King Alfonso V of Portugal, whom Henry and his council favored. They probably hoped that if Isabella married into the Portuguese royal family they could again try to secure the Castilian throne for Johanna. However, this plan failed to take into consideration Isabella's willfulness. She decided in favor of the young, stately, Aragonian heir apparent who was known to be intelligent, brave, and confident in any situation. Henry was furious and intended to prevent this marriage at all costs. Since he was away on a military campaign at the time, he had his half-sister closely guarded. He assumed that they would not be able to marry immediately, anyway, since they were related

and would first need permission from the Pope. However, Isabella was secretly preparing for the wedding with the help of the Archbishop of Toledo, and had already received the consent of many nobles and Castilian cities. Finally, in September 1469, Ferdinand signed the marriage contract that irrevocably established his role (as prince consort) in the partnership and vowed that:

"He shall take up residence in Castile and not leave the country without Isabella's permission;

He shall not form alliances or go to war without Isabella's consent, but shall proceed, with Isabella, in the Holy War against the Moors;

He shall not dispose of any property possessed by the Crown and shall, jointly with Isabella, name only Castilians for high positions of state, although she alone has the power to accept an oath of allegiance from Castilian cities or grant vassalages or titles;

He shall insure the livelihood of her mother in Arévelo and treat King Henry IV with respect and childlike obedience;

Their signatures shall both have the power to confer legal validity upon future decrees."

Miguel de Cervantes, the author of *Don Quixote*, could not have written a better tale than the one that took place a few weeks later. Since all roads to Aragón were being guarded by royal troops, the prince had to disguise himself as a mule herder to make the adventurous journey to Burgo de Osma where Isabella was waiting for him. On the way, he almost fell victim to an overzealous, stone-throwing city guard. In the end, with a forged authorization from the Pope, the wedding ceremony took place on October 18, 1469 in Valladolid.

A Queen Without a King

As a result, Henry disinherited his half-sister and again proclaimed his little daughter Johanna as rightful heir to the throne. Not too long thereafter Henry reconciled himself again

A Monk Presents Isabella and Ferdinand with His Book, 1502. Woodcarving

with Isabella. When he died unexpectedly on December 11, 1474 it was not completely certain who would be his successor and the situation in the kingdom was tense. Isabella decided to act quickly in order to ward off the Beltraneja's followers. Only two days later, on December 13, Isabella had herself anointed as Queen of Castile despite the fact that Ferdinand was still in Aragón and had not yet even heard the news of the King's death. A larger part of the nobility and clergy as well as most of the cities recognized the proclamation and pledged their loyalty to her. Still, it was a crowning without a king. Ferdinand was deeply offended. In order to take the power into his own hands, he even made the impossible decree that his kingdom would not recognize a female heir. Yet, Isabella remained victorious. The court of arbitration to which both appealed confirmed the marriage contract and simply made a few amendments to it. It was thus established that all documents had to be signed by Ferdinand first, all coins would from then on bear the likenesses of them both, and the Castilian and Aragonian coats-of-arms would be combined into one. And Isabella added the statement, "My Lord and husband, let it be known that as my spouse you are also the King of Castile and your command shall thus be obeyed in this land."

The Powerful Queen

Ferdinand, however, would remain simply prince consort until Isabella's death, for it was always she who set the standards for the political decisions of the land. Whether it was about restoring public order, rebuilding the shattered economy, consolidating state finances, establishing a Court of the Inquisition, conquering Granada or sending Columbus on his journey, Isabella was always the driving force. She conducted businesses of state with the same level-headedness and confidence that she had used to choose her husband and become Queen. Thanks to her shrewdness in matters of state, the deteriorating kingdom experienced a political and economic upswing and the return to world power. By enforcing the Inquisition, she not only gave in to the pressure of the poorer population, but also hoped to unite the country under one religion. As sole heir of the Castilian Monarchs who had launched the Reconquest from South to North, she felt that it was her duty to resume the war against the Moors and put an end to more than 800 years of Islamic rule. The decision made after four years of deliberation to send Christopher Columbus on his journey to the "New World" was not just motivated by the need to replenish the royal treasury, but also by the hope for new land and thus more subjects to convert to Catholicism. She also planned strategic marriages for her four children to help strengthen alliances with other powerful kingdoms in Europe.

Despite all of her calculated political power, Isabella also had a human side. In her testament, for example, she stipulated the preservation of "the lawful rights of the natives (in conquered territories) who are free people and not serfs." She decreed that they should

Artist unknown, Isabella of Castile (detail from a double portrait of the Catholic Sovereigns), late 15th century. Ávila, Museo de la Catedral

be treated fairly and compensated for their sufferings. Isabella's attitudes and philosophies were shaped by humanistic thought. It was she who – with the help of her advisers, the two youngest sons of the famous humanist, poet, and scholar Iñigo López de Mendoza, Marquis of Santillana (1398–1458) – made the most lasting contributions to education in her country. Through conversations with scholars and artists sought to expand her own mental horizons as well. After applying herself earnestly to the study of Latin at the age of 31, she set up grammar schools in her court for the sons of the Castilian nobility and founded a new university called Vera Cruz in Valladolid. She promoted new printing technologies and helped establish them throughout the land. In 1477, for example, she granted German printer Dierck Maertens tax exemption to practice his "art" in her country. By the end of her lifetime, approximately 50 percent of city inhabitants could read. Among the 1,000 books that had been printed by that time was the first grammar book of the Spanish language, modeled after Latin principles that Latin and grammar scholar Antonio de Nebrija (1441–1522) had presented to the Queen in 1492. This helped establish the foundations for a common language in Spain and its colonies overseas.

Her Death

One of the most decisive points in Isabella's life was the premature death of her son and heir to the throne, Juan, whom she tenderly referred to as *mi ángel* (my angel). He died shortly before his marriage to Margarete of Austria, daughter of Emperor-to-be Maximilian I, in October 1497. Juan's death left a wound that would never heal and created concerns about who would succeed to the throne. These thoughts would dominate the last years of Isabella's life.

At the age of 53 when she sensed that her death was approaching, she resolved to settle this final decision as well. Her second daughter, Juana (who was married to the Habsburger, Philip the Handsome, son of German Emperor Maximilian) exhibited signs of becoming increasingly unruly and psychologically unstable. Since Juana was now the next in line to the Castilian throne, Isabella stipulated in her testament that if Juana could not or would not assume power, the regency of Castile would fall to Ferdinand. However, he would only be acting on behalf of Juana until her son Carlos (later Charles V) was of age and could accede to the throne. With this decision, Isabella once again demonstrated her political foresight, even though Ferdinand would later choose to defy her will and warp her provisions to justify his own power-hungry, political means. (After Isabella's death, Ferdinand declared his daughter unfit to rule and had her imprisoned.) In her testament, Isabella also requested that she be laid to rest in Granada, the city of her greatest triumph, and forbid any unnecessary expenditures or the construction of a tombstone. On 26 November 1504, Isabella of Castile died. Pedro Mártir, scholar and tutor of her children, paid homage to her death with these words:

"Never before have I heard of a woman who was created by God and Nature more perfectly than she. The whole world knows of her courage, her spirit, her strength, and the zeal with which she rooted out evil to plant good."

Attributed to Michael Sittow,
The Virgin of the Catholic Sovereigns,
c. 1490. Madrid, Museo del Prado

Capilla Real

The Catholic Sovereigns wished to be buried at the site of their greatest triumph and thus, in the year 1504 only a few months before her death, Isabella I commissioned the construction of the *Capilla Real* (Royal Chapel). It was to be built right next to the cathedral which was at that time still the former mosque. Enrique de Egas was hired as head architect and he began work one year later. When construction was finished in 1521, the Sovereigns' remains were transferred from the Convento de San Francisco in the Alhambra to the new chapel. Many people at the time, Emperor Charles V in particular, criticized its striking austerity, but this was how the Queen had requested it. For unlike most other European monarchs and clergy, the most powerful rulers of the

western world did not desire an extravagant grave. The chapel was built in the form of a Latin cross with four side chapels and a trapezoidal east apse. The main entrance was once on the north side, but was later incorporated into the construction of the cathedral and now opens onto the crossing of the cathedral. Today, the Capilla Real can be accessed from the Plazuela de la Lonja. Here, visitors will enjoy a view of the Queen Isabella – style facade created by Juan García de Pradas in 1527. Above the portal is a representation of Mary with the Christ Child flanked by St. John the Baptist and St. John the Evangelist to whom the chapel is dedicated. The entablature is decorated with imperial coats-of-arms with the two-headed eagle and the emblems of the Catholic Sovereigns.

Réja

Upon entering the chapel, one immediately notice the réja, the wrought-iron grille that separates the nave of the chapel from the apse. Bartolomé de Jaén created this masterpiece which many consider the most beautiful *réja* in Spain. Royal crests, medallions, and figures of saints adorn both sides of the gilded grille. Decorative, plateresque staves with Corinthian capitals alternate with spiral- and diamond-shaped tendrils. The band stretching across the lower section represents the apostles standing under baldachins of late Gothic tracery. The Castilian coat-of-arms upheld by lions

adorns the main gate, surrounded by the emblems of the Catholic Sovereigns, oxen yokes, and crossbows. A frieze of flowing figures runs across the entire upper section of the grille depicting ten scenes from the life of Christ as well as the martyrdom of St. John the Baptist and St. John the Evangelist, all crowned by the crucifix at the top. Below the figure of St. Peter (first row, third from the left), one finds the artist's signature: Maestro Bartolomé me fecit.

The Tomb of the Catholic Sovereigns (With detail)

Positioned before the altar are the two Renaissance tombstones of the founders of the united Spanish kingdom and their first successor. In the crypt below lie the simple leaden coffins containing the remains of their bodies. The gravestone of the Catholic Sovereigns was crafted in 1517 by Florentine sculptor Domenico Fancelli and is decorated with a multitude of figures and emblems. The twelve apostles are depicted in the niches on the lower sides; griffins on the corners symbolize heathen evil which is vanquished by the four fathers of the church. The cracked pomegranate represents the conquered city of Granada; the lion in the coat-of-arms is a symbol of the kingdom of León and the small castle a symbol of Castile. One of Isabella's hands lies on top of the other and she is wearing the Santiago cross. Ferdinand is depicted with his sword and St. George medallion. Both are guarded by a lion, the symbol of strength. At the foot of the tombstone, cherubs hold up a plaque bearing the inscription *Unamines Catholici Appelati* (together named the Catholic Sovereigns).

The adjacent tombstone, which was erected in 1519/20, depicts Johanna la Loca and Philip the Handsome resting on a four-poster bed. Its sculptor, Bartolomé Ordóñez used the neighboring, Italian version as a model. In the upper corners, the Saints Andrew and Michael watch over the King, while St. John the Baptist and St. John the Evangelist attend to the Queen. Johanna's hands are folded in prayer and Philip's raised sword is daunting even in death. Johanna's head is turned away from her husband – the artist's way of alluding to the unhappy end of their marriage. Two colossal empires were united through the marriage of the heir apparent, Johanna, and the Habsburger, Philip. However after the initial happy years, Philip's infidelity led to disagreements between the two of them. Johanna was declared unfit to rule due to her supposed mental illness and was even held prisoner by her own son, Charles V, after Philip's death because he would have otherwise been forced to relinquish the Spanish crown to his mother. His son, Philip II was the one who finally had Johanna's remains moved to the Capilla Real in 1574.

The High Altar (with Detail)

The high altar, that was crafted between 1520 and 1522 by Felipe Bigarny (or Filipe de Borgoña) is one of the earliest Renaissance altar-pieces in Spain. It is dedicated to St. John the Baptist and St. John the Evangelist. The exceedingly naturalistic figures and reliefs are carved in wood and divided into picture boxes. Above the plinth, which portrays the entry of the Catholic Sovereigns into Granada and the forced baptisms of the Moors, the viewer will find reliefs that depict the Life of Christ. In the lower section, between the figures of St. John the Evangelist and St. John the Baptist, the following biblical scenes are reproduced: the The Three Kings in which the youngest king is supposed to represent Emperor Charles V, the Baptism of Christ, and John in Patmos. The middle section depicts scenes of the martyrdom, and in the upper section the viewer will find the Road to Calvary, Christ on the Cross between Mary and John and the Pietà. Angel-like figures of the Catholic Sovereigns are ascribed to Diego de Siloë, stand on both sides of the altar.

Rogier van der Weyden, The Holy Family,
Oil on wood, approx. 37 x 27 cm

15th century, for which the royal couple evidently had a special liking. Two paintings by Rogier van der Weyden (1399/1400–1464) – who besides Jan van Eyck was one of the most famous members of the Flemish School – stand out above the rest. His love of the human form and his precise, three-dimensional figures probably stem from the fact that he, just like his father, had first worked as a sculptor. The diversity and intensity of his portrayal of human emotion are also indicative of his background in sculpture. Both paintings were once part of a triptych that was intended as a glorification of Mary as she participated in the three main stages of the Life of Christ – birth, death, and resurrection. (Today, the right wing of the triptych is located in the Metropolitan Museum of Art in New York.) Each scene is framed by an arch decorated with sculpture-like figures painted in monochromatic shades of gray that, like the sculpted scenes on the capitals, complement the main themes. The panels are cut off at the top because they were fitted into the wing of an altar

In the sacristy, which contains the church's treasures and a part of the Catholic Sovereigns' extensive collection of paintings, there are numerous works from the Flemish School of Painting dating from the

during the reign of Philip IV in 1632. Originally, an angel wearing a crown hovered at the vertex of each arch. Banners unfurled from their crowns upon which Mary's virtues were extolled. These conclusions are based on an earlier version of the triptych, which is now on display in Berlin. The left wing shows the Holy Family portrayed in a manner that reflects medieval thought as larger-than-life, in a Gothic interior with an exquisite brocade tapestry in the background. Mary is wearing a white dress, as a symbol of her purity. It is hemmed with gold letters that form the words of the Magnificat. Her folded hands point towards the Christ Child on her lap, while Joseph slumbers peacefully at her side – an allusion to his dream. The sides of the arch are decorated with the statues of St. Peter and St. Luke. The scenes at the top of the arch display the birth of Christ and the worshiping shepherds while the scenes on the capitals show Abraham's sacrifice and the death of Absalom which could also be considered a foreshadowing of the Passion of Christ.

Rogier van der Weyden, Pietà
Oil on wood, approx. 37 x 27 cm

The *Pietà* on the middle panel is one of the most impressive scenes. The background consists of a landscape with green hills and a looming cross in the center. In the foreground, vivid images of Mary grieving over

Adoration of the Magi (Detail)

Errection of the Cross (Detail)

the limp body of Christ while John and Joseph of Arimathea look on, make the actual event – namely lowering the heavy body of Jesus down from the cross – take on secondary significance. The figures of St. John and St. Matthew adorn the sides of the arch and the sculptures in the archivolt recall the sufferings of Christ. The belief that he died for the sins of humanity is alluded to above this by a depiction of Adam and Eve being banished from the garden of Eden.

Hans Memling, Descent from the Cross, 1492/1494.
Oil on wood, 56.6 x 38.2 cm

Descent from the Cross and *The Wailing Women* were painted by Hans Memling (c. 1433–1494) from Hesse, who managed to gain acceptance into the relatively small circle of 15th century Dutch painters and become one of their most prominent members. Around 1465, after working for several years in Rogier van der Weyden's studio, Memling founded a large workshop in Bruges, where he also became a citizen. His style is distinguished by an excellent sense of grace and proportion, as well as beautifully harmonizing colors. Memling's expertise is clearly demonstrated by the perfection of the diptych's altar form.

These two paintings in the sacristy of the Capilla Real are also newer renditions of a diptych completed around ten years earlier with the same theme (Private Collection and São Paulo, Museu de Arte), and are attributed to his later work. Since Memling attached more importance to individual forms a tightly arranged composition and in place of movement preferred a compilation of static elements, he became a master of paintings whose themes contain no external action. Despite their actually quite dramatic themes, these paintings serve more as devotional pictures that inspire religious meditation. Thus, his *Descent from the Cross* is centered on the dead body of Christ whose arms hang limply over the shoulders of Joseph of Arimathea and Nicodemus. The painting fulfills the same contemplative function as a pietà, in which Christ's body lies across Mary's lap and the focus of devotion is the fulfillment of God's saving grace.

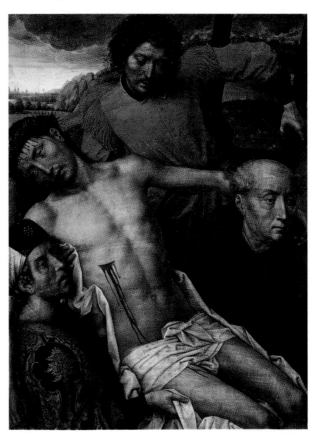

Dirk Bouts, Descent from the Cross (triptych)
Oil on wood, center panel 191 x 145 cm,
left and right wings 191 x 66 cm each

In addition to the somewhat younger Hans Memling, Dirk Bouts (c. 1415–1475) was one of the greatest painters of the Dutch School after Rogier van der Weydens. In 1457 he became the official painter of Loewen. In this triptych of the *Descent from the Cross* the viewer can clearly see the old master's influence, for Bouts was familiar with Van der Weyden's work of the same name that hung in the Liebfrauen church in Loewen. Bouts' version, however, appears more contemplative and peaceful. The scenes are set in a frame with three, arched portals that create the impression of an arch of triumph through which the observer must look to see the events on the inside. This effect is emphasized in the center panel where the crossbeam is intersected by the archivolt. Similar to Rogier van der Weyden's work, Bouts' rendition transforms a brief Bible passage into an emotionally charged scene. Joseph of Arimathea and Nicodemus hold the body of Christ, while John comforts the devastated Virgin Mary to the left. A grieving Mary Magdalene is depicted on the right. The colors red and black accentuate this meditative painting which is complemented by scenes from Genesis in the archivolts and figures of the apostles in the sides of the arches. The narrow wings of the triptych portray the Crucifixion on the left and the Resurrection on the right.

Moorish Stucco Decoration

When one enters an Islamic building, ornamental designs with recurring motifs unfold before the eyes like a tapestry, covering every surface, no matter how small. This passion for ornamental designs is an indirect product of Islamic law which, unlike Christianity, forbids any and all representations of the physical, human form. If Christian religious art captures the gaze of believers and conjures up images of a fantastical world before their eyes, the rhythmic repetition of floral and geometric motifs in Islamic art liberates believers from all conscious or imaginary constraints. It is "a parable for the declaration of divine reality, which is ubiquitous and at the center of every cosmos, so that no single being and no single thing can claim to be its sole representation." Whereas the caliphs of Córdoba still preferred the carved stonework, the Almohades favored decorations made of sculpted or cut stucco, and thus this decorative style found its way into the Moorish architecture of

Granada, Alhambra, Patio de los Arrayanes, Alcove in the North Wall

Andalusia. The primary advantage of this technique was that it could be used to cover low-quality building materials – which were often used to save time on construction – with an artistic and decorative surface. It could be applied in a multitude of ways: as an individually decorated panel or piece incorporated into an ensemble; as a decoration for vaults and arches or even entire walls and ceilings; or as the extra flourish adorning pillars or friezes over doors and windows.

Stucco also allowed a rich variety of forms: delicate squares, octagons, diamonds and stars, distinct or interwoven; stylized floral motifs – blossoms and leaves, tendrils, rosettes, and palmettes – combined with arabesques; and hieratic inscriptions set into narrow cartouches or long bands. Yet, even here the floral motifs were subject to geometric principles and were either themselves geometric or were incorporated into rigid, symmetrical patterns or grids. Once the visitor is reminded that these stucco decorations were originally painted, then he or she may begin to imagine the magnificent colors that once embellished these splendid, interlaced designs.

Granada, Alhambra, Bathhouse, detail of a Wall Decoration (Restored in the mid-19th century)

Casa del Cabildo Antiguo (Madrasa)

Inside this baroque palace, remains of a prayer room and mihrab have been preserved that were once a part of the academy built by Yusuf I. Scholars used to teach in mosques or private houses until 1349 when the Nasridian ruler had a *madrasa*, a juridical-theological academy, built right across from the Great Mosque (where the cathedral now stands). The square room is lavishly decorated with marvelous stucco designs. The upper portion of the room is formed by *muqarnas* spandrels leading up to an octagonal dome with a high row of windows crowned by a lantern and a tent-shaped, timber ceiling.

Corral de Carbón

This building's beautiful facade has a large, brick horseshoe arch which once marked the entrance to the caravansary that was built at the beginning of the 14th century near the Great Mosque. As the only remaining, intact example of this architectural style in Spain, it offers a vivid impression of Moorish commercial life. As usual, this structure is located on a street that led from the city gates to the market and served as a warehouse, trading center, and inn. The original rectangular structure, that housed stables for pack animals around the courtyard in the lower level and guest-rooms and storage space above, has been preserved. When the coal merchants moved in here during the 16th century, the building earned its present name (from the Spanish word *carbón*, or coal). After later serving as a theater and a residence, it was bought by the state in 1933 and renovated by Torres Balbás. The large patio on the inside is lined with a three-tiered gallery resting on brick pillars.

Monasterio de San Jerónimo

During the siege of Granada, the Catholic Sovereigns founded this monastery in 1492 in honor of Hieronymus, a translator of the Bible and father of the church. The ground stone was laid four years later in what is today the university district. By decree of Charles V it became a memorial to Gonzalo Fernández de Córdoba, known by the name of El Gran Capitán. This army commander who served under Isabella and Ferdinand and later under the Viceroy of Naples (d. 1515), was laid to rest here along with his wife. Their figures kneel on the side of the main altar-piece which portrays scenes from the Life of Christ and the Virgin Mary. In addition, the legendary deeds of the Gran Capitán are glorified in the reliefs on the ceiling vaults alongside representations of antique heroes and figures from the Holy Scripture. Their design is attributed to the Renaissance architect Diego de Siloë who took over the site supervision in 1528, and is the one who is actually credited with the construction of the church, begun in the late Gothic style. Next to the west facade, the two-story main patio, in particular, is exemplary of his brilliant architectural talent. He incorporated richly decorated portals into the lower level of the arcades and the upper level is trimmed with a stone balustrade. This is adorned with the initials of the Catholic Sovereigns as well as various coats-of-arms including that of the first archbishop of Granada, Hernando de Talavera.

Palacio de Almanxarra, Cuarto Real de Santo Domingo

Within this now privately owned building, the visitor will find the tower of a former Moorish palace dating from the first half of the 13th century which was part of the original fortification of the city. The palace was once owned by feudal lords and later transferred hands over the course of the Reconquest to the Catholic Sovereigns who subsequently turned it into a monastery. The chamber inside the tower is worth seeing, for it is a wonderful display of the splendor of Nasridian architecture outside the Alhambra. The entrance is a wide arch adorned with azulejos and the inscription "God is Great" in gold, Kufic lettering. The room beyond the entrance is enlarged by alcoves that are decorated with stucco lattice-work and tiles of blue, white, and gold.

Bañuelo

If visitors cross through the courtyard of a building in the Carrera del Darro 31, they will discover one of the oldest and most well-preserved Arabian bathhouses in Andalusia, dating back to the 11th century. These baths were once a standard feature of every Arabian city. The three rooms all have barrel-vaulted ceilings, supported by columns and exhibit the typical, star-shaped openings. The capitals of the columns are especially intriguing since they were appropriated mainly from Roman and Visigoth structures, but also from structures built during the reign of the caliphate of Córdoba. In those times when construction activity was florishing, parts from other buildings – the spoils – were often used to save time or construction costs.

Albaicín

On the other side of the Darro, across from the Alhambra, lies perhaps the most beautiful old-city quarter in Andalusia. With its steep, narrow streets and old, white-washed houses, it has retained much of the atmosphere of ancient, Moorish Granada. Unit the last great Moorish rebellions in 1568, the district of Albaicín was inhabited by Moors who had been forced by Christian persecutors to flee Baeza and seek refuge in Granada. It was they who supposedly gave this hill its name – *Albayyasin* (that which belongs to the people of Baeza). The name may also stem from the word *Albayyazin* (falconry) which was a popular sport among Arab peoples. Today, the district is a picturesque residential area which is again home to a Muslim community.

The Art of Islamic Calligraphy

In every work of Islamic art, whether displayed on walls, textiles, vases, weapons or tiles, one finds – often stylized into fantastical forms. Calligraphy (the art of beautiful handwriting) was one of the most noble forms of art in a world where there was no printing press until the 18th century. The calligrapher was superior to other artists and was held in high esteem by Muslim rulers. The importance of writing in the Islamic world stemmed from the fact that Muslims regarded the ability to write as a gift and even a blessing from God. The first revelation that Mohammed received was, "Read in the name of the Lord, ... He taught His people how to use the pen; He taught them that which they did not know before." Arabic was the sacred language, for it was in Arabic that God spoke to Mohammed and in Arabic that His Word was recorded in writing. Thus, only those who have learned

Arabic can truly comprehend the revelations. From the very beginning, the religion's greatest mission was to preserve and spread the word of God. In the religion of Islam, God is believed to be beyond any human image and any physical representation of God is strictly forbidden (in one interpretation it is a sin to create a representation of God because it would have no soul). Thus, artists used calligraphy to create a highly decorative form of art, for in the words of Mohammed, "beautiful script reveals the truth."

The Arabic Alphabet

Arabic did not become the official language of the Islamic empire until the late seventh century during the reign of the Umayyad. Then, regardless of their cultures or national pasts, subjugated peoples were fused into one homogenous union. As the God-given language of the Koran, Arabic, which was already the language of worship and law, now became the language used in literature, science, and government. The Arabs most likely derived their alphabet from the Syrian one and then modified various letters with

Page from the Koran in Kufic Script, Abbasside Dynasty, 9th century. Iraq, Mrs. Bashir Mohamed Collection

A Calligrapher at Work, al-Kazwini, The Miracle of Creation, 16th century. Turkish handwriting, London, British Museum)

diacritical marks to distinguish them from one another. The Arabic alphabet is essentially cursive in form, contains no capitals, and is read from left to right. It is composed of 28 consonants that are written differently depending on their position in the word – namely at the beginning, in the middle or at the end. The consonants are represented by specific signs ordered along a horizontal line with vowels and diacritic marks and other

The Arabic Alphabet

alif (a)

bā (b)

tā (t)

tā (t, th)

ǧīm (ǧ, j)

ḥā (h)

ḫā (h, kh)

dāl (d)

ḏāl (ḏ, dh)

rā (r)

zāi (z, s)

sīn (s)

šīn (š, sch)

ṣād (ṣ)

dād (d)

ṭā (ṭ)

ẓā (ẓ)

ᶜain

ḡain (g, gh)

fā (f)

gāf (q,k)

kāf (k)

lām (l)

mīm (m)

nun (n)

hā (h)

wāw (w,u)

yā (y, ī)

hamza

special signs arranged above and below them. In addition to the 28 consonants, the first letter of the alphabet, called the alif, functions as the standard which dictates the size of all the other letters.

The Forms of Arabic Script

Due to the cursive characters of Arabic script, scribes soon began to develop its calligraphic form. The simple, geometric design of the letters made it possible to write and connect many of them with one stroke of the pen. Over the course of the centuries, many school and styles evolved. Each country developed its own, unique methods. Sometimes individual styles were reserved for specific materials or were only used for a certain subject, like verses from the Koran, poems or official documents.

One of the oldest script forms is *kufi*, which was named after the city of Kufa. It is based on angular elements that are always written horizontally and often have a pronounced base. Because of its ceremonial and monumental appearance, this was the predominant, priestly script form used since the beginnings of Islam for the Koran and other texts of high religious value. Parallel to the introduction of rag paper, which was much easier to write on than the brittle papyrus, as well as the use of the quill pen, a new form of writing began to develop. Founded in the eighth century, this scripts characters were formed by a series of loops. In the tenth century, *nashi* – a script similar to stenography and thus better suited to bureaucratic and private use – was elevated to the rank of Koran script and ultimately replaced the older *kufi*. This new style gave birth to a multitude of rounded script forms like the Andalusian-Maghrebian style in Andalusia, whose slimmer, softer lines and smaller spaces between words distinguish it from *nashi*. However, the old *kufi* letters continued to be an especially dignified decorative style reserved for sacred monuments and holy texts.

Calligraphy and Architecture

One of the most essential aspects of Islamic architecture is calligraphy which, in combination with floral arabesques and geometric designs, covers the walls of mosques, palaces, and mausoleums. Calligraphy's extraordinary wealth of characters, their harmony and the rhythmic movement of their composition create an opulent interplay of light and shadow, that accentuates nuances of color and form. As the manifest form of language and the written word, calligraphy glorified the hidden countenance of Allah. Set into a geometric framework, it was used to record verses from the Koran that praise God and the prophets, recall religious laws, creeds and prayers, laud rulers, preserve poets' greatest litererary works or commemorate architects and reasons for a building's construction. While *kufi* was used well into the 11th century exclusively for epigraphic texts, *nashi* subsequently found its way into Islamic architecture because its cursive structure offered artists more creative possibilities. This innovation led to a constant development process, and the letters of this script form underwent many changes as they were adapted to the dimensions and materials used in architecture.

Kufic Inscription, Alhambra, Sala de los Embajadores

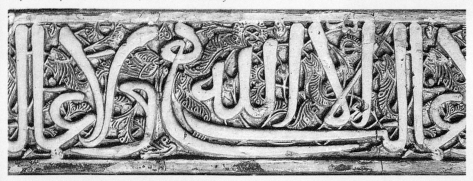

Monasterio de la Cartuja

This Carthusian monastery, famous for its baroque sacristy, once stood in the middle of the countryside, outside the city. It was established in 1506 by an endowment from the Gran Capitán who is said to have won a battle against the Moors on this site. However, construction of the monastery was not completed until the 18th century.

Above the portal with the simple facade framed by listels stands a statue of the founder of the monastic order, St. Bruno. His followers lived here in solitary cells until the monastery was severely damaged by the French in 1824. The entrance hall leads into the cloister with ambulatories surrounding an orange grove. The adjoining rooms are worth a visit, for they hold paintings by lay brother Juan Sánchez

Cotán 1560-1627) and artist Vicente Carducho (1578–1638), as well as a compilation of the history of the order and pictures illustrating the martyrdom of the Carthusians in England during the reign of Henry VIII.

Upon entering the monastery's single-aisled chapel completed by architect Cristóbal Vilches in the first half of the 17th century, struck by the lavish, imaginative stucco decor, which makes the Cartuja a masterpiece of baroque architecture. The room is divided by a wrought-iron gate into two sections, one for monks and one for laypeople, and on each side is an altar designed by Juan Sánchez Cotán, one depicting the Baptism of Christ and the other the Flight into Egypt. The latter includes an impressive still life of bread and cheese which represents the meager provisions of the Holy Family. The patron saint of the monastery, María de la Asuncíon, is revered in seven works painted by Pedro Atanasio Bocanegra that depict scenes from the life of the Virgin (1670). The focus of the entire room, however, is the baldachin altar in the choir, crafted in 1710 by architect and sculptor Francisco Hurtado Izquierdo. It stand on a pedestal of red and black marble and is supported by six gilded columns decorated with floral patterns and inlaid mirrors and is crowned by a painting of the Virgen de Asunción.

and statues, the sagrario is a masterpiece of high baroque art. The cupola painted by Antonio Palomino displays the Trinity in its center, and below that a portrait of St. Bruno with the globe, and representations of the four Evangelists in the pendentives.

Sacristía

The highlight of every visit to this monastery is the *sacristía* (sacristy), begun in 1727, which is exemplary of the baroque style in Spain, and forms a sharp contrast with the colorful splendor of the Sagrario. Above a base of colored, grained marble, the sacristy's walls are covered with a rich, lacy and contoured, decorative layer of white stucco. The architectural structure of the room almost dissolves in the convoluted flourishes which seem to fluctuate according to the play of light. Cabinets inlaid with wood, ivory, tortoiseshell, and silver add to the effect. The polychromatic marble altar-piece is dominated by a statue of St. Bruno who is portrayed meditating on a skull in his left hand. Saints and archangels adorn the cupola, while paintings of the saints of the Carthusian order adorn the walls.

El Sagrario

Hurtado Izquierdo is also credited with the construction of the square *Sagrario* (1704/1705), or sanctuary, which is dominated by a multicolored marble altar-piece in its center. With gilded woodcarvings, luminous frescoes and a wealth of marble

Guadix

Catedral Santa María de la Encarnación

Famous for its white-washed houses, this city is considered by many to be the cradle of Spanish Christianity because its inhabitants are said to have converted to Christianity after a miracle performed by St. Torcuato. Upon the foundations of the former mosque, a large Renaissance cathedral was built. Construction began in 1510 and was not actually completed until 1796, but the decisive work was done in 1549 by Diego de Siloë. Using the cathedrals of Málaga and Granada as his models, de Siloë designed a new choir and a tower which were ultimately added on in the course of the 17th century. The monumental facade which contains baroque as well as early classical elements is the result of remodeling work done in the 18th century by Vicente de Acero, the architect of the cathedral of Cádiz.

Lacalahorra

Castillo

Nestled into the background of the nearby Sierra Nevada mountain range, these thick walls with their four round corner towers topped with tiny cupolas are a magnificent sight. Built in 1509–1513, this structure presents itself as a solid fortress on the outside. However, on the inside visitors will discover a brilliant, Italian Renaissance palace. Architects, sculptors, and craftsmen from Italy, and in particular Michele Carlone of Genoa, were all involved in the design of the interior, for which architectural elements of Carrara marble were custom-designed in Italy and then brought to Spain. The palace complex became especially important for the development of the plateresque style, although its decor first brought the characteristic elements of the Italian Renaissance to Andalusia. Lacalahorra was actually a gift that the margrave, a son of the famous cardinal of Mendoza, presented to his first wife. The showpiece of the palace, however, is the two-story courtyard with Latin inscriptions and coats-of-arms that represent the alliance between the margrave's family and that of his second wife.

The Province of Jaén

The Province of Jaén

"Fields, nothing but fields – and white farmhouses scattered between olive trees." This is how Spanish poet Antonio Machado (1875–1939) described the province that he endearingly referred to as "silver Jaén." Indeed, the landscape here is covered by endless groves of olive trees that stretch like a green net over the light or red colored hills and spread a silver glow in the sunlight. The few urbanized areas, like the beautiful Renaissance cities of Úbeda and Baeza or the capital city (with the same name as the province) that interrupt this image only serve to underscore the fact that this infrastructurally poor region is completely economically dependent on the mono-culture of the olive tree industry. Only the eastern part of the province provides a break from this monotony. Spain's largest national park is located here, at the headwaters of the Guadalquivir and Segura rivers. Owing to their extraordinary diversity of flora and fauna, the Sierra de Cazorla and Sierra de Segura are a favorite travel destination. But despite the enthusiasm that many visitors feel for the province, the city of Jaén has for centuries remained a mere stopover, in which few tourists choose to tarry. As in the times of the Moors, who named the city Giyen or *Geen* ("way of the caravans"), it still lies at the intersection of many roads leading from the north to the coast. The Carthaginians were the first to recognize how strategic this location was, and referred to it as Aurigii because of its silver mines. The Romans elevated it to the status of city under the name of Flavia, and after the fall of the caliphate it became the capital of one of the many *taifa* kingdoms. Because of its strategic position, the region was the scene of many fierce battles during the Reconquest. The mountain pass *Desfiladero de Despeñaperros* ("bottleneck pass of the falling dogs") became famous as Castile's gateway into Andalusia, for it is said that at this seemingly impenetrable pass a shepherd showed the army of Alfonso VIII the way down. This established access to Andalusia and thus, after conquering the Almohades near Navas de Tolosa in 1212, Alfonso VIII could commence his Christian campaign against the Moors. Other historical battles were carried out near the pass as well, for example the defeat of Napoleon's troops near Bailén in 1808. However, Jaén, which was conquered in 1246 by the Christian Ferdinand III, was only important for a very short time as an outpost in fight against Granada and still suffers today under its fate of insignificancy. Culturally, though, it represents an interesting conversion of Castilian and Andalusian art and architecture.

Jaén, La Guardia de Jaén

Jaén

Museo Provincial,
Paseo de la Estación 29, p. 370

Baños Árabes, Plaza de
S. Luisa de Marillac, p. 365

Also worth seeing:

1 Palacio Episcopal,
  Plaza de Santa María

2 Iglesia de San Bartolomé,
  Plaza de San Bartolomé

3 Arco de San Lorenzo,
  Almendros Aguilar

4 Iglesia de San Andrés,
  Calle de San Andrés

I. Figueroa

C. Muñoz Garnica

Bernabé Soriano

Hurtado

Pescadería

Plaza de San
Francisco

Campanas

Flores

1 Plaza de
Santa María

Maestra

Almendros

3

Plaza de
la Merced

Capitán Aranda Alta

Carretera al Castillo y Neveral

Catedral, Plaza de Santa María,
p. 366

Castillo de Santa Catalina, p. 364

Castillo de Santa Catalina

This castle was named after St. Catherine, for it was on her name day that the city of Jaén was conquered in 1246. On the ruins of the Arabian *castillo*, one of the most fortified and impenetrable of its time, the Christian ruler built a new structure with the help of Moorish construction workers from Granada. It remained the bastion of Christianity in Spain for a long time.

which contained the warm water bath. Finally, they would finish with a bath in a smaller side room with cold water in large clay jugs.

An underground tunnel led from the baths to the building complex of the Santo Domingo monastery whose beautiful courtyard occupies the site where the Moorish Royal Palace once stood.

Baños Árabes

In 1913, the remains of an Arabian bathhouse were discovered underneath the 16th century Palacio de Villadompardo. At 5,057 square feet (470 square meters) in size, it was one of the largest in all of Spain and is impressive testimony to Andalusia's highly developed bathing culture. It is also referred to as the Baños de Alí after a taifa king who ruled over the city in the 11th century and, according to legend, was murdered here. The arrangement of the rooms provides a good and lasting impression of Arabian bathing culture, which was primarily a social event. In the first room people would shed their clothes and then enter the steam bath with its star-shaped openings in the ceiling to provide fresh air and light. Hot water canals under the floor heated the rooms and turned the water being sprinkled into steam. From there, bathers would enter the large, domed central room

Cathedral

The West Facade

One of the most exquisite Renaissance churches in Andalusia rises above the roofs of the houses in the old city. Whether one views at it from afar or close up, the balance and proportionality of this massive, square structure is awe inspiring. On the site of the former mosque and a previous Gothic structure, construction of this three-aisled, hall church began around 1540 according to plans drawn up by native architect Andrés de Vandelvira. After over 150 years of work, the cathedral was ultimately completed around the beginning of the 18th century. The facade on the west side with its twin towers was designed in the last phase of construction by Eufrasio López de Rojas. Adorned with columns and statue decorations in the style of a baroque altar-piece, it softens the building's otherwise austere appearance. Opening onto the Plaza de Santa María, its three portals are set between Corinthian columns on high pedastals beneath a monumental attic level. Here, sitting high on a throne in a gabled alcove among evangelists and fathers of the church, is Jaén's conqueror, Ferdinand III, with a sword in one hand and an imperial orb in the other. His gaze is purposely directed at the former Moorish fortress. All sculptures, like the figures of Peter and Paul in alcoves on the lower level, are the work of Pedro Roldán.

The Floor Plan

Modeled after the Cathedral of Seville, the church was constructed as a rectangle with a nave and two aisles of equal height, each with adjoining side chapels. In the middle of the cathedral lies the choir with elaborately carved choir stalls from the 16th century and the Capilla Mayor. The Capilla Major holds the cathedral's most precious treasure in a golden shrine: St. Veronica's veil with the true image of Jesus Christ.

Sacristía

The most remarkable room on the interior is the *sacristía* (sacristy) which was designed by Vandelvira. Pairs of columns, with alternatingly small and large arcades reminiscent of the Mosque of Córdoba, subdivide the barrel vaulted room. In the alcoves are chests that hold the chasubles and liturgical instruments. The sacristy leads to the museum of the cathedral which exhibits many art treasures, including paintings by José de Ribera and Valdés Leal.

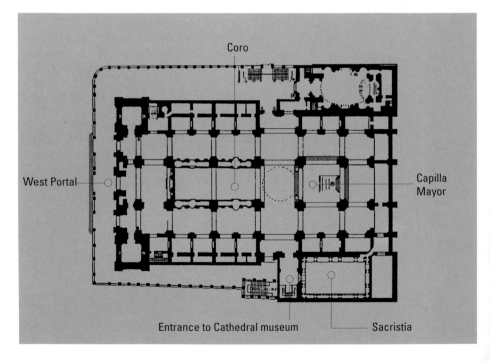

Coro

West Portal

Capilla Mayor

Entrance to Cathedral museum

Sacristía

Museo Provincial

Torso of a Horseman from Porcuna

This torso of a horseman is part of an extensive archeological find discovered at the ancient city of Obulco (today's Porcuna). It may be regarded as a unique example of the influence of Greek art on Iberian culture in the fifth century B.C.

More than 40 of these almost life-size sculptures chiseled out of local stone, all crafted in the same workshop, were apparently crushed to pieces and buried around 400 B.C. The sculptures – battle and hunting scenes, mythological creatures, gods and goddesses, priests, eagles, lions, bulls, and sphinxes – imply that the statues were once displayed in a holy place as votive offerings or played a role there in the cult of the dead.

Early Christian Sarcophagus of Martos

Some of the most beautiful and precious examples of early Christian art of the late Roman Empire in Spain are these stone sarcophaguses. They were quite evidently modeled after artistic examples of the sort in the capital of Rome. In the niches of the columned sarcophagus from Martos, scenes from the New Testament are depicted: the Miracle of the Loaves and Fishes, the healing of the Canaanite woman's demon-possessed daughter, Peter's Denial of Christ, the healing of the blind and the lame, and the Wedding in Cana.

Baeza and Úbeda

Unlike other places in southern and western Andalusia, the two cities of Baeza and Úbeda, only 5.6 miles (9 kilometers) away from each other and near the Castilian border, are not primarily characterized by their Moorish history. Instead, visitors here will feel as if they had gone back in time to the Renaissance. Here, sandstone-colored churches and palaces from the 16th century dominate the scene, yet still blend in harmoniously with the timeless of white houses of the "Twin Cities'" Moorish-Arabian past. Both cities boast a long and eventful history. In 1013, at the site of the Roman *Beatia* (blessed city), one of the most important centers of Baetica, King Bayyani founded an independent empire in Baeza. Úbeda, an Iberian settlement, had already made a name for itself in Moorish times as Ubdalat

Úbeda, Casa de los Salvajos (with Detail)

al-Arab and was famous throughout all Andalusia for its ceramic and *ubedíes* (carpets made out of spun esparto grass). Ferdinand III conquered Baeza in 1227 and Úbeda in 1234 putting and end to Moorish rule. In the years that followed, both cities played important roles as outposts in the conquest of the Kingdom of Granada. They flourished economically and culturally in the 16th century when numerous nobles who had participated in the Reconquest settled there. These nobles had a multitude of churches and palaces built, whose magnificent facades flaunted the wealth of their patrons.

Baeza was lauded by Antonio Machado, who was a teacher there for several years, as a "beautiful city, half Moorish, half La Mancha, whose venerable stones speak of its glorious past." In 1542 it became a university city and was also a diocesan town for many centuries. Úbeda's fate and fortune during the Renaissance lie primarily in the hands of two men: Francisco de los Cobos y Molina, under secretary of Charles V, and his nephew Juan Vásquez de Molina, who served Philip II. They are credited with fostering the brilliant career of architect Andrés de Vandelvira (1509–1575) whose work is evident in many buildings in Baeza and Úbeda.

Baeza, Fuente de Santa María

Baeza

Plaza del Pópulo, p. 376

Palacio de los Marqueses del Jabalquinto, Calle San Juan de Ávila, p. 387

Catedral de Santa María, Plaza Santa María, p. 386

Puerta del Toledo

Plaza de Cervantes

Cipriano Alhambra

Maestro Palomino

Platerías

Camino Real

C. M. Garcerán

La Yedra

Sta. Catalina

C. de San Gil

P.ª S

Plaza del Arcediano

Antigua Carnicería,
Plaza del Pópulo, p. 377

Fuente de los Leones,
Plaza del Pópulo, p. 377

Cipriano Tornero o del Rojo

Jurado de la Parra

Concepción

avides

San Pablo

Plaza de
España

Obispo Narváez

Compañía

Callejón Sta. Cruz

Sacramento

Juan Bautista

0   200 m

N

Plaza de Sta. Clara

Fuente de Santa María,
Plaza Santa María, p. 373

Also worth seeing:

1   Casa del Pópulo, Plaza del
    Pópulo

2   Seminario de San Felipe Neri,
    Plaza Santa María

3   Universidad, Calle Beato Ávila

4   Ayuntamiento, Calle Cuesta
    Buenavides

Plaza del Pópulo

Considered by many to be the most beautiful square in the city, the Plaza del Pópulo is framed on three sides by Renaissance buildings. The two-story Casa del Pópulo, built between 1535 and 1540, was originally a civil court and chancellery. Thus, the building was also referred to as Audiencia Civil e Escribanías. The offices of the city scribes were once located behind the six entrances to the lower level. Today, these rooms house the tourist information office. The building's name refers to the Virgen del Pópulo, whose sculpture once

The Fuente de los Leones

The focal point of the square is the 16th century *Fuente de los Leones* (Fountain of the Lions) whose sculptures and columns came from the Roman, formerly Carthaginian, city of Cástulo (near Linares, in the province of Jaén). According to legend, the female statue standing on a column with the four lions at her feet is the Iberian princess, Imilce, the wife of Hannibal.

The Antigua Carnicería

Given the prestigious facade of this Renaissance building next to the Fuente de los Leones, no one would guess that it was originally a butcher's shop. Above the ground floor with its low ceilings, a gallery displays the massive coat-of-arms of Charles V between its middle columns. Today this building, which was completed in 1550, functions as the municipal archive and museum.

stood on the right balcony of the plateresque facade next to the coats-of-arms of Charles V and of the city. Ever since the Christian conquest of 1227 when the first mass was celebrated in front of this cloaked figure of the Virgin, soldiers have prayed here to the Madonna for protection before going into every battle.

Connected to this building are the Puerta de Jaén, a memorial gate which was constructed in 1526 for the occasion of Charles V's visit, and the Arco de Villalar. This arch was built in 1521 as a memorial for the imperial victory over the *Comuneros* – the insurgent Castilian cities – in the Battle of Villalar, in which many nobles of the city took part.

Reyes católicos
(Catholic Sovereigns)

Ox yokes and sheaves of arrows joined by the letters F (for Fernando) and Y (for Ysabella) adorn the outer walls of the Capilla Real in Granada. These emblems are symbols of the unusual ruling couple that reigned as Isabella of Castile (1474–1504) and Ferdinand II of Aragón (1479–1516) over both of their kingdoms as husband and wife and in 1496 received the honorary title of *Reyes Católicos* (Catholic Sovereigns) from Pope Alexander I. Their reign was marked by radical changes in domestic and foreign policy and is considered to be the turning point in the history of modern Spain. However it is also one of the country's most controversial epochs. The Sovereigns came into power when the country that was in economic and political ruins and created a united nation under the sign of the cross, and laid the groundwork for Spain's rise to hegemonic power under Charles V and Philip II. One essential factor that led to the royal couple's success was the personal harmony that existed between them that – despite some differences of opinion and uneven distributions of power – provided ultimately for uniform and coherent policies. *Tanto monta, monta tanto Isabel como Fernando* (Of equal power, hand in hand, Isabella and Ferdinand) was their motto.

Their marriage in 1469 at the ages of 17 and 18 signified the end of the century-long power struggle between the two biggest kingdoms in Spain, Castile and Aragón. But although their marriage was considered to be the union of two people of equal birth, Castile was the greater and more powerful kingdom with six to seven million inhabitants and a surface area three times that of Aragón, which had only about half a million inhabitants. Although the thought of combining the two kingdoms may have played a role in the marriage, the individual interests of each country stood in the foreground. Aragón was primarily interested in obtaining support against France

Granada, Capilla Real, Facade, Details: Ox Yoke and Sheaves of Arrows

Granada, Capilla Real, Statues of the Catholic Sovereigns

and the insurgent Catalans and also hoped to gain back some of the land it had lost to Castile, while Isabella's adviser regarded the union as the most appropriate and prudent for the heir to the throne. Since the ruling King, Henry IV, still favored his daughter Johanna as his successor, Castile and Aragón intended to pool their resources, while at the same time retaining their unique state and social institutions, their traditions and even their respective languages. The marriage may have ultimately been the catalyst for the founding of modern Spain, but the visionary idea of a united nation was never the motivating factor. In hindsight it is clear that this fusion of the kingdoms on the Iberian peninsula only became possible through the timely synthesis of complex, internal political processes.

Spain – On the Road to Power

Thanks to clever foreign policies and strategic alliances, the Catholic Sovereigns would make Spain the leading power of the western Mediterranean during the course of their 35 years of joint rule. But the road leading up to this was long and full of obstacles.

The first strategic move in foreign policy was the successful conclusion of the Castilian War of Succession in the year 1479, which was provoked by Portuguese King Alfonso V's claim to the Castilian throne. At the price of significant economic concessions concerning the agreements on the delimitation of their respective spheres of interest in the Atlantic the Catholic Sovereigns attained Portugal's relinquishment of all inheritance claims. Moreover, Isabella and Ferdinand made an

alliance with their most formidable rival on the Iberian peninsula and secured it with the marriage of their oldest daughter to the grandson of the Portuguese King.

Their second foreign policy triumph would be the seizure of Moorish Granada which brought the 700 year Reconquest – the recapturing of originally Spanish territory from the Moors – to an end. Although this wealthy, culturally, and economically flourishing emirate had long been obliged to pay tributes to the Castilian Crown, the two enjoyed close diplomatic relations and lively trading. Nonetheless there were frequent border disputes which continually required the deployment of Castilian troops. Moreover, there was the danger that Granada would ally itself with Castile's enemies, since it already maintained alliances with the Islamic pirates of North Africa who had repeatedly plundered Castile's coastal regions. Although the Moorish Kingdom was weakened and split by internal disputes between its factions – which would have made a military attack seem opportune – it was border skirmishes that eventually provoked the war. Isabella, who demanded the final conquest of the last Moorish bastion in Andalusia continued to wage the war. Ten years passed in which the Catholic Sovereigns had to mobilize an enormous army and come up with large sums of money, until they could finally march victoriously into the city in 1492. They were heralded in all of Europe as

Philip I of Castile, dubbed "the Handsome,"
Pedro Maranello shows his works to the
Sovereigns

"Crusaders of the Faith" and received the honorary title from the Pope.

In the same year, the expansion and exploration of America began. After the fall of Granada, there seemed to be enough available resources to challenge Portugal as the leader in exploring the oceans. So, of course, when Portugal learned of the safe and happy return of Christopher Columbus in the spring of 1493, they immediately claimed their contractual rights to the newly discovered islands. However, Isabella and Ferdinand were able to convince Pope Alexander VI to suggest a new dividing line for the bilateral spheres of interest. An imaginary dividing line was established which divided the Atlantic west of the Cape Verde Islands so that all lands west of the line belonged to Castile's sphere of influence and all lands east of the line went to Portugal; and each country received exclusive shipping and colonization rights in their territories. For Spain, this meant the beginning of the Conquista, the conquest of the New World, which brought the country magnificent amounts of gold and silver during the reign of Charles V.

The final foreign political venture, which was guided by Aragonian interests, actually took place on Italian soil. In 1503, Ferdinand, who was also the King of Sicily, was successful in freeing to free southern Italy and Naples from the French occupation. He added the Kingdom of Naples to the Spanish Crown, thus securing and extending Spain's supremacy in the western Mediterranean.

By the end of the reign of the Catholic Sovereigns, Spain had become a powerful

Main Altar in the House Chapel of the Catholic Sovereigns, 1504. Seville, Upper Palace of the Alcázares Reales

country. The far-reaching changes which have left their mark on the history of Spain, Europe, and even the world become clear when one compares the territorial possessions of Spain at the time of Ferdinand and Isabella's marriage with the political map at the beginning of Charles V's reign (1516-1556).

The Inner Peace

The country's rapid rise to power was accompanied by fundamental, radical changes on the domestic front as well, for the civil uprisings during the reign of Henry IV and the War of Succession had shaken the internal structure of Castile and seriously impaired trade and the economy. When Isabella and Ferdinand took over the business of the state, they found the country on the verge of financial and political ruin. Although their rule extended over a wide, territorial area – from Asturias on the northern coast to the Andalusian cities of Seville and Cádiz, and from Extremadura in the west to Murcia on the Mediterranean coast – their actual domain of power was limited to their small, inner-Castilian possessions, while the other territories were ruled by powerful nobles and princes of the church. The royal couple was dependent on the favor of the grandees and the cities, as well as their tax revenues to fill their empty treasury. In addition to all of this, attacks of all kinds ranging from rival parties to bands of thieves were an everyday occurrence at that time.

Thus, the Catholic Sovereigns were confronted with two urgent tasks: besides restricting the nobles' power and influence in favor of the Crown, the re-establishment of public order was first priority. A number of measures took care of these problems in a short amount of time. For example, they reformed the justice system, strengthened the *Consejo Real* (Royal Council) and the supreme court, instituted *chancillerías* (independent courts) and founded the *Santa Hermandad* (the holy brotherhood), whose function was to set up permanent troops in all cities to take over the duties of the police and fight local uprisings and organized crime. The Santa Hermandad was also an important means of asserting royal authority, because they defeated the bands that were often commissioned by the nobles, thus radically diminishing the grandees influence.

The Sovereigns also managed to increasingly weaken the powerful nobles through a strategic personnel policy. By filling all the decisive positions in all departments of the administration with men who had nothing to do with the nobles, they created a wide following for themselves. Thus, they could rely on the support of the people and were eventually able to pull all the nobles over to their side. A further domestic issue was the policy on religion. The more the Catholic Sovereigns were able to strengthen their position of power, the more urgent it seemed to subject the autonomous power of the church with its far-reaching social influence and expansive economic potential to their authority as well. By exercising their full power over the influential orders of the

knights, they were slowly able to achieve this goal and thus lay the groundwork for the Spanish church state. However, the most drastic measures within the framework of their policies on religion were the introduction of the Inquisition and the expulsion of peoples of a different religion, which are two of the most controversial decisions taken during their reign.

Plate with the Coat-of-Arms of Ferdinand and His Wife Isabella of Castile, c. 1469/1479. Spanish-Moorish ceramic, glazed, London, Victoria and Albert Museum

The Catholic Sovereigns, Initials of a Manuscript, 1494. Valladolid, University

The Inquisition

Relations between Christians and Jews had been aggravated since the 14th century when repeated pogroms forced many Jews to convert to Christianity. Thus, there was a large number of *conversos* who were suspected of only pretending to be Catholics. This numerically strong minority was regarded by Spanish Catholics as a serious threat to Christianity. For this reason, as early as 1748 the Sovereigns were able to convince Pope Sixtus IV to convoke the Court of the Inquisition to examine the converts. Although the Inquisition was primarily motivated by the desire to maintain the purity of the Christian faith, there were also social and economic reasons behind it. Jews and *conversos* were one of the major forces in the economy and belonged to the wealthier classes of society which, of course, aroused envy in the common people. However, the methods of the Inquisition were not undisputed. One of its toughest opponents was Bishop Hernando de Talavera, who believed that religious minorities could only be converted by persistent missionary work. One of his most bitter adversaries was the powerful Archbishop of Toledo, Francisco Jiménez de Cisneros, father confessor of the Queen, who also used the Inquisition as a means of making reforms within the church in order to re-establish morals and discipline in clerical institutions and protect the church from the influence of the Reformation.

The Expulsion of the Jews and Moors

Because the Jewish minority, which often had close ties and maintained economic relations with the *conversos*, continued to pose a problem for the Catholic state, the Catholic Sovereigns issued a decree on March 31, 1492 that would have serious consequences. All Jews were ordered to be baptized within four months or leave the country. Around 200,000 Jews chose exile, whereby the urgency of the situation often forced them to sell their property at far less than its worth. Thus, the only remaining religious minority was the Moors, who had been assured of religious freedom by the Sovereigns before they annexed Granada. Still, the Grand Inquisitor Cisneros demanded that they be subjected to the same conditions as the Jews were, and after a Moorish uprising, the Sovereigns gave in to his pressure. A royal decree on February 11, 1502 left the Moors with only two alternatives: conversion or exile. With the expulsion of the Jews and the Moors, Isabella and Ferdinand had established religious unity in Castile, which was an important step towards their goal of a unified country. However, at the same time the land had lost a great number of citizens who had played a prominent role in intellectual and economic life. Moreover, the Moors who were forced to convert, the Moriscos, represented a new trouble

spot, since most of them had only converted to Christianity on paper – in their hearts they were still Muslim.

When Isabella died in 1504, the Catholic Sovereigns could credit themselves with having established royal power as an absolute, uncontested authority, creating a nation united under one faith, and obliging the church to become an instrument of its governmental policies. Through their farsighted foreign policies and alliances they transformed Spain into a new and powerful nation which made it possible for it to become a world power. However, their rigid persecution of peoples of a different faith and the Inquisition throw dark shadows on their otherwise glorious reign.

Sword and Scepter of the Catholic Sovereigns, Granada, Treasure Chamber of the Cathedral

Catedral de Santa María

Baeza's history as a diocesan town goes as far back as the seventh century. It was not until 1248 that the archbishopric was transferred to Jaén. The Plaza de Santa María, with its Fuente de Santa María (1564) in the shape of an arch of triumph, is dominated on one side by the Renaissance facade of the cathedral. This great hall church with one aisle on either side of its nave was constructed on top of the ruins of the old mosque and a previous Gothic structure and completed in 1593 based on the plans of Andrés de Vandelvira. Remnants of the previous Moorish structure can still be seen at the base of the bell tower and in the cloister. The oldest parts of the Christian structure can be found on the west facade. The Puerta de la Luna exhibits late 13th century forms with its

Mudéjar, slightly pointed and notched horseshoe arch, while the tracery window above it dates from the end of the 15th century. On the inside of the cathedral, a point of interest is the artistic *réja* (grille), attributed to the master Bartolomé de Jaén, in the Capilla del Sagrario.

strewn with diamonds. Only the gallery with five arcades which was added in the 16th century alters the original appearance of the palace which was built in the late 15th century by Juan Guas who was commissioned by Juan Alfonso de Benavides Manrique, a cousin of Ferdinand III.

Palacio de los Marqueses del Jabalquinto

With its charming court-yard, this Renaissance palace is probably the most beautiful in Baeza. It is impressive for its facade in the purest Isabellan style. Semi-circular pillars, each holding a small pulpit in their stalactite-like capitals, flank the middle section, which in turn is distinguished by an interesting contrast between rigid, Gothic lines and playful Moorish ornamentation. Stone bands, fine ledges, tiny reliefs, and delicate twin windows lend contour to the surface of the walls. In the shimmering sunlight, the *picos* (the protruding, pointed ashlars) make the wall appear to be

Úbeda

Sacra Capilla del Salvador

On the east side of the Plaza de Vásquez de Molina hemmed with elegant palaces and churches, stands the *Sacra Capilla del Salvador* (Church of Salvation) which was constructed by some of the greatest Andalusian architects. The plans were drawn up by Diego de Siloë and in 1536, Andrés de Vandelvira and Alfonso Ruiz began construction. The results of their work are reflected in the plateresque west facade done in the Renaissance style. The tall, middle section is framed by buttresses and a triangular pediment, while half-sized, round towers with pagoda-like tops border the smaller side sections. Reliefs fill the empty spaces. Above the portal, two figures representing faith and justice hold an inscribed plaque. A detailed frieze depicting the expulsion of the Israelites from Egypt adorns the entablature and above that is the large relief portraying the transfiguration of Christ, flanked by St. Peter and St. Paul. On the side walls of the lower level as well as at the top of the buttresses, the coats-of-arms of the patrons Fran-

cisco de los Cobos y Molina and his wife Maria de Mendora are displayed. They had commissioned the Capilla as their private chapel and are buried in its crypt. The interior of the church is also spectacular. Besides the wood altar-piece crafted by Alonso Berruguete in the mid-16th century, which was severely damaged in the Spanish Civil War, it also contains a classic Renaissance sacristy with lavish atlas and caryatid sculptures designed by Vandelvira.

Palacio de las Cadenas

The north side of the Plaza is dominated by one of the most magnificent Renaissance palaces which was named for the *cadenas*, or chains, that originally linked the pillars of the forecourt. The unadorned, austere facade is distinguished by a balanced proportion of horizontal and vertical lines. The three horizontal levels, separated by pronounced ledges, are divided vertically by Corinthian pillars on the first level and Ionic ones in the middle; the upper level is divided by caryatids instead of the canonical Doric pillars. Stone lions guard this building that Andrés de Vandelvira created in the mid-16th-century as a residence for Juan Vásquez de Molina. His coat-of-arms, along with the Catholic Sovereigns and the Lions of Aragón, decorate the arches between the columns of the patio. From 1566 to 1873 the building served as a Dominican convent after which it became the *ayuntamiento*, or townhall, of Úbeda.

The Province of Córdoba

The Province of Córdoba

Córdoba, Puente Romano

Situated at the foot of the Sierra Morena, the province of Córdoba is divided by the Río Guadalquivir into two parts: the mountainous region in the north and the Campiña, a landscape of evenly rolling hills and fertile fields, in the south. In the center lies the capital city of the same name that was once famous throughout the world as a caliph residence and a mecca for science. It was also, along with Baghdad, a capital of the Islamic world. Graced with the Medina az-Zahara and *La Mezquita* (Great Mosque), Córdoba was praised by German poet Roswitha von Gandersheim in the tenth century as being the "ornament of the world." Today, when walking through the old quarter of the city, visitors will still be able to envision the hustle and bustle of this once great, ancient Moorish city, even though now, with 300,000 inhabitants, it seems provincial compared to Andalusia's other famous cities, Seville and Granada. Not much remains of the former splendor, but the few remnants that do are impressive enough, and without rival in the European world.

Córdoba's history begins with the rule of the Phoenicians during which the city is said to have had great economic significance. From 200 B.C. on, while the city was in Roman hands under the leadership of Augustus, Corduba (as it was then called) became the capital of the Roman province of Baetica until Hispalis (Seville) took over this role in the fourth century A.D. Great Roman poets and philosophers, like Seneca and Lucanus, were born here. After being conquered in the sixth century by the Visigoths, the city became a diocesan town. However, its glory days did not begin until 756 when Abd ar-Rahman I made it the capital of his emirate. Not only did he bring the pomegranate tree and the date palm to Córdoba, he also paved the way for the introduction of Arabian art and architecture. He and his successors set extensive construction projects in motion that would transform the city into the prestigious center of the Umayyad dynasty. Under Abd ar-Rahman III, Córdoba was the largest city of the Mediterranean world with over 300 mosques, 300 official baths, 50 hospitals, 80 public schools, 20 public libraries and 17 colleges. But the decline of the caliphate also initiated the downfall of the metropolis. In 1013, religiously fanatical Berber troops destroyed the magnifi-

cent residence city of Medina az-Zahara and in 1031 Córdoba became the seat of one of the many taifa kingdoms. In the 12th century the city again experienced a brief period of intellectual prosperity – the philosophers Maimónides and Averroes are the most famous representatives of this epoch – until 1236 when Ferdinand III and Christian rule moved in. The Reconquest opened the doors to a great wave of immigration from the Castilian north. Córdoba became a trading center for cloth and silk. But the expulsion of the Moorish and Jewish population, the economic crises in the 16th century, the plague, and uprisings in the 17th century all led to the decline of this once glorious city.

Water mill on the Guadalquivir near Córdoba

Medina az-Zahara

When walking through the ruins of Medina az-Zahara about 5 miles (8 kilometers)
west of Córdoba, visitors will get an idea of
the luxurious lives that Arabian princes led
in their amazingly enormous palaces. For
almost 40 years (starting in 936), a countless number of artists and craftsmen were
involved in building this palace city with
an area of 2,450.8 x 4,921.5 feet (750 x
1500 meters) for Abd ar-Rahmans III.
Sources say that the caliph named his new
residence after his favorite wife, *az-Zahara*
("flower"), whose statue is said to have
adorned the main portal. Other sources,
however, believe that this statue was of
antique origin. Monstrous sums of money,
some say 1.8 million gold dinars, went into
the construction of this complex. The ruler
also had 4,313 columns – 140 of them from
Constantinople – and 12 gold statues inlaid
with pearls brought in for the bedchamber.
His son al-Hakam was in charge of super-
vising the work and had the new residential and administrative center enlarged
considerably after the death of his father.
Four years after the consecration of the
mosque in 941, the entire royal household
and administration moved in to the new
palace. However, this power and glory
would not last for long. As early as the
beginning of the 11th century, rioting
Berber troops had reduced Medina az-
Zahara to a mound of rubble. After that,
the ruins were used merely as a quarry.

Medina az-Zahara

The complex is built on a hillside in three terraces and is surrounded by a tremendous, defensive wall. The upper terrace was composed of the caliph's palace and the nobles' residences. Official reception halls and administration buildings were located on the middle terrace while the village area, complete with a mosque, workshops, lodgings for the cavalry, a mint, and even a wild game preserve, occupied the lower terrace. One remarkable feature of the complex is the ingenious system of canals that Abd ar-Rahman had installed to supply the palace with water, which was pumped into the complex from the mountains through 9.3 miles (15 kilometers) of aqueducts and tunnels. A system of underground passages with covered galleries also ran through the entire palace city. However, these were reserved for the caliph and his servants.

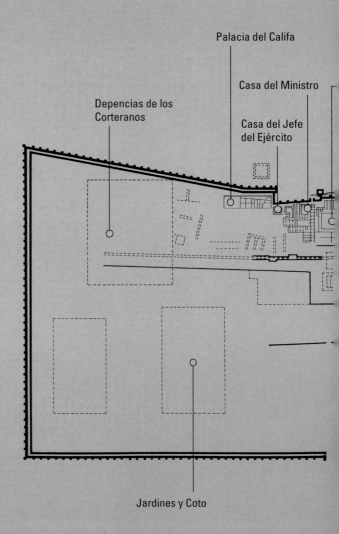

Palacia del Califa

Casa del Ministro

Casa del Jefe del Ejército

Depencias de los Corteranos

Jardines y Coto

Army Residence
p. 398

East Assembly Hall

Sala del Trono

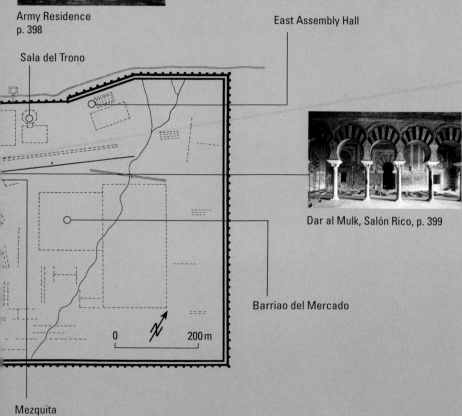

Dar al Mulk, Salón Rico, p. 399

Barriao del Mercado

0   200 m

Mezquita

Army Residence

The army residence located on the upper terrace has a very unusual groundplan. Whereas the civil servants' buildings were arranged according to the traditional Arabian groundplan with several rooms grouped around a central courtyard, here the rooms lie next to each other and are connected on their shorter side by the powerful pillar arcades of a portico. They open to the south, whereas the ruler's throne was set up against the north wall. This is probably evidence of the influence of Slavic military slaves, who held high positions in the court of the caliph. For these nomadic tribes of eastern Europe, north was the direction that was considered to be most sacred. The portico separated the building from the great training grounds where the caliph's 1,200 guards would do their exercises. Very little remains of the caliph's palace, but ancient sources tell of its unending splendor. Two fountains in gold-plated bronze that were a gift from the Byzantine emperor stood in the courtyards. The caliph received his guests in an octagonal throne room whose vaulted ceiling was decked in ebony and ivory and whose walls were inlaid with gold, jewels, jade, and colorful marble. However, the caliph apparently had a cupola torn down that was made of gold- and silver-plated bricks and glittered in the sunlight. The story goes that when he asked his courtiers for their opinion on the decor of the room, one of them accused him of being a non-believer because of his addiction to luxury. He referred to a verse in the Koran which says to condemn "everyone that blasphemes against Allah Most Gracious and builds silver roofs for their houses, and silver stairways on which to go up."

Dar al Mulk, Salón Rico

One of the most magnificent palaces in the whole city is the Royal Residence on the middle terrace which is referred to as Salón Rico because of the opulence of its decor. It is composed of a large hall with three high, vaulted aisles that probably served as a reception room for Abd ar-Rahman III, and smaller adjoining rooms to accommodate distinguished guests. Colorful building materials, filigree floral ornaments, and numerous inscriptions decorate the walls. One inscription says that the hall was constructed between 953 and 957. Five horseshoe arches frame the view from the main entrance that once led out to a series of gardens and pools, one of which, according to sources, held twelve animal statues from Córdoba. On the south side of the great hall was a rectangular pool that was in those days allegedly filled with quicksilver which would reflect light to shine into the hall in the evening. Foreign guests would be treated to the spectacle of slaves stirring up the water with staffs to make reflections dance on the ceiling.

The Last Sigh

On January 2, 1492, Boabdil, the last ruler of the Moorish Kingdom of Granada, rode off into the Alpujarra hills with his followers. Before reaching the top of the first pass he looked back once more with tears in his eyes at the city and the walls and towers of the Alhambra shimmering red in the winter sun. "Do not cry like a woman for that which you could not defend as a man," were the admonishing words of his mother Aisha. In remembrance of this day, the pass has since been referred to as the *Puerto del Último Suspiuro del Moro* (Pass of the Last Sigh of the Moor).

Boabdil, whose real name was Abu Abdallah, has probably received more negative criticism than almost any other ruler in the history of Spain. No other ruler has fascinated poets and writers as much as this tragic figure of the last Nasrid who conceded to the end of almost 800 years of Moorish rule in Al-andalus. Indeed, he did not have much choice, unless he wanted to let them destroy his palace – just like they had destroyed the city – and take his followers prisoner.

Ever since the kingdom of Granada was founded in 1246, and throughout the course of the Reconquest where one taifa kingdom after another fell to the Christian conquerors, the Nasrids had been able to assert their rule through a combination of armed force and extremely strategic propaganda to resist Christian invasion. However, when Boabdil's father, the venerable Caliph Muley refused to pay new tributes in 1481 and attacked the Castilian city of Zahara, the Catholic Sovereigns began a military campaign that would last for over ten years. In 1482, as a countermove to the attack on Zahara, the duke of Cádiz moved deep into Moorish territory and conquered the fortress of Alhama in a surprise attack. This fortress was near Granada – only five hours by foot – and controlled the connecting road to Málaga, the second largest city with the only harbor in the empire. The capture of such a key position was the chance that the Catholic Sovereigns had been waiting for. Instead of simply destroying the fortress as usual, they quickly gathered their troops there to defend it against the Muslims. Then, the fight to conquer the final remaining pockets of Moorish rule on Iberian soil began, from which Ferdinand and Isabella would emerge victorious. Internal power struggles in Granada also contributed significantly to the Moors' defeat. The warring factions were not able to set their differences aside in order to team up against the common threat.

A Tragedy in Five Acts

The complex events of these ten years seem like a tragedy with five main characters playing in five acts:

José Moreno Carbonero, The Surrender of Granada to the Catholic Sovereigns, Madrid, Palacio Senado

The First Act

The first act features the aged Caliph Muley and his mistress, a Christian slave named Zoraya, who tries to do everything in her power to bring her own sons to the throne. She prophesies that the kingdom will be destroyed under Boabdil, whereupon his own father has him thrown in prison. But when Muley is called away to the outer limits of his kingdom because of a Christian attack, the people call upon Boabdil to be their new ruler.

The Second Act

Boabdil is now the new ruler of Granada. He has married the daughter of the most distinguished general in the city and leads a happy life. But since he is often accused of being cowardly and idle, he decides to attack the Christian city of Lucena in 1483, while his repudiated father and younger brother are defending the kingdom against the Christians in Málaga. His military campaign is a failure and he is taken prisoner by the Catholic Sovereigns.

Felipe Bigarny, Boabdil King of the Moors Hands Over the Keys to the City After Surrendering Granada, 16th century. Wood relief, Granada, Capilla Real, High Altar

The Third Act

Boabdil's capture brings Muley back onto the stage; he returns to Granada and resumes his role as king. However, Muley's newly found rule does not last for long, as his brother El Zagal ousts the old, weak caliph from the throne.

The Fourth Act

Ferdinand takes advantage of the situation and uses it to divide the Granadine forces. He sets Boabdil free after concluding a peace and vassalage treaty with him. After years of fighting, Boabdil can finally return to the Alhambra –

but only at the price of being a puppet to the Catholic Sovereign. Not only did Boabdil guarantee them sovereignty over Granada and give up the title of emir (which the Spaniards considered to be the same as king) so that they could become rulers of parts of the old kingdom. He also betrays his uncle El Zagal and lets him fall into the hands of the Christian troops. At the same time he looks on as Málaga is conquered and its people are sold into slavery.

The Fifth Act

The fifth and final act takes place in Granada. In the winter of 1490, when the Catholic Sovereigns march into the city to lay claim to that which Boabdil had promised them, the people revolt. After a long, one-year siege during which the Castilians set up an encampment near the city walls that they called *Santa Fé* (Holy Faith), the inhabitants of Granada finally agree to resume negotiations. After Boabdil is assured the safety and religious freedom of his people, he agrees to surrender. As he leads the procession of Moorish nobles to the place where he will hand over the keys to the city, his mother Aisha takes a last look at the Alhambra and says reproachfully, "Look you upon it, all of this that you intend to abandon. And remember, too, that all of your forefathers died as kings of Granada." No less humiliating is the act of surrender itself. Boabdil dismounts from his horse and tries to kiss Ferdinand's hand but is brusquely rebuffed. He then kisses several large keys and says, "My Lord, these are the keys to your Alhambra and your city. Come hither, My Lord, and take possession of them." Then he leaves the city through a gate that is, at his request, walled up behind him. In 1493 he leaves the Alpujarras and moves to North Africa where he is said to have perished in 1527.

Boabdil or Mohammed V's dagger with arabesque engravings, Madrid, Museo del Ejército

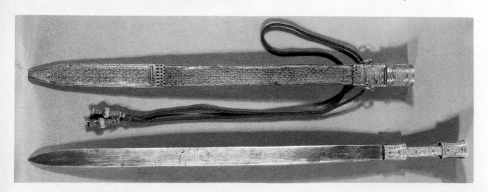

Almodóvar del Río

On a 229.7 foot-(70 meter)-high, rocky hill far above the fertile plains of the Guadalquivir, a fortress can be seen from miles around that is one of the most well-preserved in all of Andalusia. It seems to be the perfect example of a medieval castle. It also seems that no other location could be more suited for an impregnable bastion at the gates of Córdoba. This tin-crowned, Mudéjar structure with its colossal keep (Torre Albarrana) and five towers was built under Pedro I in the mid-14th century. However, its beginnings evidently go much further back than that because Roman, Visigoth, and Arabian remnants have been found under its foundation. It is also a famous historical site, for it was in front of these gates that the regent of the taifa kingdom of Baeza died. He was killed in a battle against his own troops because he intended to relinquish several fortresses in Andalusia to Ferdinand III.

Lucena

Torre del Moral

Lucena is more famous for its history than its architecture. It was here that Boabdil was held captive after he had been taken prisoner by the *Conde de Cabra* (Count of Cabra) during his attack on Lucena in 1483. He was set free again after signing a treaty of neutrality and paying tributes, but nine years later he was driven from his throne for good by the Catholic Sovereigns. The only remaining testimony to these events is the eight-sided Torre del Moral, the last remnant of the Moorish fortress.

Cabra

San Juan Bautista

In Cabra – the birthplace of Don Juan Valera (1824 – 1905), one of the greatest Spanish romantics of the 19th century – a steep cobblestone road leads up to one of the oldest churches in Andalusia. From an inscription on a stele in the facade we learn that the *baselica* was consecrated in the year *E 628* (590 A.D.). It exhibits the simple architectural style of a Visigoth church. During their reign, Cabra was the seat of one of the ten dioceses of *Baetica* (Andalusia). Its ancient holy water font with floral motifs is an especially noteworthy masterpiece.

Priego de Córdoba

This little town of Roman origin with its beautiful baroque architecture is one of Andalusia's most frequently overlooked treasures. Next to the old, Moorish quarter that has remained almost unchanged since the 15th century, there is a "new" part of town with numerous parks, fountains, villas, and churches that were all built during the reign of Charles III in a wave of construction that followed the devastating earthquake of 1755. Thanks to its silk and textile industry, the city experienced a period of vibrant rebound which is reflected in the extravagance of its numerous old buildings.

Fuente del Rey

One of the town's most exquisite works of art is the *Fuente del Rey* (Fountain of the King), a baroque composition of pale sculpted stone framed within the setting of a park-like promenade. Bubbling, clear water cascades down from one elegantly curved pool to the other. The main pool is

Priego, one of the great Andalusian rococo masters, added a sacramental chapel. Commissioned by a wealthy citizen of the city in 1784, the octagonal chapel is lavishly adorned with latticed stucco designs and crowned by a cupola whose windows flood the sanctuary with light. Delicate, baroque gold work completes the picture. Pedrajes also designed other churches in the city, like the Carnarín de San Pedro, the Sagrario de San Francisco, the Santa María de las Angustias, and the *sagrario* of the Capilla de la Aurora, which all exhibit his masterful style.

fed by 139 spouts set into the inner wall of the basin. The extensive fountain complex is graced by two groups of sculptures crafted around 1800 by José Álvarez y Cubero, who later worked with Antonio Canova in Rome. The sculpture in the upper pool depicts a lion fighting with a snake and the lower pool contains sculptures of the sea god Neptune and his wife Amphitrite being pulled through the water in a chariot drawn by seahorses.

Santa María de la Asunción

Near the Castillo which was built by Christians in the 13th century using parts of a previous Moorish structure, there is another masterpiece of the Spanish baroque, the Santa María de la Asunción. This three-aisled parish church underwent a decisive transformation in the 18th century when Francisco Javier Pedrajes of

Córdoba

Synagogue, Calle Maimónides,
p. 415

Mezquita, Calle Herreros, p. 430

Puente Romano, p. 458

Also worth seeing:

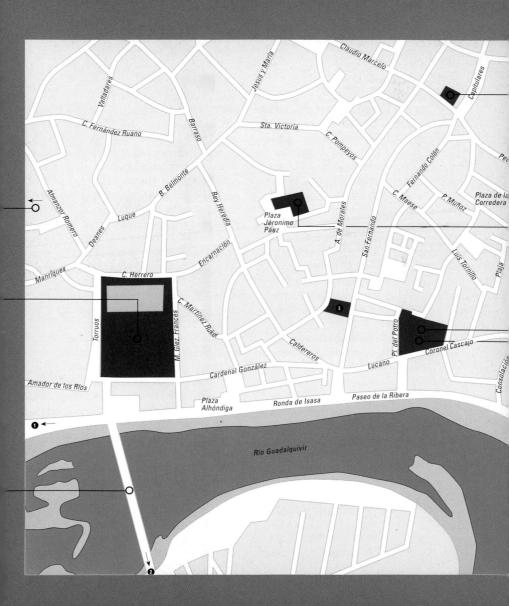

Claudio Marcelo

Capitulares

Valladares

C. Fernández Ruano

Jesús y María

Sta. Victoria

C. Pompeyos

Barraso

Fernando Colón

Pe

B. Belmonte

C. Maese

P. Muñoz

Plaza de la
Corredera

Almanzor Romero

Luque

Rey Heredia

Plaza
Jéronimo
Páez

A. de Morales

San Fernando

Luis Tornillo

Plaja

Deanes

Encarnación

Manríquez

C. Herrero

Torruos

M. Glez. Francés

C. Martínez Rükek

3

Pl. del Potro

Coronel Cascajo

Consolación

Caldereros

Lucano

Cardenal González

Amador de los Ríos

Plaza
Alhóndiga

Ronda de Isasa

Paseo de la Ribera

1 ←

Río Guadalquivir

2

Roman Temple,
Calle de Claudio Marcello,
p. 418

Museo Arqueológico Provincial, Plaza Jerónimo Páez,
p. 420

0   100 m

Museo Provincial de
Bellas Artes, Plaza del
Potro, p. 422

Museo Julio Romero
de Torres, Plaza del
Potro, p. 424

Lucas Valdés, Auto-da-fé, Seville, Iglesia de Santa María Magdalena

Semitic theories of the fourth Lateran council. This marked the beginning of the Catholic church's rigorous fight against Jews and Muslims alike, which for them meant either forced baptism or expulsion. Jews who opted for the forced baptism were referred to as *Marranos* or *Conversos* which is what new Christians have been called since the 16th century. However, they, too, avoided persecution for only a short time, for the Inquisition that was founded in 1478 in Seville took up the fight against all those who were not of "pure blood." Only the true Christians had the right to live in the nation that was to be united under one faith by the Catholic Sovereigns. The multicultural nation that had endured on Spanish soil for more than 800 years ceased to exist. The year 1492 marked the beginning of the mass expulsion of the Sephardim from Spain. True to the motto of the Catholic Sovereigns, "One people, one nation, one faith," up to 200,000 Jews were driven out of the country, and an ancient, flourishing culture was obliterated forever. Four-hundred years would pass before it was again legal to build synagogues in Spain (1909), and in 1968 the law of expulsion was officially rescinded. After almost 500 years, the Spanish government finally passed a law in 1990 that granted Jews and Protestants the same rights as Catholics.

caliphate, and it grew to be a center of intellectual and social life. Since laws and taxes hindered Jews from owning or working the land, most of them lived in the cities where they worked as doctors, interpreters, merchants, and craftsmen. A labyrinth of narrow winding streets and small, enchanted city squares still bears witness to the Jewish quarter that once extended to the west of the Arabian city walls. Visitors will be pleasantly surprised by the occasional view that unfolds between white-washed walls of shadowy patios lavishly filled with flowers.

Judería

Ever since the destruction of the temple of Solomon in 586 B.C. and on through to the persecution by the Almoravides in the 12th century, Jews streamed into Andalusia. In Córdoba, the Jewish community was the largest during the time of the

Synagogue

Only a few yards from the Maimónides memorial stands the only intact synagogue in southern Spain which was built under Christian rule near the former entrance gate to the Jewish quarter, the Puerta de Almodóvar. The building can be entered through a courtyard that leads to an anteroom. From here, a stairway leads up to the upper level that was reserved for women, who were excluded from the synagogue service. Above the entrance is a Hebrew inscription, "Open the gates for the just and the faithful." The walls are richly decorated with Mudéjar stucco designs composed of floral and geometric motifs as well as inscriptions of the Psalms. In the east wall there is a niche for the tabernacle with an inscription next to it that mentions the architect, Isaac Mejeb, and the date of completion, 1315. The opposite wall to the west exhibits a seven-ribbed arch in which the remains of a cross can still be detected. The Christian symbol here dates back to the time after 1588 when the shoemakers guild used the building as the Chapel of St. Crispin, their patron saint. After the expulsion of the Jews in 1492, the building had first served as a rabies hospital. In 1885 it was declared a national monument.

Maimónides und Averroes

Córdoba, The Averroes Memorial

Schools and libraries in Córdoba had been the center of intellectual life for the Jews, Christians, and Muslims since Umayyad rule. These buildings remained standing even after the decline of the caliphate. But in the 12th century when the dogmatic regime of the Almohades, who were rigid advocates of Islam, came to power, the times of tolerance were over, and were replaced by the persecution and severe oppression of all people with dissenting views. Two of Córdoba's greatest sons – one Jewish, the other of Islamic faith – fell victim to this religious war.

Mosche ben Maimon, better known as Maimónides (b. March 30, 1135 in Córdoba – d. December 13, 1204 in Cairo) had to flee to Morocco with his family in 1149/50. In 1165 he settled in Egypt where he became the personal physician of Sultan Saladin and the leader of the Jewish community. His literary writings, that were translated from Arabic into Hebrew and were thus known in the mosques and synagogues in Andalusia, focused on explaining biblical and talmudic literature from the perspective of philosophy, mathematics, astronomy, and medicine. He was most famous for his philosophical treatise on the Jewish order of faith (*Guide of the Perplexed*) in which he sets reason against the belief in miracles and correlates central elements of the Jewish faith with the antique philosophies of Aristotle.

The memorial in the Plazuela de Maimónides depicts the great scholar as an older man in a seated position wearing a turban and a robe. Behind the memorial, a column on the corner of the square bears an inscription in Spanish and Hebrew, *Córdoba for Maimónides*. The inscription also records the date according to both calendars, 1964 and 5724.

In one of the gates of the old city wall near the Puerta de Almodóvar stands a memorial for another great scholar of the city, Averroes (Ibn Rusd), who was born the son of a judge in Córdoba in 1126. This jurist, doctor, and philosopher of religion was a supreme court judge of Seville and Córdoba for a period of time. But the fanatical Almohades banished him to the old Jewish town of Elisana (Lucrena). His philosophical works were banned and burned. It is said that he was forced to stand before the mosque's Puerta del Perdón so that the zealots could splt on him. After his rehabilitation, he was summoned to the court at Marrakech where he died a short time later in 1198. Averroes was very famous in the Islamic and Christian world during his lifetime, although his teachings were often quite controversial. But since the Arab world rejected his assertion that the teachings of philosophy in religion must be accompanied by pictures for the common people, he and his theories were quickly forgotten after his death. At the beginning of the 13th century his writings were translated into Latin and Hebrew and found their way into European universities. However, Christian Europe also contested his teachings because he, like his greatest role model Aristotle, did not believe that the soul was immortal. Instead, he believed that humans should do good for their own sake and should strive for a higher ethic than that which is motivated by fear of judgement in the afterlife. Nevertheless, his writings on Aristotle's philosophies were read by all intellectuals in Europe and were regarded by Christian scholars until the Renaissance as the key to Aristotle's teachings.

Córdoba, The Maimónides Memorial

Santa Marina

This three-aisled Gothic basilica is the oldest church in Córdoba. Construction on it began immediately after the Reconquest in 1236, and it was remodeled in the 18th century. Reinforced by buttresses, the massive outer walls resemble those of a fortress, although their austere appearance is softened by the pointed arch portal and rose window. The north portal is outstanding for its weathered capitals with human and animal masks that are exceedingly rare in Andalusia. Inside the church, visitors will still be able to admire the Mudéjar decor in the 15th century Capilla de los Orozcos, which is today the sacristy. Elaborate arabesques twine around shields bearing the Maltese cross next to a stalactite vault.

Roman Temple

After the Romans had conquered Córdoba in 206 B.C., it became a resplendent metropolis and capital of the Roman province. In 151 B.C., the Roman praetor Marcus Claudius Marcelus established a Roman colony here that was destroyed during the civil war and rebuilt under Augustus. Still standing today as testimony to this Roman past is a podium erected on large ashlars with the reconstructed columns of a temple right near the Roman city wall. It was built in the first century A.D. and was probably dedicated to the emperor. Archeological findings suggest that the structure was made primarily out of marble and was an example of exceptional architectural design which can still be seen in the Corinthian capitals of the columns. A model of the original structure is housed at the city's archeological museum.

Iglesia del Carmen

Juan de Valdés Leal, Elijah Altar, 1658
Oil on canvas, 567 x 508 cm

Near the Puerta Nueva lies the *Convento de las Carmelitas Descalzas* (the Convent of the Discalced Carmelites) that dates back to the end of the 16th century. Here one finds the Mudéjar church, Iglesia del Carmen, which houses one of the most famous works of Juan de Valdés Leal. Between the years 1654 and 1658, the artist, who was headmaster of the Seville School of Painting, created this altar-piece which is composed of twelve paintings and is dedicated to the glorification of the prophet Elijah. Scenes from the life of the prophet as well as portraits of the patron saints of Córdoba and the Virgen del Carmen frame the middle section, which depicts Elijah's ascent into heaven. With the simple use of shading techniques and very few colors, Valdés Leal created a masterful representation of this visionary event. With his beard streaming in the wind, the first great prophet of Israel rides towards heaven in a golden chariot above flaming clouds. An angel steers the four white horses in red harnesses that make them look like a blazing flame. Below on the right, Elijah's successor, Elisha interrupts his work to catch Elijah's coat as it falls from the sky. This scene is interpreted to be a prefiguration of the resurrection of Christ.

Museo Arqueológico Provincial

The beauty of the complex alone makes a visit to the archeological museum worthwhile, for it is housed in the former palace of the Cordobán noble family Páez de Castillejo. Lavishly adorned with statues, the plateresque facade was designed by Hernán Ruiz II in 1543. The entrance way leads into the first patio which is lined with shrubbery and has a fountain in the middle. In keeping with the style of old Cordobán estates, the rooms of the palace are constructed around a second patio. On the lower level, in addition to exhibits from prehistoric and Iberian times, many examples of Roman and West Gothic art are displayed. The upper level contains a collection of Moorish art that is one of the most renowned in all of Spain.

Mithras Killing the Bull

Among the Roman sculptures, one second century marble composition stands out. It depicts the god Mithras killing the primordial bull – a sacrifice that is ritually repeated by the god's followers. A dog and a snake lap up the blood of the bull that flows down from the wound made by Mithras' dagger and a scorpion stings the bull's genitals. Like all oriental divinities, Mithras, the Indo-Iranian god of victory and heavenly light, was very appealing to the Romans and especially to the Roman soldiers. They worshiped him as the god of light who could vanquish the powers of darkness. Therefore, the sculpture also represents the mythical image of the moon, symbolized by the bull, being killed by the "sun," Mithras.

Museo Provincial de Bellas Artes

The *Plaza del Potro*, whose name means "Foal Square," was originally used as a place to trade horses and mules. This is reflected in the stone sculpture of a foal that crowns the square's 16th century fountain. On one side of the square is the famous old 15th century inn, Posada del Potro, that Miguel de Cervantes mentions in his narrative, *Don Quixote*. Across from this, the Catholic Sovereigns erected the Hospital de la Caridad, which today houses the city's art museum. It contains a remarkable collection of works by Cordobán painters and sculptors from the 14th to the 20th century.

Alejo Fernández, The Flagellation of Christ, before 1508

Alejo Fernández was one of the most prominent Andalusian painters of the early 16th century. Evidence of his work first appears in Córdoba in 1496. When the cathedral chapter in Seville commissioned him to design the cathedral's high altar, he moved to Seville with his brother, the sculptor Jorge Fernández Alemán. This painting is indicative of Fernández' role within Andalusian art during the transition from Gothic to Renaissance. The powerful scenario of Christ tied to a column after the denial with St. Peter praying on the right exhibits late – Gothic elements, for example the little figures of the patrons and the drapery. But Renaissance elements, like the opulent architectural details of the column bases and capitals that recall the times of the caliphate, also prevail. In the background on the right, a little scene depicting one of Peter's three denials recalls the theme of betrayal.

Juan de Valdés Leal, Virgen de los Plateros, 1654-1656.
Oil on canvas, 217 x 202 cm

In this painting, Juan de Valdés Leal attempted to imitate the aesthetic ideals of Bartolomé E. Murillos. The painting, which was probably commissioned by the goldsmiths' guild, portrays the Virgin Mary standing on a half moon floating above a pedestal. Her head is encircled by a wreath of stars and she is accompanied by a host of angels. Her gaze is directed at the gray-bearded St. Eligius, the patron saint of the goldsmiths. On his richly decorated cloak that is held together in the front by an artistically crafted gold clip, the Annunciation, the Birth of Christ, and the apostles John and Matthew are all depicted. On his right, an angel holds his miter and another in the bottom left corner holds his crosier. On the right side of the picture, St. Anthony of Padua kneels on the ground with the Christ child in his lap. The golden pedestal looks like a triumphal chariot seen from the side and its lavish decor is also reminiscent of the art of the goldsmiths.

Museo Julio Romero de Torres

Across from the Museo Provincial de Bellas Artes, the museum dedicated to the famous Cordobán painter Julio Romero de Torres (1874–1930) is established in the former home of the artist's family. As opposed to other great painters like Picasso, he was not one of those artists who played a decisive role in the transition to the modern period. His pictures did not represent any radical break from the prevailing styles of art, and instead display the typical bourgeois realism style of the early 20th century. His work often recalls past Spanish and Italian painting styles as well.

La Chiquita Piconera (The Little Coal Trader), 1930

This Cordobán is praised as the "painter of the black-brown girls," an expression that comes from an old Andalusian folksong. No other painter could portray the beauty and melancholy of an Andalusian woman with such vividness and intensity. In this painting, which was his last, he takes a critical look at the situation of many young Andalusian women which was characterized by poverty and hopelessness. The woman's mechanical, almost powerless gesture can be interpreted as a sign of resignation, while her childlike face expresses the will to maybe someday find a way out of her situation.

El Poema de Córdoba (with detail), 1914

De Torres composed his *El Poema de Córdoba* (Ode to Córdoba) in the form of a three-part altar piece that lauds the city's greatness through realistic portraits of women with various monuments in the background. With statues of the Gran Capitán, the poet Luis de Góngora and the Jewish philosopher Maimónides, the left wing recalls Córdoba's former significance as a dazzling center of politics and science. The middle section represents Córdoba's goldsmiths, the city's patron saint Raphael, and Roman past, which is symbolized by the Roman philosopher and political leader, Lucius Annaeus Seneca. In the right wing, the monasteries are represented by a depiction of the facade of the Capucin church, and the tradition of bullfighting is symbolized by a reproduction of the memorial dedicated to torero Rafael Molina.

Flamenco – The Dance of Life and Death

Georges Bizet, "Je vais en ton honneur danser la Romalis...," c. 1905 Photo postcard, colorized, Paris

Tablaos (flamenco clubs) can be found all over Andalusia, the home of flamenco. With clapping hands, spinning skirts, and stamping feet, brightly dressed *bailadoras* (female dancers) captivate the audience, while their male counterparts accompany them by drumming thun-

derous staccatos into the floorboards of the stage with their high-heel shoes. Their shrieks and ecstatic song mingle with the cords of the guitars which keep the beat. However, such productions actually have very little to do with the real flamenco, one of the oldest forms of Spanish music which is an expression of spontaneous inspiration and intimate passions. Real flamenco can only be experienced in a small group of aficionados when one of them begins to sing a few *coplas*, traditional or individually adapted lyrics, and the others join in to urge him or her on. Flamenco does not try to entertain. Instead, it is in its original form a lament. When the *duende* (demon) possesses the *cantaor* (singer) the *quejido* can be released – a lament coming from the very depths of the soul, a hoarse, guttural, liberating song whose strange tonal patterns and unique rhythms make it fundamentally different from any other form of European music. With wails and screams, this *cante jondo* expresses feelings. It relates the pain of unrequited love, loneliness, and hopelessness. Flamenco can last for hours, even days. The listeners sustain the ecstasies of the singer, they urge him or her on, and set the rhythm. They applaud *brazadas* (expressive arm and body movements) by clapping their hands (*palmas*) and stamping their feet (*zapateado*). Other *cantaores* join in, perform their *coplas* and reach their own state of ecstasy through song and dance. Thus, flamenco is above all a group experience in which laments – but also feelings of great happiness, optimism, and love of life – can be harmoniously expressed through music and dance.

No one really knows where the word "flamenco" comes from and what it actually means. Some believe it is derived from the Arabic words for folksong, *fellah* and *mangu*. Others associate it with the Spanish word for Fleming or Flemish man, *flamenco*, an allusion to the Flemish followers of Charles V who were characterized as being arrogant and behaving in an especially haughty and conceited way. In any case, flamenco originated within the triangle of Seville, Cádiz, and Ronda, among the *Gitanos*, the gypsies that lived in Andalusia. When they came through southeast Europe to Andalusia – probably from India – in the middle of the 15th century, the songs and dances from their Indian homeland intermingled with the traditions of other cultures in southern Spain. Therefore, flamenco contains elements of ancient Indian and Byzantine liturgical music, Moorish and Mozarabic songs, and Jewish synagogue hymns that were all passed on by the Gitanos for centuries. It is essentially and originally the music of an oppressed people who were refused the right to an autonomous way of life by the Catholic government. It was not until the situation of the Gitanos improved in the 18th century and Bizet's opera *Carmen* introduced flamenco to the world that the music received belated recognition. *Cafés cantantes*, meeting places for flamenco aficionados, sprang up everywhere and even *pasos*, non-gypsies, learned the art, this triad of *cante* (song), *toque* (guitar), and *baile* (dance) that has retained all of its liveliness and passion throughout all these centuries.

Spanish Dance Scene, c. 1850. Color lithography

Alcázar de los Reyes Cristianos

In 1327/28, Alfonso XI had his residence built on the grounds of this Moorish fortress. In the late 14th and early 15th century, the residence was expanded to include gardens and baths. After the Catholic Sovereigns resided here from 1482–1490 during the war against Granada, it became the headquarters for the Inquisition. It served as the city prison from the early 19th century till 1951. The rectangular complex rises above a grove of palm trees in the north and compromised an octagonal residential and defensive building to the east, the Torre del Homenaje, and three other towers: the round, three-story Torre del Río on

the south, the Torre de la Vela on the north and the Torre de los Leones with its square groundplan on the west side, which serves as an exhibition hall for the fragments of buildings and ornaments from the original complex and the Roman remnants discovered here. Beneath the mosaic room, visitors can view baths dating back to Arabian times. Especially enchanting are the magnificent gardens with their numerous pools and fountains. The Paseo de los Reyes is flanked by the statues of all the kings who have lived in the Alcázar. At the very end of the promenade is a small square with the statues of the Catholic Sovereigns and Columbus, who had journeyed here many times to report to the Queen.

Polyphem and Galatea (Mosaic)

In the Salón de los Mosaícos, Roman mosaics from the 2nd and 3rd centuries are on display. One of these portrays the myth of Polyphemus and Galatea with rocky cliffs in the background. Galatea is depicted on the left holding a strand of her hair in one hand and sitting on the back of a sea monster. She looks towards Polyphemus who is seated on a rock to the right, trying in vain to woo the Nereid with his love.

Marble Sarcophagus

The Alcázar's most famous exhibition is a marble sarcophagus dating from the mid-3rd century that shows the deceased at the gates of the kingdom of the dead. In the middle section is the door to Hades, standing slightly ajar and decorated with the heads of lions and rams which are symbols of a happy life after death. Accompanied by the muse Calliope, protectress of epos, philosophy, and rhetoric, a woman on the left raises her right hand in prayer. The man, who is probably a senator judging from his clothing, is being led by a knight to an official ceremony. Members of the Roman upper class enjoyed having themselves portrayed on sarcophaguses next to the likenesses of philosophers and muses in order to flaunt their education. Thus, the knight resembles an antique philosopher. Pegasus, on the narrow side of the sarcophagus, symbolizes poetic inspiration.

Mezquita

The *Mezquita* (Great Mosque) rises up out of the heart of Córdoba's old city. Its architectural style reflects the history of the Umayyad dynasty from the beginnings of the emirate and the glory days of the cali-

phate up until its abrupt end. Visitors standing on the outside of this fortress-like, rectangular complex will not even begin to imagine the splendor that awaits them on the inside. Considered to be the largest in the Islamic world, the mosque covers a surface area that is approximately 574 feet (175 meters) long and 420 feet (128 meters) wide, surrounded by sandstone walls crowned with tin and reinforced with buttresses. Decorative portals are the only elements that soften the austerity of the walls.

According to one anonymous source from the 14th or 15th century, there had never been anything in the Islamic world that could rival the Mezquita's importance, size, splendor, and perfection. Originally, a Roman temple stood on this location, and later, the Visigoths used the temple's foundation to erect a Christian basilica dedicated to St. Vincent. When the Arabs made Córdoba their capital in 711, they needed a new place of worship for the Islamic community. Initially, they transformed one half of St. Vincent's church into a mosque and left the other half for the Christians. However the Muslim population grew so rapidly that in 785, Abd ar-Rahman I took over the Christian half as well and began construction of the new mosque. His successors would continue to expand and supplement this original structure to meet the requirements of the constantly growing population.

Mezquita, View of the Outer Wall, fifth truss from the left

Abd ar-Rahman III – The First Western Caliph

When Abd ar-Rahman III (912– 961), Emir of Córdoba from the dynasty of the Umayyads, accepted the title of caliph in 929, Arab civilization on the Iberian peninsula reached the height of its splendor. Had this western caliphate – which provided the empire with its own political and intellectual center – not been established, Islamic culture would have possessed far less magnetism and power.

As caliph – which comes from the Arabic word *khalifa* and means "representative" as well as the successor of the prophet Mohammed – Abd ar-Rahman III was the religious as well as political leader of the Muslims, since Islam does not differentiate between secular and religious law. He was a shrewd and just statesman as well as a successful army commander. When the Umayyads came to power in Córdoba in 912, the empire was threatened by independence movements lead by Arabian clan and tribal leaders, and revenues had dwindled. The new ruler subjugated his opponents quickly and decisively. In only twenty years he was able to eliminate his political rivals, drive back the increasingly powerful Christian kingdoms in the north and ward off the attacks of the Fatimids in northern Africa. Given this time of peace on the home front, agriculture and trade once again began to flourish, and huge sums of money began to flow back into the state treasuries. Abd ar-Rahman III soon became one of the wealthiest rulers of his time. Raising his empire to the status of caliphate in 929 was just the next logical step in the process. For one thing, the

Court of a Caliph, miniature from the Siliman Namé, Istanbul, Top Kapi Saray Library

Umayyad dynasty had always been independent from the Abbasside caliphate in Baghdad anyway, even if it had recognized their ruler as the religious leader of Islam up until that point. For another thing, the Shiite Fatimids in northern Africa had in the meantime established their own caliphate which posed a threat to the Sunnite Umayyads. As the new caliph of the West, he made a political statement and emphasized the fact that from then on he intended to have full sovereignty over his empire. This is reflected in the title that he chose for himself as caliph, *an-Nasir li Din Allah*, which translates to the "Protector of the Religion of Allah."

From this point on, Abd ar-Rahman strove to live up to this title and to create obvious physical signs representing it. This led to a display of splendor in his capital city that would outshine Baghdad in every way. Eloquent testimony for the splendor and glory of his court was the palace city Medina az-Zahara at the gates of Córdoba with its inexhaustible number of multicolored marble columns, walls inlaid with gemstones and pearls and arches decked in ebony and ivory. "Az-Zahara's superiority over all other palaces in the world is comparable to the superiority of the dynasty that built it over all other dynasties," said Arabian poet Ibn Suhais in praise of the impressive beauty of this monumental structure.

Although the grandeur of the ruler's residence may conjure up images of the ancient tradition of the Persian god-kings, Abd ar-Rahman III still felt beholden to the first caliphs, who had lived in modesty. "Before me, as representative of the prophet, you are all insignificant," he is said to

Christians Kneeling Before the Caliph of Baghdad, c. 1412. French manuscript of "Livre des Merveilles du Monde" from the Atelier of the Boucicaut Masters

have proclaimed, "but before God even I am nothing." The extent to which his interpretation of the role of ruler was characterized by this dualism between grandeur and modesty is reflected in a report by a historian of his time: "A legation of Spanish Christians from the north came to negotiate with the caliph. He wanted to fill them with fear by flaunting the magnificence of his kingdom before their eyes, so he had a double row of soldiers stand on both sides of the road from the city gates of Córdoba to the entrance of the Medina az-Zahara, a distance of one parasang – approximately 3.5 miles or 5.5 kilometers. The soldiers held their shiny, wide, and also very long swords high so that their tips met in the middle like the beams of a roof. At the ruler's command, the legation was led through these rows of soldiers as if they were being led down a covered walkway. The fear and respect that this magnificence aroused in them is indescribable. The caliph also had the road – all the way from the city gate to the place where he would receive his guests – covered in brocaded cloth. But at certain points along the way, he planted dignitaries that one might think they were kings, for they sat on luxurious chairs and were clothed in brocade and silk. Each time the legation saw one of these dignitaries they would fall to their knees before him thinking he was the caliph. Then they would be told, 'Rise to your feet! That is only a servant of his servants!' Finally they arrived at the court. Here, the floor was strewn with sand and the caliph sat in the middle of the room wearing crude, short robes. Everything he had on was not worth more than four dirhem. He sat on the ground with bowed head. In front of him were the Koran, a sword, and a fire. 'This is the ruler,' the legation was told, and they threw themselves to the ground. Then the caliph raised his head, and before they had a chance to say a word, he said to them, 'God has ordered us to summon you people so

Julian Köchert, Harun al-Raschid Receives the Legation of Charlemagne in 786, 1864, Oil on canvas, 354 x 195, Munich, Maximilianeum Foundation

Córdoba, La Mezquita, ornamental inscription above the Gate of the Imam

that you might submit yourselves to this.' And with these words he pointed to the Koran...".

In this way, tales of the splendor and glory of the court of Abd ar-Rahman III spread throughout the whole world. His palace became a cultural and political center that attracted multitudes of scientists, scholars, and artists. Powerful empires like Byzantium, the Normans and the Franks also sent ambassadors to his kingdom. In 961, when Abd ar-Rahman died at the age of 73, he left a great legacy behind him. One historian proclaimed later that, "Never was the Islamic empire happier and the true religion more triumphant than it was under his rule."

Puerta del Perdón

The main entrance to the mosque is located on the north side right next to the bell tower, which stands on the spot where the minaret once stood – a masterpiece of its time that was emulated in all Islamic countries of the world. The name *Puerta del Perdón* (Door of the Pardon) stems from Christian times, when the church court would meet under the archway where they could release defaulting debtors from payments or penalties. Henry II of Trastámera had the gate – which is modeled after a gate of the same name in the cathedral of Seville – constructed in 1377 in the Mudéjar style. The archway is completely covered with a relief of stylized arabesques and the arch's spandrels are adorned with Christian coats-of-arms. The heavy wooden doors are covered by pounded metal plates engraved with both Gothic and Arabic lettering, *Deus* and *Al Mulk Lilah* (The power is in God alone).

Puerta de San Esteban

On the western side is *Puerta de San Esteban* (Stephen's Gate) which is the oldest, intact portal of the whole complex. Large parts of it date back to the original structure of Abd ar-Rahman I. The inscription on the tympanum, which indicates that the gate was completed in the year 855 under Mohammed I, refers to a restoration of the horseshoe arch. It has alternating voussiors of brick and pale sandstone, the latter being decorated with arabesques in relief. Called Portal of the Viziers in Moorish times, this gate still exhibits the original division into three, and the two-level structure. Above the rectangular entrance way, the facade is decorated with blind arch niches. Upon these rest consoles with a kind of rolled leaf decor that support a protruding ledge. On the sides, which are covered with delicate arabesques, the visitor will see the window openings that are equipped with stone grilles. The upper border is formed by four-level merlons.

Mezquita

Under Abd ar-Rahman I, a mosque was built with 11 naves of 12 trusses each and an open courtyard in front. From 833–852 under Abd ar-Rahman II, the first addition to the prayer room was made that extended it by eight trusses to the south beyond the *qibla* wall (wall indicating the direction of Mecca). Abd ar-Rahman III (912–961) enlarged the mosque's courtyard and erected a new minaret. In 961, Al-Hakam II had the prayer room expanded on the south side by an additional 12 trusses and had a cupola built over the front mihrab room and both flanking trusses. Since the Guadalquivir prevented any further expansion to the south, al-Mansur had the prayer hall enlarged from 8 to 19 naves on the east in 987/88 and enlarged the forecourt accordingly. In the 16th century, after they had conquered Córdoba, the Christians had a massive cathedral built in the middle of the prayer room.

Patio de los Naranjos, p. 446

Puerta del Perdón, p. 436

Puerta de San Esteban, p. 437

Bell tower, former minaret

Puerta de los Deáne

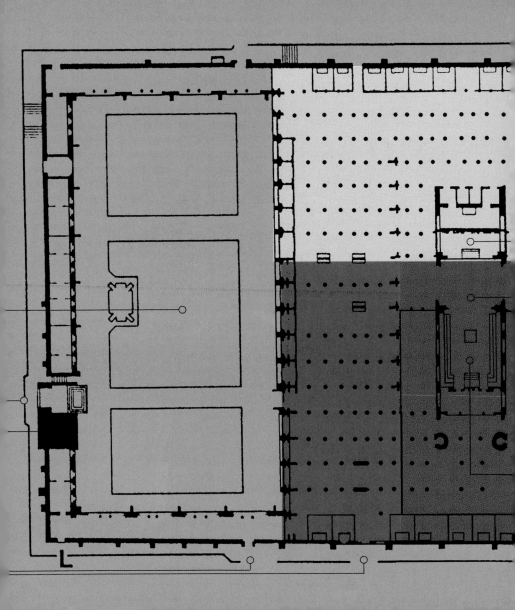

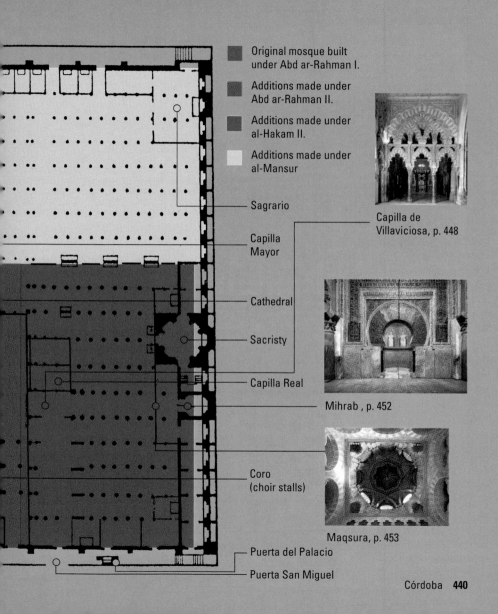

Original mosque built
under Abd ar-Rahman I.

Additions made under
Abd ar-Rahman II.

Additions made under
al-Hakam II.

Additions made under
al-Mansur

Sagrario

Capilla
Mayor

Cathedral

Sacristy

Capilla Real

Mihrab , p. 452

Coro
(choir stalls)

Puerta del Palacio

Puerta San Miguel

Capilla de
Villaviciosa, p. 448

Maqsura, p. 453

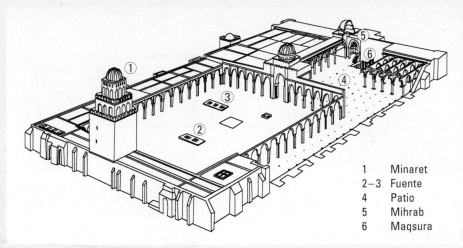

1	Minaret
2–3	Fuente
4	Patio
5	Mihrab
6	Maqsura

Great Mosque in Cairuan, Tunisia

Koran. In a Christian church, on the other hand, God and the saints are personified in pictures and sculptures that inspire believers to worship them. Christian churches also always have a central focal point – believers are crowded close together inside and directed towards the high altar which dominates the room. For Muslims, however, every place where they pray is equally close to Allah, the only requirement is that they face Mecca. Wherever they happen to be praying becomes the middle of the room, even the middle of the world. This is reflected in the structure of prayer rooms with their endless repetition of identical pillars and arches – they have no focal point. In an endlessly wide forest of densely set columns, the worshiper's gaze is not pulled in any one specific direction, it is free to wander. This forest of columns is a symbol of

God's infinity and the equality of all believers who stand before him. Even in the very first mosque that Mohammed and his followers had built in Medina, this was symbolized by the trunks of palm trees whose leaves served as the structure's roof.

A Visit to the Mosque

Despite all differences in size and furnishings, mosques are always built according to the same plan. From the minaret, which towers above the shady arcade of the courtyard, the muezzin calls believers to prayer five times a day, crying, "God is greater! Come and pray! Find salvation! I affirm that there is no other god than God and I affirm that Mohammed is his prophet. God is the greatest! No other god but God!" They can pray in any place, but all male, adult Muslims of sound mind are required to go to the mosque on Friday for midday prayer. At these services there is also a sermon. Before entering the prayer hall, believers must take off their shoes so as not to soil or desecrate the

Mohammed and the First Mosque: The Prophet Gives a Sermon in the Mosque, miniature from the Turkish manuscript "Siyer i Neb" (The Life of the Prophet), 16th century

floor, and they must wash their face, hands, and feet at a basin in the courtyard. This is the ritual cleansing for prayer. However, if a believer happens to be in a state of "great impurity" which could, for example, be caused by sexual intercourse, he must wash himself completely. A mosque will often have special facilities for this. Should Muslims fail to perform this ritual purification, then the subsequent prayer will be in vain. In the prayer room, believers gather and praise God with their face turned towards Mecca. The direction is indicated by a niche in the *qibla* wall, the mihrab, which is the most important part of every mosque. Unlike the Christian altar, the mihrab is not sacred; it only indicates the direction of Mecca. This is so important to Muslims that they will even design their graves, washrooms, and bedrooms to face Mecca.

Originally the mihrab was only a shallow niche, sometimes marked by a lamp, that a blind man could feel on his way along the wall to orient himself towards Mecca. Later, however, it was transformed into a magnificent room that worshipers would circle seven times on their knees, in order to realize the ritual circling of the Kaaba in Mecca. The mihrab is the place where God reveals himself and thus it is here that the imam, the prayer leader, recites the words that God has revealed in the Koran. He leads the communal prayer at specific times, and believers repeat the words he utters in loud or quiet voices, depending on the rule. They mimic his gestures, his bows and his prostrations. A believer can also pray in any other part of the mosque at any time and become a prayer leader for anyone who wants to join him.

For, unlike Christianity, there is no priestly hierarchy in Islam. In many capital city mosques there is a separate room near the mihrab, the *maqsura*, that is reserved for the ruler or governor and his entourage. On the right side of the mihrab is the *minbar*, or pulpit, from which the imam gives his Friday sermon in the name of the ruler. In larger mosques, a *dikka*, or podium is located a little bit in front of the prayer niche to provide a place for the respondent. The respondent's function is to repeat the prayer style of the imam and give the appropriate responses so that the intervals of the prayer can be communicated to a large congregation. Next to the podium is the *kursi*, the lectern with the Koran.

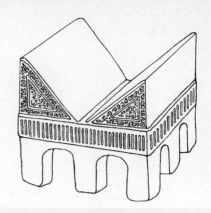

Kursi, lectern

The Mosque in the Middle Ages – A Place of Science and Jurisprudence

In the Middle Ages, the mosque was not just a place of prayer. Outstanding scholars would usually be entrusted with a lifelong "chair," like in a university, and the opportunity to attend their lectures was open to everyone. Outside of the established prayer times, the scholars would sit under the arcade of the courtyard, each one at the foot of his designated column, in order to teach students, visitors, and other people who might be interested in the sciences connected to religion. Drawing on their great wealth of knowledge, they would hold open discussions or comment on fundamental texts in order to instruct their listeners about the Arabic language, in which the Koran was revealed, and about law, which was solely derived from religion, since secular law does not exist in Islam. There were also specific times set aside for the supreme judge, accompanied by a few advisers and court clerks, who would meet in another area and hold sessions of court. But the judge did not always pass an irrevocable judgement, for, if the case was disputable and no serious wrong was being perpetuated, he would simply leave the judgement up to God.

Patio de los Naranjos

The Puerta del Perdón leads to the *Patio de los Naranjos* (Orange Courtyard). Cypress, laurel, and olive trees, as well as fountains that worshipers used for ritual purification before prayer once stood in this wide courtyard ringed with arcades. The orange trees were planted later on by the Christians, who also had the mosque's 19 arcades walled up, drastically changing the interior lighting. In Moorish times, scholars sat under the arcades and gave lectures, doctors gave medical advice and administered *qadi* law. Today, remains of the mosque's old Moorish wood ceiling can still be seen here. When worshipers wanted to go in to pray, they would go through the *Puerta de las Palmas* (Palm Gate) which led directly into the main nave and the oldest part of the mosque.

The Interior

Upon entering the Mezquita, visitors will notice that the original impact of an absolutely infinite forest of columns has been marred, to a great extent, by the changes made by the Christians. Before, the interior was crowned by a wood ceiling with carved and exquisitely painted cross-beams (the light – colored vaulting that can mostly be seen today stems from the 18th century). It was illuminated by the open arcades on the north side and thousands of burning oil lamps. Although many columns fell victim to the addition of the cathedral, 800 of them, made of marble, granite, and jasper, still support the horseshoe and pointed arches of the prayer room. In the oldest part of the mosque, architects found an ingenious way of making the interior appear loftier despite the insufficient height of the materials that were used and which were primarily spoils from Roman and Gothic structures. They laid imposts on top of the columns' capitals and extended horseshoe arches from them to the neighboring supports. On top of these they added massive pillars that lengthen the columns below them and support a second level of round arches. Both levels of arches were constructed with alternating brick and pale sandstone voussoirs. To even out their varying lengths, some of the columns were placed on pedestals and others were sunk into the floor. The symmetrical arrangement of the supports and the alternating red and white colors of the arches produce a sense of rhythm and the feeling of weightlessness. The two levels of arches resemble the tops of date palms and seem to make the ceiling unfold like a fan. In all extensions that were later added to the mosque, architects strove to preserve this overall picture by adopting the two-level structure and the two-tone color scheme.

three arches are again topped by others and are finally all enclosed under one large arch. The intricate arches reflect the two-tone color scheme of the prayer hall in that their voussoirs are decorated with alternatingly smooth designs and filigree arabesques designs.

Dome

As the first of the four skylight cupolas that provided ample light for the addition built on by al-Hakam II, the Capilla de Villaviciosa deserves much admiration. Without having anything to use as a model, the architects who designed this masterpiece in the ninth century found an original and unique way to build a domed ceiling over a large room. Using ribs to create an artistic network of triangles and squares, they divided up the area that needed to be covered, so that the middle could be closed off with a marble scallop shell. Between the vertical sections of the ribs, tiny cloverleaf and horseshoe arch windows open up to let in the light.

Capilla de Villaviciosa

The Capilla de Villaviciosa, also called the Lucernario, was remodeled in the 15th century to become the altar room of the first Christian church. Its two-level arch system once provided a wonderful prelude to al-Hakam II's magnificent prayer room, which was intended to surpass the splendor and beauty of all previous Islamic structures. Rising above four Corinthian columns,

Catedral

In 1523, the church chapter authorized the construction of this cathedral – which juts out of the mosque's low saddle ceiling – against the will of the people who were worried that it would destroy the harmony of the mosque. Just like the bishop's palace that was built in place of the Moorish royal residence, this invasive structure in the middle of the Muslims' prayer room was supposed to demonstrate Christianity's victory over Islam. Although the city council threatened architects and craftsmen with the death penalty if they began work on the cathedral, 63 columns were torn down almost immediately. Hernán Ruiz Sr. created a cruciform church whose choir lies between the transept and the nave. It is said that when Charles V visited Córdoba three years later, he cried out, "You have destroyed something that was unique to this world and replaced it with something that can be seen everywhere."

Capilla de la Encarnación Pedro de Córdoba, Anunciación (The Annunciation), 1475

East of the mihrab in the Capilla de la Encarnación – one of the over 30 side chapels of the cathedral – one can view the principal work of Pedro de Córdoba, the eminent Andalusian painter of the late Gothic period. Signed and dated in 1475, this panel painting is one of the most prominent examples of the Hispano-Flemish style which became popular in Spanish painting in the 15th century. It was characterized by the combination of Moorish ornamental designs with the realism of Flemish art. Here, garments, attributes, and architectural details are reproduced in exacting detail, and the tracery is similar to late Gothic goldsmith work. Small figures of the work's commissioner and the artist kneel beneath the scene of the Annunciation.

Mihrab

Under the Umayyads, Córdoba had risen to become a famous pilgrimage center and therefore needed a splendidly decorated mihrab that was representative of its new, important position in the Islamic world. Following the example of the architect of the mosque in Damascus, al-Hakam II asked the Byzantine emperor to send him a mosaicist that would train the local artists in the technique. The specialist came to Córdoba, along with 16 tons of stone and cube material. The entrance to the mihrab is formed by a horseshoe arch resting on two pairs of demi-columns – taken from the mihrab made under Abd ar-Rahman II – and crowned by blind arcades. It is framed by a square decorated with polychrome tesseras laid together on a golden background to form floral patterns and inscriptions that praise Allah and al-Hakam II.

The inscription on the impost of the arch indicates that construction was completed in the year 965. The mihrab itself is an octagonal alcove crowned by a scallop-shell -shaped cupola cut from one block of marble and richly decorated with stucco lattice work. In Islam, the shell symbolizes the heart in which Allah lays the pearl, which is his Word.

Maqsura, Dome

The cupola in the room in front of the mihrab, the *maqsura*, displays its wealth and splendor. It is covered in mosaics of geometric and floral patterns on a golden background. A system of transecting ribs form an eight-pointed star with what looks like the cross-section of an orange in the middle. The ten-pointed star at the zenith of the cupola symbolizes the celestial globe.

Ziryab – A Singer Sets Standards

At the court of Abd ar-Rahman II (822 – 852) lived a minstrel named Ziryab who had a greater influence on the music and lifestyle of medieval Andalusia than any other. *Ziryab* (which means "black bird," his real name being Abul Hassan Ali Ibn Nafi) moved from Baghdad to Córdoba after a disagreement with his master. His biographer, Ibn Khalliqan, recorded the events surrounding the move. He relates that one day in Baghdad, Caliph Harun ar-Raschid (786–809) asked his court musician Ibrahim if he might know of a new singer who could perform for him. Ibrahim suggested one of his pupils, and the caliph had the pupil summoned immediately. It was Ziryab, and he gave the ruler the choice of hearing a song and singing style that he had developed himself, or one that he had learned from his master. Harun ar-Raschid opted to hear Ziryab's song and summoned a servant to bring Ibrahim's lute. However, Ziryab refused this, saying that he could only play on his own lute because he had equipped it with an additional string. The hymn of praise that Ziryab sang to the caliph pleased him so much that he reproached Ibrahim later for keeping such an original and talented singer a secret from him for so long.

This reproach enraged the master and he admonished Ziryab, saying, "You have betrayed me by concealing your real talent from me and only showing it off in front of the caliph! I know now that you are plotting to become the ruler's favorite. But take heed! I swear it will cost you your life if you try to swindle me out of my position with the caliph! If you cherish your life, accept travel money from me and disappear to the ends of the earth where neither I nor the caliph will ever hear from you again."

Ziryab decided to leave Baghdad with his family and ended up at the court of Abd ar-Rahman II. He quickly won the ruler's favor, who later refused to hear any other singer but Ziryab. They would talk for nights on end about history, poetry, and all other arts and sciences. Ziryab is said to have been well versed in all of these subjects and to have known more than 10,000 songs. He was thus able to attract the sages of Persian music to Córdoba who would continually leave their mark on every style of Andalusian music, even flamenco; and he also introduced the five-stringed lute. He founded a school for music and voice in Córdoba which propagated Persian traditions throughout all of Europe. Moreover, Ziryab is credited with making Seville a leader in the manufacturing of musical instruments.

Music at the Court of a Caliph, miniature from the Siliman Namé, Istanbul, Top Kapi Saray Library

Alias Scheferscher Hariri, The Wine Tavern of Anah, Arabic manuscript, Baghdad 1237. Paris, Bibliothèque Nationale

Ziryab, however, was not just a talented singer but also a gentleman of the court and a skilled conversationalist. He brought all the courtly customs from the cosmopolitan city of Baghdad to Córdoba and set standards in etiquette and taste. Up until that point,

Cordobáns had maintained a simple, traditional Arabian lifestyle. But Ziryab introduced them to the new style, a new etiquette, new social rules, new table manners and foods, new fashions and interior designs. It is said that before his arrival, the nobles wore their hair long and parted, they ate from gold and silver tableware, used linen tablecloths, and all foods were brought to the table at once. However, under Ziryab's influence, all the men started shaving their heads, and everyone began to use crystal tableware and tablecloths of fine leather. He also established an order of dinner courses that included dessert at the end; taught the Cordobáns how to eat asparagus, and invented many new dishes. Ziryab also played an important role in the transmission of Islamic culture from the Arabian East to the Far West of the Islamic world, possessed the authority and influence to break with long-standing tradition, and decisively change the Andalusian way of life. When

Paul Louis Buchard, Les almées (traveling female dancers and singers), 1893. Oil on canvas, 160 x 133 cm, Paris, Musée d'Orsay

Ziryab died in 845, he left behind eight sons and two daughters who were, like himself, minstrels who contributed to the development of Andalusian music.

Puente Romano

On the southern side of the only residence city of the Spanish caliphs lies a 787.4 foot- (240 meters) long bridge that spans the Río Guadalquivir. This bridge, supported by 16 arches was built in Roman times by Augustus as a part of the Via Augusta, the main transportation route of Baetica. For a long time it was the only access to the city and was thus the scene of many fierce battles. In the course of the centuries, it underwent so many changes that now, little more than the foundation of the original structure remains. Gracing the middle of the bridge is a statue of the archangel Raphael, the patron saint of Córdoba, which was erected in 1651 after an outbreak of the plague. The bridge offers an excellent view of the ruins of the Arabian mills and the rebuilt water wheel of the

water mill called La Albola-fia on the banks of the river. This used to supply water to the nearby gardens of the Alcázar. At the city end of the bridge is the *Puerta del Puente* (Bridge Gate), which was designed like a Roman victory arch with the Castilian coat-of-arms. It was once part of the old city wall and was built in the place of a previous structure in 1571 by Hernán Ruiz III, commissioned by Philip II.

Torre de la Calahorra

Towering above the southern end of the Puente Romano, across from the old quarter

of the city stands the tin-crowned fortress whose name, Calahorra, is probably derived from the Arabic words *kalat* (fortress) and *horr* (free, outside). In 1325, Alfonso XI had this twin-tower complex built upon the ruins of the former Moorish structure. In 1369, Henry II of Trastámara had it expanded by a third tower in the middle which accounts for its T-shaped ground-plan. He had this third tower built and the walls fortified after the old defensive structure proved to be too weak to hold up to

the attacks by his half-brother Pedro I, the Cruel. The pointed tops of the towers and the walkway around the battlements date back to the 15th century. Today, the rooms of the complex house the Museo de las Tres Culturas, a museum designed by French philosopher Roger Garaudy. It provides visitors with information about the intellectual life of the city during the Middle Ages and displays models of the mosque and the Alhambra in Granada.

The Patio – A Secluded Oasis Within the Home

When walking along the narrow winding streets in the old quarters of Córdoba, Seville, Granada, and the many little towns of Andalusia, visitors will not be able to resist peering into the beautiful, flower-filled courtyards, which are the pride and joy of every Andalusian household. Intrica-

García Rodríguez (1863–1925),
Andalusian Patio

tely beautiful wrought-iron grilles referred to as *cancelas* invite visitors on the street to peer through the forecourt into the patios with their white-washed walls. These patios have been the setting of family and social life for centuries. Shady arcades, pebbled walks, a fountain in the middle, brilliant azulejos, orange and lemon trees, and a sea of flowers transform the patios into an oasis. In baroque and Renaissance palaces the entrance way also usually leads through one or sometimes several inner court-yards. Surrounded by two-story arcades and walls adorned with azulejos and Mudéjar stucco designs, embellished with antique statues and exquisite fountains, these patios are unusually magnificent.

The rich tradition of patio architecture can be traced back to Andalusia's Moorish past. In Moorish houses, the living and sleeping quarters were arranged in right angles around a courtyard that would allow light and fresh air to permeate the rest of the house and provide cool shade in the summer as well. In those times, however, the forecourts did not open up onto the street, and the gray walls with only a very few, high-set windows did not reveal whether poverty or riches were hidden within.

This curious contrast between the rather stern facades and the magnificent patios and interior rooms was an architectural expression of the Moorish way of life, in which private life was conducted behind closed doors, in the secure

Seville, Casa de Pilatos, Patio Principal

and protected interior space which was considered to be sacred. The fountain also had special significance since bodily cleanliness plays such an important role in Islam. Thus, all Muslims placed a high importance on having a sufficient supply water in their houses that could be drawn from pipes, wells or cisterns. Today, this aspect of cultural life is threatened with extinction as more and more old houses are torn down and replaced by modern, luxury apartments. In order to encourage the preservation of these patios, the city of Córdoba sponsors a contest in which the most beautiful courtyards receive awards and are opened for the public to view.

461

Appendix

Overview of Andalusia's History

Prehistory

Andalusia is the scene of an event in mythological prehistory. According to later Greek tradition, it was here, where the sun sinks into the ocean, that one of the Twelve Labors of Hercules took place: the theft of the famous herd of oxen from the three-headed monster Geryon. Before Hercules killed the giant Geryon and stole his herd, he had set up two great columns between heaven and earth, the mountain of Moussa on the African and the Rock of Gibraltar on the European side.

c. 20,000 B.C. Prehistoric graves and rock paintings (e.g. Cueva de la Pileta near Benaoján, 18 miles (30 km) west of Ronda/Málaga Province, Cueva de Nerja near Veléz Málaga/Málaga Province) are witnesses of the earliest human occupation of the area.

Tarifa, Gibraltar

4,000 – 1,800 B.C.   Agricultural ways of life arise as a result of several waves of colonisation from the Near East.

after 2,500 B.C.   Andalusia becomes a center of megalithic culture: new forms of burial in dolmen, chamber and passage tombs arise (e.g. Cueva de Menga near Antequera/Málaga Province).

2,500 – 1,800 B.C.   Starting in Andalusia, the Beaker culture (named after the bell-beaker earthenware with geometric designs or naive depictions of animals) spreads into the rest of Europe (Los Millares 15 miles (25 km) north of Alméria).

c. 1,800 – 1500 B.C.   Flowering of the El Argar culture (named after the township of El Argar near Antas/Alméria Province), which played a leading role in bronze working and produced jewelry and weapons.

End of the 2nd millennium B.C.   Immigration of the Phoenicians who founded the legendary kingdom of Tartessus, the precise location of which has not yet been determined. It probably lay at the mouth of the Guadalquivir (which was called the Tartessus until 200 B.C.) and is probably identical to the Tharshish mentioned in the Old Testament. Many writers have equated it with the legendary city of Atlantis that sank beneath the waves. Productive ore deposits and the production of bronze enable Tartessus to develop great wealth. Thanks to its tin, copper and silver exports, the region becomes extremely important. It maintains trade links with Crete, Phoenicia and Carthage. Its greatest period of prosperity takes place in the centuries from 800 to 500 B.C. At this point it appears to have been destroyed, for it is no longer mentioned in sources.

c. 1100 B.C.   Phoenicians from Tyre and Sidon found their first trading settlement on the Atlantic coast, called Gadir (now Cádiz, the oldest city in Spain), possibly as a trade center for the tin and silver trade with Tartessus. It is soon followed by further important trading colonies such as Malaka (Málaga) and Sexi (Almuñécar).

c. 700 B.C.   The rich metal deposits finally also cause the Greeks to become trading partners with Tartessus. They found trading bases such as the town of Mainaké (near Málaga).

from 700 B.C.   The Phoenician daughter colony of Carthage drives out the Phoenicians and Greeks, takes over the Phoenician settlements and sets up further settlements.

from 237 B.C.   Carthage, which has risen to become the leading sea and trading power in the western Mediterranean, fights with Rome for supremacy. After the loss of Sicily, one of its bases, to the Romans in the First Punic War (264 – 241 B.C.), the Carthaginians start to extend their area of influence on the Iberian peninsula, led by General Hamilcar. In 226 B.C., in a treaty with Rome, the river Iberus (Ebro) is named as the border between the two spheres of influence.

Roman Rule

218 – 201 B.C.   Hannibal's attack on the city of Saguntum (near Valencia), which is allied with Rome, starts the Second Punic War. During its course, P. Cornelius Scipio defeats the Carthaginians in 206 B.C. at the Battle of Ilipa and founds the veterans' town of Itálica. After the defeat of Carthage, the Iberian peninsula is divided into two provinces, Andalusia becoming part of Hispanie Ulterior.

27 B.C.   Under Augustus, the Spanish provinces are redivided into Tarraconensis in the north and east, Lusitania in the west, and Baetica in the south. Baetica, named after the large river, Baetis (Guadalquivir), and with its seat of government in Corduba (Córdoba), corresponds to present day Andalusia. Thanks to a flourishing agriculture and valuable mineral deposits, it rises to become a wealthy province of the empire.

from 409   During the course of the migration of the peoples, Vandals, Suevi and Alans sweep down into Andalusia, until they are finally subjugated by the Visigoths.

Marble sarcophagus (Detail), Alcázar, Córdoba

Kingdom of the Visigoths

507   After the Visigoths are driven out of southern France, they shift their kingdom to the Iberian peninsula. Their capital is Toledo.

589   At the 3rd Council of Toledo, the Christian faith is adopted as the state religion.

1st half of 6th century   Internal struggles for power and arguments over succession to the throne leads to Baetica occasionally being ruled by Byzantium.

7th century   The Visigoth kingdom is increasingly weakened by the social contrasts between the propertied upper classes and the mass of dependants and slaves.

710   Beginning in 661, the Islamic empire is ruled by the Omayads. According to Muhammad's

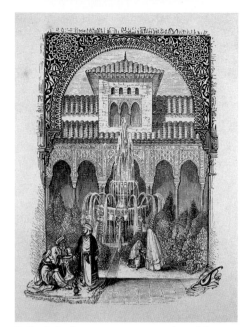

Patio de los Leones, copper engraving of the Alhambra

the Straits of Gibraltar and, in the valley of the Río Barbate, defeats the army, 90,000 strong, of the Visigoth King Roderick.

The Age of Islamic Rule

In a wave of conquest, the Arabs pushed forward as far as southern France, before being forced back in 732 at the battle near Tours and Poitiers by Charles Martel.

722   The Battle of Covadonga (Asturia), in which the Visigoth Count Pelayo conquered an Arab expedition, is considered to be the start of the Reconquista. During the that years followed, the first Christian kingdom was established in the north.

750   In Damascus, the Abbasids (750 – 1258) manages to overthrow the Omayad dynasty. The last survivor, Abd ar-Rahman, succeeds in fleeing to Andalusia.

(died 632) instruction to spread Islam, they extend their rule to India and West Africa. After the subjugation of the former Roman provinces in North Africa, the Omayads are led by the Berber prince Tarif in an initial raid and scouting expedition to the southern tip of the Iberian peninsula. The place where the prince lands is called Tarifa.

711   In response to the command of the Arab governor of North Africa, General Tarik ibn-Ziyad leads an army of 7,000 Arabs through

Omayad Rule

756   Abd ar-Rahman I (731 – 788) founds the independent emirate of Córdoba, whose capital city rises to become a flourishing metropolis (in 785 construction of the mosque of Córdoba started). By the end of his reign, which is characterized by revolts and conspiracies, he has created a united Islamic state in which the religions of the non-Islamic population are tolerated.

822 – 852 Under Abd ar-Rahman II, Andalusia enjoys a highpoint in cultural activity. At the court poets, musicians, philosophers and scientists in particular are encouraged. The best-known is the Persian singer and musician Ziryab, who introduces the five-stringed lute to Andalusia and founds a school of music in Córdoba.

Baths, Alhambra, Granada

929 Abd ar-Rahman III (891 – 961) appoints himself Caliph, and therefore also relinquishes his ties with Baghdad in religious matters. Under his leadership, the Omayad dynasty reaches its height in Spain (construction of the palace city of Medina az-Zahara near Córdoba from 936). Córdoba, with more than half a million inhabitants, is now the largest city in Europe apart from Constantinople, and has countless mosques, public baths, schools, libraries and colleges.

997 The unstoppable decline starts under his successors, al-Hakam II (961 – 976) and Hischam II (976–1031). During his extended campaigns, the imperial administrator al-Mansur destroys the city as well as the cathedral of Santiago de Compostela.

1031 Following the death of al-Mansur, a civil war over the succession to the throne breaks out between the Omayads and the descendants of the imperial administrator. During the course of revolts and unrest, the political unity of the caliphate disintegrates. Numerous smaller partial kingdoms (taifas) arise around the larger cities; they attempt to outdo each other and fight each other. Due to their quarrels with each other, they are no match for the power of the united Christians advancing from the North. Many of them even have to pay tribute to Christian rulers.

View of the ruins of Medina az-Zahara

The Reconquest

1023 – 1091 The Abbadids rule in Seville, now the leading city of the empire.

1035 Following the unification of the northern kingdoms to form the kingdom of Castile under Ferdinand I the Great, the Christians start to advance into the south.

1085 When Alfonso VI of Castile (1072 – 1109) conquers Toledo, the despairing Moors ask the Almoravids, a warlike and fundamentalist Berber tribe, for help.

1086 The Christian advance is stopped by the victory of the Almoravids over Alfonso VI near Sagrajas.

1089 – 1145 After the capture of Seville in 1091, the Almoravids rule the empire. Andalusia becomes a province in the Almoravid empire, its capital being Marrakech.

1145 – 1230 The Almoravids are succeeded by the Berber dynasty of the Almohads.

1195 The Almohads defeat the Christian King Alfonso VIII (1158–1214) in the Battle of Alarcos (Province of Ciudad Real).

1211 Pope Innocent III proclaims a Crusade against the Moors.

1212 The decisive turning point in the Christian battle for the Moorish empire comes at the Battle of Las Navas de Tolosa (near Jaén), in which Alfonso VIII inflicts a heavy defeat on the Almohads. During the course of the following decades, the major part of Andalusia is subjugated by the Christians: in 1236 Córdoba falls, Jaén in 1245, Seville in 1248 (which the Christian rulers choose as their residence), Cádiz in 1262 and in 1292 the Straits of Gibraltar.

1340 In the Battle of the Río Salado near Jerez de la Frontera, the Moorish forces are again defeated.

1238 – 1492 Only the Nasrid emirate in Granada is able to survive, as a vassal state of the kingdom of Castile. Its founder, Muhammad I, starts the construction of the Alhambra.

1349 – 1369 Peter I (the Cruel) resides in Seville as king of Castile.

1479 After the marriage of Isabella of Castile (1451–1504) and Ferdinand of Aragon (1452–1516) in 1469, the Catholic kings rule both kingdoms jointly.

1480 The Inquisition, introduced in 1478, starts operating in Seville.

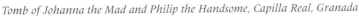
Tomb of Johanna the Mad and Philip the Handsome, Capilla Real, Granada

1492 The rule of the Moors in Spain ends with the cession of Granada to the Catholic kings. Andalusia becomes part of the Spanish national state, which rises to become a world power. Christopher Columbus leaves the harbor of Palos de la Frontera in order to seek a sea route to India. The discovery of America creates the conditions necessary for the foundation of a Castilian colonial empire in the New World, whose gold and silver brings immeasurable wealth to the Spanish motherland. In the same year the rigorous battle against the Jews and Muslims begins, by means of which the unity of Church and state is to be enforced.

1499 Cardinal de Cisneros orders the burning of all Islamic manuscripts and the enforced baptism of Muslims. Many Jews and Muslims flee the country. Thus it loses its most capable doctors, administrators, financiers, agricultural experts and craftsmen.

1503 Seville is granted a monopoly on trade with the New World.

The Habsburg Era

1516 – 1556 Through the marriage of Johanna, daughter of the Catholic rulers, to the Habsburg Philip the Handsome, two enormous European empires are united. In 1516, her son becomes the king of Spain as Charles V. He uses the riches flowing into Spain from the New World to finance his military campaigns against Turkish power in the Mediterranean, and to fight Protestantism in central Europe.

1529 In Granada increasing numbers of Inquisition trials of conversos (Christian converts) and Moriscos (Moors forcibly baptised) take place.

1556 – 1598 Under Philip II Spain reaches the height of its power. However, the large-scale expulsion of the Jews and Muslims leads to a collapse in the crafts and agriculture, as well as the decline of art and the sciences.

1568 The Moriscos revolt after Philip II reinstates the law forbidding Arabic language and dress, which Charles V had repeated for 40 years. The Moors who had remained in Spain after Arabic rule fight for two years. Their revolt is defeated by the Christians.

1571 The united Christian armies defeat the Turks at the Battle of Lepanto, breaking the Turkish supremacy in the Mediterranean.

1588 The defeat of Philip II's Armada at the hands of the English marks the beginning of the empire's political decline. In 1640 Portugal declares its independence, and in 1648 Spain has to acknowledge the independence of the Netherlands.

1609 All Moriscos are driven out of Spain.

Titian, Portrait of Charles V, 1533,
Oil on canvas, 192 x 111 cm, Museo del Prado,
Madrid

The Modern Era

1704   During the course of the Spanish War of Succession, Gibraltar is lost to the English.

1714   As a result of the Peace of Utrecht, the Spanish royal throne is promised to the Bourbons. Philip V's policies of reform create an economic upturn. Spain is now administered centrally, the separate kingdoms lose their autonomy. The foundation of the Royal Academies (1750 Royal Academy of Surgery in Cádiz, 1752 Academy of Literature in Seville) gives new impetus to spiritual and cultural life.

1717   Cádiz takes over the monopoly on trade with foreign colonies.

1808   After Napoleon forces the Spanish king Charles IV to abdicate and French troops occupy the country, the Spanish War of Independence breaks out (1808 – 1814). In the Battle of Bailén (Jaén Province), Napoleon suffers his first defeat. In 1809, however, Andalusia also comes under French rule. Only Cádiz remains as the sole unoccupied enclave.

1812   The original national assembly, the Cortes, met in Cádiz and proclaimed Spain's first liberal constitution. Two years later, it was abrogated by Ferdinand VII upon his return to power in Spain.

1820   When the people's revolution forces Ferdinand VII to take an oath on the liberal constitution, he appeals to the French for aid. In 1823 the liberal government is forced to flee and the reforms decided upon are retracted. What follows is the "Decade of Absolutism" with the brutal suppression of all liberal ideas.

1816 – 1824   During the occupation of Spain by the French, the battle for independence begins in the New World.

1833 – 1839   War-like struggles over the succession to the throne unsettle the entire country (Carlist wars).

1844   The police force, called the Guardia Civil, is established. Big landowners use the police against revolting farm laborers.

1873   The First Republic is proclaimed and brought to an end by the military one year later. Alfonso is proclaimed king.

1892   Despite the secularisation of church properties and the sale of ecclesiastical land (called the *demortización*, from 1836), the stark contrasts between the propertied and impoverished classes remain. The social tensions vent themselves in various revolts: in 1840 a farmers' revolt near Casobermeja (Málaga Province), in 1863 in Loya, and 1892 in Jerez de la Frontera.

1898   In the Spanish-American War, Spain loses its last foreign colonies.

1913 – 1918   Spain remains neutral during the First World War. This gives it an edge over the warring nations in world trade.

1923 – 1930   Under the dictatorship of General Primo de Rivera, the economic upturn continues, its most visible expression being the Ibero-American exhibition in Seville in 1929.

1931 – 1936   After the victory of the Republicans in municipal elections, the Second Republic is proclaimed. Agricultural reforms fail due to resistance from conservatives. Many churches and monasteries fall victim to the unrest and anticlerical riots.

1936 – 1939   When the majority of the left-wing parties are successful in the 1936 elections, the right wing carries out a coup led by General Francisco Franco. This triggers the Spanish Civil War, during the course of which many works of art are destroyed.

1939 – 1975   General Franco's dictatorship.

1960s   In the coastal regions, tourism starts to develop into an important economic factor.

1975   Juan Carlos I is proclaimed king and Franco's successor. Thus restoration of democracy in Spain starts; in 1977 the first free elections take place, in 1978 the country receives a democratic constitution governed by a parliamentary democracy, in 1982 it joins NATO and in 1986 the EU.

1982   Andalusia receives partial autonomy as a Comunidad Autónoma.

1992   The world's fair Expo 92 is held in Seville, providing Andalusia with a route into Europe.

Glossary

Abbadids, Arabic dynasty in Seville (1023 – 1091), founded by Mohammed ibn Abbad.

Abbasids, dynasty of caliphs (750 – 1258). Descendants of Abbas, an uncle of the prophet Mohammed, who moved their caliphs' capital from Damascus to Baghdad in 763.

Aedicule (Lat. *aedicula*, "little house"), the frame around portals, windows and niches using two columns, pillars or pilasters, carrying an entablature and a triangular or segmental arch pediment.

Main portal, Iglesia San Pedro, Seville

Alabastron (Gk.), small Greek ointment container, originally made of alabaster, later also of clay or bronze; in shape long or spherical with a narrow neck.

Alcazaba (Arab. *al-kasbah*), fortified area, citadel.

Alcázar (Arab. *al-kasr*, "castle"), fortified Moorish ruler's palace, frequently taken over and extended by Christian kings.

Alfiz, rectangular relief frame of arches.

Alicatado (Sp. "tiles [in the Arabic style]"), term dating from the Moorish period (712–1492) denoting panels with faience mosaic which were used as wall coverings. Up to the beginning of the 16th century, Spanish alicatados had an almost exclusively geometrical pattern, though this was later replaced by Renaissance patterns. In contrast, North African alicatados, some of which are still produced today, retained the geometrical tradition.

Alcove (Sp. *alcoba*, "bedchamber"; Arab. *al-qobbah*, "vaulted chamber"), windowless recess in a room which is connected to the main room by a large opening in the wall; usually used as a bedchamber.

Allegory (Gk. *allegoria*, "depict differently"), a work of art which represents some abstract idea or content by depicting them in a symbolic manner, usually by means of personification (the figures of people) or groups of objects and figures.

Almohads (Arab. *al-Muwahhidun*, "who proclaim the unity of God"), Berber dynasty which became established as a result of the religious movement of the ascetic scholar Muhammed ibn Tumart. They ruled in Morocco (1147–1269) and Spain (1147–1224).

Almoravids (Arab. *al-Murabitun*, "men of the Ribat"), Berber dynasty (1089 – 1145) created by a religious brotherhood founded to convert the Berbers to Islam. Starting in Morocco, they extended their rule into North Africa and Spain (from 1086), until they were overthrown by the Almohads in 1145.

Amphitheater (Gk. *amphitheatron*; from *amphi*, "on both sides, around", and *theatron*, "theater"), open air theater on an elliptical groundplan with rising rows of seats; used mainly for fights between gladiators.

Amphitrite, Greek sea goddess, the wife of Poseidon and mother of Triton.

Amphora (Lat. *amphora*; Gk. *amphoreus*, "container with a handle on both sides", from *amphi*, "on both sides", and *pherein*, "carry"), bulbous storage container used by the Greeks, with two handles and up to 3 feet (1 m) in height.

Apostle (Gk. *apostolos*, "messenger, pioneer"), the twelve disciples of Jesus, who were chosen by him from amongst his followers in order to continue his work and preach the Gospel.

Appian (born c. 100 A.D.), Roman historical author who wrote a history of Rome compiled from various sources.

Apse (Lat.; Gk. *hapsis*, "connection, arch, vaulting"), a niche built on a semi-circular or

Inmaculada, Granada Cathedral

polygonal groundplan or vaulted with a semi-dome and which can contain an altar. When connected to the main part of a church, or the choir reserved for the clerics, it is also called the exedra or chevet. Small side apses are often found in the ambulatory, transept and side aisles.

Aqueduct (Lat. *aquaeductus*, "water system"; from *aqua*, "water", and *ducere*, "lead"), water conduit in the form of a bridge of arches carrying a water channel.

Arabesque, Salon Rico, Medina az-Zahara, Córdoba

Arabesque (Fr. *arabesque*, "Arabic ornamentation"; It. *arabesco*, "Arabic"), decoration consisting of leaves and vines that is very similar to its plant models. It has been known since Hellenistic art and in classical times was used to decorate pilasters and friezes. It was once more used on a larger scale during the Italian Early Renaissance, thus gaining entrance to later periods in Western art.

Arch, vaulted structure in a wall opening which carries its weight or transfers it onto pillars or columns. The highest part of the arch, with the keystone, is the crown. The rise is the vertical distance between the crown and the springing line between the imposts (the layer of stone between the wall, pillar or column, and arch). The inner surface of an arch is called an intrados.

Archivolt (It. *archivolto*, "front arch"; Gk. *archein*, "begin, rule" and Lat. *volutus*, "rolled, twisted"), a continuous decorative moulding framing the face of an arch, which can be viewed as a semi-circular architrave (main beam carrying the weight of the building above) leaning on a jamb (vertical surface of a wall opening).

Arianism, teachings of the Alexandrian priest Arius, according to which Christ is not identical in nature with God but a creature created out of nothing by God; condemned by the council at Nicaea in 325. Emperor Constantine II (337 – 361) helped to spread the teachings; supported by Goths, Vandals, Burgundians and Lombards until the politically superior Franks, supporters of the Roman-Catholic church, finally stopped these teachings in the 7th century.

Arcade (Fr. *arcade*, "strainer arch"; Lat. *arcus*, "arch, bow"), an arch or row of arches resting on piers or columns.

Artesonado (Sp. "paneling"), ornamented coffered ceiling consisting of several woods, arranged together in geometrical patterns.

Ashlar, accurately squared stones with smooth parallel faces or rough sides.

Athena or Pallas Athena, Greek goddess of war and victory, but also of wisdom, city life, patroness of the arts, sciences and crafts; daughter of Zeus having, according to legend, sprung from his forehead.

Attic (Lat. [*columna*] *attica*, "Attic [pillar]"), in architecture a low self-contained strip of wall above the main cornice of a building, frequently used to conceal the roof; can be decorated with inscriptions, reliefs or statuees.

Attis, god of the ancient country of Phrygia in Asia Minor, and part of the retinue of Cybele (mother of the Olympian gods). Attis makes a promise of chastity to the goddess who loves him. After he breaks his promise, she sends him into such a mad frenzy that he castrates himself and then commits suicide.

Attribute (Lat. *attributum*, "added"), a symbolic object which is conventionally used to identify a particular person, usually portraying a characteristic moment from the person's life.

Augustus (63 B.C. – 14 A.D.), first Roman emperor.

Ayuntamiento (Sp.), town hall.

Azulejos (Sp.; from *azul*, "blue"; Arab. *azzuleycha*, "glazed, colored stoneware"), colored glazed tiles made of fired clay, introduced to Spain by the Nasrids at the end of the 13th century.

Bacchus (Gk. *bakchos*) or Liber, Roman god of wine, equated with the Greek god Dionysus.

Baldachin (It. *baldacchino*), a textile canopy above a throne or bed; a canopy supported by poles at the four corners carried at processions; in architecture, a permanent ornamental canopy made of wood or stone above a throne, bishop's throne, altar, catafalque, chancel or statue. The name derives from the valuable silk material with gold thread that was made in Baghdad (It. *Baldaccho*), which was used to make the first canopies in Italy.

Balustrade (Gk. *balaustion*, "flower of the wild pomegranate"; It. *balustra*, "banister"), A railing or balcony supported by short pillars called balusters.

Baroque (from Port. *barocco*, "little stone, irregularly round"), European stylistic epoch that followed on from the end of Mannerism (c. 1590) and ended with the beginning of the Rococo period (c. 1725). The term originally derives from the goldsmiths' trade, where *barocco* is the term used for an irregular pearl.

Barrel vault, type of ceiling whose cross-section is usually a semicircle or arc; more rarely it has a pointed or parabolic cross-section.

Base (Gk. "step, walk, foundation", then "walked-on floor"; *banein*, "walk"), in architecture the projecting and usually shaped bottom course of a column or pillar which spreads the weight of the column onto a larger surface and forms a point of transition to the plinth; in sculpture, the plinth that a statue or relief stands on.

Basilica (Gk. *stoa basilike* , "king's hall"), generally a church building pointing to the east, flanked by two or four lower side aisles. A transept between the nave and choir, which was reserved for the clerics, was sometimes used to extend the building. The basilica was originally an ancient Greek government building, and in Roman times a long hall designed to accommodate markets and legal courts.

Christianity adopted the basilica as a community meeting place. The term derives from the official seat, in the marketplace in Athens, of the highest judge Archon Basileus.

Bay, part of a vault within a sequence of similar vaults; the part of an area that accords with, and is assigned to, a section of a vault.

Berber (probably from Gk. *barbaroi*, "stutterer, incomprehensible speaker"; Lat. *barbari*, "non-Roman"), name of a northern African Mohammedan tribe.

Bishop (Gk. *episkopos*, "supervisor"), high ecclesiastical dignitary. Amongst early Christians, he was the head of a community, later the successor of the Apostles and highest church dignitary in a bishopric, diocese or parish. He is fully empowered as a teacher, priest and shepherd, and is furnished with a mitre, crosier and gold bishop's ring.

Blind ornament, a blind architectural motif that is added to a building for the purpose of decoration and creating structure, but does not support the structure in any way; examples are blind windows and blind arcades.

Bodegón (Sp. "tavern"), in painting, a Spanish type of genre painting of kitchen interiors whose subject is mainly still life.

Booty piece, piece of a work of art or building used in another.

Buttressing, arch and pillar which, in addition to the walls, carries the pressure of the vault and weight of the roof on the outside of the building.

Caesar, Gaius Julius (100 – 44 B.C.), Roman statesman and general at the end of the Roman Republic.

Caliphate (Arab. *halifa*, "successor, representative"), the office, title and area ruled by a Caliph (title of Muhammad's successors as rulers of the Islamic empire).

Camarín (Sp.), chapel which normally houses the wardrobes for the statues of the Madonna and saints, and is usually placed behind the altar.

Campanile (from It. *campana*, "bell"), an Italian belfry, often detached from the main building.

Capilla Mayor (Sp.), main chapel, sanctuary.

Capital (Lat. *capitulum*, "little head"), top of a column or pillar. They can be decorated in various ways, either as figural capitals, or capitals with leaf and flower motifs.

Capitol (Lat. *capitolium*, "main temple of Jupiter"), name of the old fortified hill in Rome above the Forum Romanum.

Caravanserai (Pers. *karwan sarai*, "building where caravans stop"), public building in town on trade routes used as inns by travellers and merchants with their pack animals and goods. The building is usually arranged around an open arcade courtyard, with stables and storerooms on the ground floor and bedchambers arranged along wooden galleries in the one or two storeys above.

Caravel (Fr. *caravelle*; Port. *caravela*, "large ship"; from Lat. *carabus*, "woven basket"), sailing ship with three masts and a high stern.

Carthusian order (Lat. Ordo Cartusiensis), Catholic order of hermits founded in 1084 by Bruno of Cologne (1032 – 1101). The order's ideals are a combination of hermit and community life. In the 14th and 15th centuries, new

Capital, Bañuelo, Granada

Carthusian monasteries (with individual houses) were created, open to the Late Medieval mysticism, the *devotio moderna* ("new devotion"), and Humanism, the striving for genuine humanity.

Cartouche (It. *cartuccia*, "small piece of paper"; from Lat. *charta*, "paper"), shield-haped frame of a coat-of-arms, inscription or picture which is made up of a framework of scroll ornaments which roll up at the ends or edges; particularly popular element for decorating surfaces during the Baroque period.

Cartuja (Sp.), Carthusian monastery; a special form of monastery developed by Carthusian monks in which the monks' small individual houses with small gardens are next to the cloister and only the chapterhouse and church are used by all together; the abbot's and guests' houses are outside the enclosure (accessible only to monks).

Caryatids (Gk. *karyatides*, probably derived from the priestesses in the Temple of Artemis at Karyai in Laconia), female figures used as architectural supports.

Cathedral (Med. Lat. *ecclesia cathedralis*, "church belonging to the cathedra [bishop's throne]"; Gk. *cathedra*, "bishop's throne"), term used to denote a bishop's church.

Central plan building, a building whose parts are of equal proportions, with a groundplan that is normally a circle, ellipse, square or Greek Cross type. Models for centrally planned buildings in the Italian Renaissance were drawn from the Classical period, including the Roman Pantheon.

Ceres, Roman goddess of agriculture and all food plants, and also the goddess of marriage and death; since the 6th century B.C. equated with the Greek goddess Demeter.

Chancel screen or rood screen, balustrades or walls which separate off the choir which is reserved exclusively for the prayer or singing of the clerics. They often feature pictorial ornamentation.

Chapel (Med. Lat. *capella*, "small cloak"), small independent space for worship within churches; small church without parish status used for special purposes, such as baptismal or mortuary chapels. The term is derived from a small prayer room in the royal palace in Paris in which the cloak of St. Martin of Tours (316/17–397) has been kept since the 7th century.

Chapter house, assembly room of the chapter (body of clerics) in a monastery, usually situated on the east wing of the cloister. It was used for daily readings of chapters from the order's Rule and the Holy Scripture.

Chevet or apse, the eastern end of a church's choir (reserved for the clerics), which consists of a wall recess and semidome.

Choir stalls (detail), Málaga Cathedral

Choir (Lat. *chorus* and Gk. *choros*, "round dance, group of dancers and singers") or chancel, usually raised and separate space within the interior of church which is reserved for the communal worship of the clerics and singing of the choir. Since Carolingian times the term used for the extension of the nave which extends beyond the transept (which crosses the main part of the church) and which includes the apse (wall recess with a semidome) often found at the far end.

Choir stalls (Lat. *chorus* and Gk. *choros*, "round dance, group of dancers and singers"; Sp. *sillería*), the rows of seats set up on either side of the choir for the use of the members of a cathedral or colle-

Cloisters, Santillas del Mar

giate chapter or a community of monks. The choir stalls consist of a lower and upper row of seats with a rear wall rising up behind; the individual stalls have arm rests and folding seats, the front edge of which was widened to be used as a support (known as a misericord) when standing. High side walls complete the structure.

Christogram (Gk. *christos*, "the anointed", and Late Lat. *monogramma*, "symbol consisting of several letters"), the Greek first letters of Jesus Christ's name, *chi* (C) and *rho* (R), written on top of each other.

Church aisle, interior space of long sacred buildings. The different aisles are the nave, the side aisles that run parallel to it, and the transept that crosses it.

Cicero, Marcus Tullius (106 – 43 B.C.), Roman politician, philosopher and orator.

Cistern (Lat. *cisterna*), subterranean walled container for collecting and storing rainwater.

Claudius (10 B.C.– 54), Roman emperor (41 – 54 A.D.).

Cloister, a vaulted arcade which forms a square around the monastery courtyard and opens out onto it, usually with a balustrade on the south side of the monastery, the other sides being taken up by the walls of the monastery's main rooms, in accordance with strict rules.

Coffering, means of structuring the intrados (inner surface) of an arch, or a flat or vaulted ceiling, with rectangular, box-shaped recessed panels. Coffered ceilings were already known in classical times and were revived in Renaissance palaces and churches.

Collegiate church, church belonging to a diocese which possesses both its own property and legal status and likewise a chapter of priests but no bishop's see.

Columns, normally elements for supporting architectural strucutres with a circular cross-section that taper towards the top; they can consist of a base, shaft and capital. Most names refer to the type of shaft involved, so that monolithic columns consist of a single piece of stone, drum columns consist of drum-shaped pieces, and likewise fluted columns have vertical grooves.

Compound pier, in Gothic architecture a group of smaller and larger three-quarter columns (strong and weak shafts) arranged around a core pillar; in High Gothic, the group is condensed to the point where the core pillar is either almost or completely invisible.

Conquista, discovery and conquest of Central and South America.

Console (Fr. *consola*, "base", from Lat. *solidus*, "firm"), bracket, often shaped or with figural ornamentation, which projects from the wall as a support for arches, entablatures, balconies and figures.

Corinthian column, like Ionic columns consisting of a richly shaped base and a slim shaft fluted with fillets; its capital and abacus, however, are decorated with acanthus leaves (large prickly thistle-type leaves curled up at the tips). It is part of the Corinthian order of columns (Greek architectural system).

Cornice, horizontal moulding projecting from the wall which structures the horizontal sections of a building.

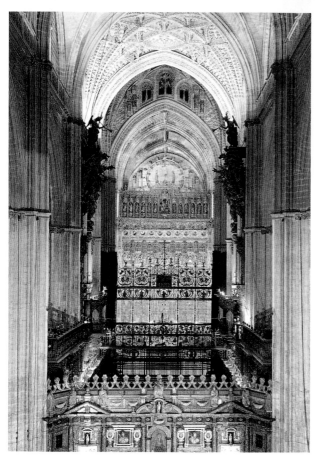

Interior, Seville Cathedral

Coro (Sp.), choir.

Council (Lat. *concilium*, "meeting"), gathering of high ecclesiastical dignitaries, such as bishops.

Crenellation, a rectangular, tooth-like notched parapet on a wall, usually in a row.

Crossing, part of the church interior where the nave and side aisles intersect the transept.

Crucifix (Lat. *crux*, "cross", and *fixus*, "fixed"), sculptural or painted representation of the crucified Christ.

Crypt (Lat. *crypta* and Gk. *krypte*, "covered walkway, vault"), subterranean space for worship or burial, usually beneath the choir, reserved for the clerics, of a church.

Cubism (Lat. *cubus*, Gk. *kybos*, "cube"), modern art movement which came into being between 1908 and 1910 as a reaction to Impressionism, and which elevated the values of a cube to form a structural principle for representing it on a surface. This means that all three dimensions of a depicted object are represented, merged together, on the surface by placing the front and sides above and next to each other.

Cuenca (Sp.), *azulejo* (colored glazed tile) with (clay) fillets to border the individual ornamental fields

Cueva (Sp.), cave.

Cufic, an older form of Arabic calligraphy named after the city of Cufa (near Baghdad).

Diptych (Lat. *diptychum*; Gk. *diptychos*, "folded twice"), in classical times a folding writing tablet; in the Middle Ages, an altarpiece (whether sculptural or painted) comprising a pair of panels hinged together, without a fixed central part.

Dolmen (Breton *dol*, "panel [or New Breton *toul*, "hole"], and *men*, "stone") or cromlech, a stone table; prehistoric burial site with four to six unhewn large stones erected in the form of a rectangle or polygon, and covered with another large stone and a mound of earth.

Dome, a type of ceiling or roof, evenly curved over a round, rectangular or polygonal base. The transition from a square groundplan to the round base of the dome can be achieved in a number of ways: 1. in sail vaults, the base of the dome forms an imaginary circle that surrounds the square of the groundplan. 2. In the case of domes resting on pedentives, an imaginary sail vault is cut off horizontally above the arch, the circular surface thus created carries a semidome; the spherical triangles thus created are called pedentives. In cross-section, domes can have any of the configurations of an arch.

Dominican Order (Lat. *Ordo Fratrum Praedictatorum*, "Order of Preaching Brothers"), order of mendicant monks founded by St. Dominic (1170 – 1221) in Toulouse in 1216, to spread and extend the faith by preaching and tea-ching. In 1232, the Pope put the Dominicans in charge of the Inquisition, the Church's judicial institution for seeking out heresy.

Doric column, vertical architectural element without a base that is part of the Doric order of columns (Greek architectural system), with sharp arris stonework, a fluted shaft and a capital (undecorated) consisting of an annuli (ring moulding), echinus (cushion-like torus) and square abacus (top slab).

Drum, cyclindrical architectural area between the building below and the dome. It usually contains windows and is used to raise the height of the structure.

Eaves, horizontal projecting edge on the long side of a roof where rainwater runs off.

Emir (Arab. *emir, amir*, "commander"), title of the Arabic ruler of an emirate (Islamic principality).

Entablature, the upper part of one of the orders of architecture (classical architectural system), including the architrave (the main beam carrying the weight of the building above), the frieze (horizontal wall decoration) and cornice (projecting strip of wall below the roof.

Ephebe (Gk. *ephebos*, "youth"), in classical Greece a young man between the ages of 18 and 20 who was fit for military service.

Estofado sculpture (Sp. *estofar*, "dressed up"), naturalistic, colourful and frequently folk form of colouring and fashioning in Spanish Baroque sculpture.

Exedra (Gk. "exterior seat, isolated seat"), niche containing a seat at the end of a colonnade; also term used for an apse, the altar

Entablature, Monasterio S. Jeronimo, Granada

niche at the end of the choir, or any other semi-circular niche.

Faience (Fr. *faience*, from the Italian city of Faenza) or majolica, earthenware that has been fired once and then coated with an opaque usually white tin glaze treated with heatresistant underglaze pigments.

Flamboyant style (fr. "flamed"), ornamental motif consisting of flame-like shapes found during the French Late Gothic.

Foil, in Gothic architecture a circular shape which occurs in tracery; depending on the number of circular forms (with equal diameters) which intersect to make cusps (projecting tips), they are called trefoil, quatrefoil or multifoil.

Forum (Lat. "marketplace"), the marketplace in a Roman town, where judicial procedures and public affairs were also carried out;

Dome of the Maqsura, Mezquita, Córdoba

usually a long rectangle surrounded by public buildings which were later combined together by colonnades (rows of columns with an architrave).

Fresco (It. *fresco*, "fresh"), wall painting that is applied to moist plaster in so-called *giornata* (the amount of work done in one day).

Frieze (Med. Lat. *frisium*, "Phrygian work" or "fringe"), sculptural or painted strip-likecontinuous wall ornamentation in a horizontal format, used to decorate, structure or brighten up a wall surface.

Frontispiece (Fr. *frontispice*, "front side [of a building], title page"; Med. Lat. *frontispicium*; from Lat. *frons*, "front", and *spicere*, "look"), triangular pediment above the central protruding facade bay of a building, and also above doors and windows.

Gable, the upper part of the wall at the end of a saddleback roof; also used above doors, windows or niches.

Galatea (Gk. *galateia*, "milk-white"), one of the Nereids (the 50 daughters of the sea god Nereus and the Oceanide Doris) who was loved by the Cyclops Polyphemus, though his love was not returned.

Gallery, 1. an upper storey like a balcony in a church constructed in order to produced additional space for worshippers or in order to separate particular groups (women, courtiers); in hall churches, carried by free-standing supports; in central plan buildings above the ambulatory, in basilicas above the side aisles, rarely place above the west bay or in the transept; 2. a long room used to connect several spaces; 3. an arbour attached to houses and military buildings that is open to one side; 4. covered passage.

Glory (Lat. *gloria*, "fame, splendor, heavenly magnificence") or gloriole, light painted as emanating from God the Father, Christ, the Holy Spirit, Mary or a saint and surrounding the entire body.

Gothic (It. *gotico*, "barbaric, not classical"), medieval European period of art which started in northern France in about 1150. It ended there in about 1400, though continuing in other parts until the beginning of the 16th century. The term is derived from the Goths, a Germanic tribe. Specific characteristics are the introduction of pointed arches (broken at the crown), rib vaults (created by the intersection at right angles of two barrel vaults of the same size) and the use of flying buttresses (arches and pillars to help the walls carry the pressure of the vault and weight of the roof. Gothic buildings are very tall; the walls are broken up and lit by large windows, which determine the overall impression of the building. The cathedral is the determining feature of Gothic architecture. Gothic sculpture was closely connected to the architecture. An idealistic conception of nature is a typical feature: bodies and robes – usually stretched disproportionately long – are an important part of the expressiveness of the design. Gothic painting was mainly restricted to panel paintings, illuminated manuscripts and stained glass windows.

Grisaille (Fr. *gris*, "grey", and *grisailler*, "paint grey"), grey on grey painting, a type of painting which deliberately avoids colours and restricts itself to stone colours, using shades of brown or grey. It is particularly suited to imitating sculptural works in paintings.

Grotesque (It. *grottesco*, "wild, fantastic"), a kind of ornament from the Hellenistic and classical Roman periods which consists of fantastic plant and animal shapes. In the 16th century, the term was derived from the subterranean spaces (It. *grotta*, "grotto") where these ornaments were found, and which are now known as the Baths of Titus or the Golden House of Nero.

Hades, Greek god of the Underworld; term used for the Underworld itself.

Hadrian (76 – 138), Roman emperor (117–138).

Hall church (gk. *kyriakon*, "that which belongs to the Lord"), a long church whose nave and aisles are of equal height and contained under one roof. There is usually no transept.

Hercules (Gk. *Herakles*), most important Greek hero; son of Zeus and Alcmene; his deeds, particularly the 12 Labors which he had to carry out for King Eurystheus, have frequently been depicted in both classical and later art.

Horseshoe arch, arch in the shape of a three-quarter circle that narrows at the bottom.

Immaculada (Sp. from Lat. *immaculata*, "the immaculate one"), doctrine of the Immaculate Conception of Mary which was supported by the Franciscans in the 15th century and later became part of the dogma of the Catholic Church.

Impost, layer of stone between the wall, pillar or column, and arch or vault, which is frequently emphasized by a projecting, shaped impost block.

Intarsia (from It. *intarsiare*, "do inlay work"; Arab. *tarsi*, "to stud"), a type of marquetry in wood, though also using ivory, mother of pearl, tortoise-shell and metal. The patterns are either raised above the wooden body and filled with other materials, or put together out of small pieces and glued onto it.

Intrados, the vertical interior surface of wall openings such as arches.

Ionic column, supporting element comprising a shaped base, a slim shaft that is fluted using fillets, and a capital with an egg and dart pattern, volutes (scroll-shaped ornament) and abacus (top slab), and part of the Ionic order of architecture (Greek architectural system).

Isabelline style (Sp. *estilo Isabel*), stylistic term for a special Spanish form of Late Gothic, named after Isabella I (1451 – 1504), which developed from the last third of the 15th century into the early 16th century. It is characterized by a decorative style that combines projecting and rampant flamboyant (flame ornament) forms with Mudéjar elements.

Islam (Arab. *islam*, "state of grace, surrender to the will of God"), monotheistic religion founded by the Prophet Muhammed in the 7th century.

Jamb, the vertical, frequently decorated or stepped inside surface of windows or portals.

Janus, classical Roman god of doorways, though also of entrances and exits in both literal and figurative senses; usually depicted with two heads, facing both right and left.

Jasper (Gk. *iaspis*, Hebr. *jaspeh*, Assyr. *aspu*), semiprecious stone consisting of very fine grain, opaque and usually intensively coloured quartz mineral; widespread brown, yellow, red and grey shades, rarely blue and black ones. Since classical times, used in crafts as an ornament for small items, boxes, dishes, vases, table and wall mosaics and cameos.

Juno (Lat. *iuvenis*, "life force [of young women]"), Roman goddess of women and female life as a whole, in particular childbirth; worshipped as a triad together with Jupiter and Minerva on the Capitol in Rome.

Jupiter (Lat. *Diespater* and *Diespiter*, "father of light"), Latin name for the Indo-germanic father of the gods who corresponds to the Greek Zeus; god of the weather who sends forth lightning, thunder and rain; protector of justice and virtue who defends marriage and oaths; god by whose name oaths were sworn. Together with Juno and Minerva, he was worshipped as Jupiter Optimus Maximus on the Capitol in Rome as the embodiment of the Roman state.

Kline (Gk.), couch for reclining.

Koran (Arab. *qur'an*, "reading"), sacred scripture of Islam; collection of the revelations of Allah which were made known to the Prophet Muhammed and which he wrote and proclaimed in Arabic from about 610 to 632.

Lantern (Lat. *laterna* and Gk. *lamptera*, "lamp, light"), in architecture, a round or polygonal turret with openings above a dome or vault, used to light the space below.

Latin Cross, a cross with a lower shaft which is longer than the other three shafts. It is the preferred type of groundplan for medieval Western sacred buildings.

Lesene (Fr. *lisière*, "border strip, edging"), slightly projecting vertical wall moulding used to structure a wall surface and frequently topped with blind arches or friezes with round arches.

Loggia (It.), open arcade or hallway supported by columns or pillars.

Lonja (Sp. "forecourt", also a long hall where merchants gathered in the Middle Ages), stock exchange.

Lucanus, Marcus Annaeus (39 – 65), Roman epic poet, nephew of Seneca; from Córdoba.

Lunette (Fr. *lunette*, "little moon"), a semi-circular space, sometimes a window, over doors and windows, and usually containing figural decorations.

Mannerism (It. maniera, "manner", from Lat. *manuarius*, "of the hands"), term describing European art in the period between the Renaissance and the Baroque, c. 1520/30 to 1620. In Mannerism, the harmonious ideal forms, proportions and compositions developed during the Renaissance were set aside. Typical features of Mannerist art include scenes that are more dynamic, elongated human bodies positioned in anatomically contradictory fashions, compositions that are excessively complicated, irrational and theatrical lighting, and the use of color in a way less restricted to the object it represents.

Maqsura (Arab.), a separate space close to the Mihrab that is reserved for the ruler or governor; frequently closed off by an artistic grille. The maqsura is only found in mosques in capital cities; it first arose during the Omayad period, presumably to protect the ruler from attacks.

Marcus Aurelius (121 – 180), Roman emperor (161 – 180).

Marquetry (Fr. *marqueterie*, "inlay work"), technique of inlaying woods into wooden objects.

Martyrdom (Gk. *martyrion*, "blood proof"), torments, torture and sacrificial death suffered for one's faith or convictions.

Medina (Arab. *Madinat*), city.

Megalithic culture (Gk. *megas*, "large", and *lithos*, "stone"), neolithic culture (4th millennium – 2000 B.C.), the characteristic features of which were sacred buildings and graves made of large stone blocks.

Mensa, the table of an altar.

Mezquita (Sp.), mosque.

Mihrab (Arab.) or qibla, concave and usually richly decorated prayer niche in the wall of a mosque facing Mecca.

Minaret (Arab.), turret of a mosque with a platform from which a muezzin calls the faithful to prayer five times a day.

Minerva, Roman goddess; protector of Rome, patroness of craftsmen, poets and teachers, and as Minerva Medica of doctors; from the end of the 3rd century B.C. equated with the Greek goddess Athena.

Mirador, 1. view point, 2. open or glazed roofed turret, usually above the corners of a building.

Misericord (Lat. *misericordia*, "mercy"), small supporting bracket, frequently decorated with carvings, on the front edge of the folding seat in a choir stall, for clerics to lean against when standing.

Mithras, ancient Persian sun god who the Greeks equated with Apollo-Helios and depicted with a glory, barsom (bundle of twigs) and Parthian dress; entered Roman religion at an early stage and reached the provinces with the army. The god usually appears in cult images killing a bull.

Monstrance (Lat. *monstrare*, "show"), *custodia* in Spanish, liturgical container made of precious metal which exhibits the consecrated Host behind glass and held in a crescent-shaped holder *lunula*.

Moors (Late Gk. *mauroi*, "black", Phoen. *mauharin*, "western"), Roman name for the Berbers from the Atlas regions whose country was called Mauritania. After the Arabs conquered North West Africa, the name was applied to the mixed population, consisting of Berbers and Arabs, of the towns in the Atlas region, and following the Arabic invasion of 711, was indiscriminately applied by the Spanish to all Arabs and Berbers (*los moros*).

Moriscos (Sp.), Moors that converted to Christianity.

Mosque (Arab. *masgid*, "house of prayer"), Islamic place of worship usually consisting of a forecourt with fountains for ritual washing, a minaret and a prayer hall with a mihrab.

Mozarabs, Christians living under Arabic rule.

Mudéjars (from Arab. *mudayyan*, "allowed to stay"), term used from the 13th century for Moors living under Christian rule.

Mudéjar style, stylistic term introduced in the 19th century for the architectural and ornamental forms used by Moorish artists and craftsmen, widespread from the 14th to 16th centuries. The buildings, mainly constructed for Christian masters, contain a mixture of Late Gothic and Islamic stylistic elements.

Muqarnas (Arab.), prismatic, three-dimensional ornamental elements of varying sizes made of plaster, which can be combined in various ways.

Muses, female goddesses of poetry, music, dance and the sciences; appear as a group of nine sisters, with each one having a particular function in relation to the arts.

Muslim, one who practices Islam.

Mythology (Gk. *mythologia*; from Gk. *mythos*, "story", and *logos*, "teaching"), knowledge and interpretation of myths (holy teachings) and legends of the gods and heroes of a group of people.

Nasrids (Arab. *an-Nasriyyun*), Arabic dynasty of Granada (1238 – 1492) founded by Muhammed I.

Nave and side aisles, the part of a church between the west end (facade) and the crossing (where the nave and side aisles and transept intersect) or the choir. One-aisled churches contain no side aisles, and basilicas and hall churches can contain several aisles.

Necropolis (Gk. *nekros*, "dead one", and *polis*, "city"; Sp. *necrópolis*), area of tombs laid out outside the city walls during the classical period and early Christianity.

Neoclassicism (from Fr. *classique* and Lat. *classicus*, "exemplary"), style of decoration from 1750 to 1840 based on the model of classical antiquity (5th – 4th centuries B.C.).

Neptune, Roman god of flowing water, and later of the ocean; equated with the Greek god Poseidon.

Net vault or reticulated vault, Late Gothic form of vault in which the ribs (load-bearing parts of the roof) form a network so that the division of the vault into bays is less obvious.

Octagon (from Gk. *octo*, "eight", and *gonia*, "corner"), an ancient Middle Eastern and

Nécropolis Romana, Carmona

classical symbol for the perfection of the universe; in architecture it is a central plan building with an octagonal groundplan.

Oeil-de-boeuf, a round or elliptical window.

Oeuvre (Fr. "work"), entire works of an artist.

Omayads, Arabic dynasty of caliphs in Damascus from 661 – 750; one grandchild of Caliph Hischam escaped the bloody extermination by the Abbasids, and in 756 as Abd ar-Rahman I he founded the Omayad kingdom of Córdoba.

Orant or orans (Lat. *orare*, "pray, speak"), a praying figure in painting and sculpture.

Oratory, small space or chapel for prayer and services. Initially reserved for clerics or princes. From the 16th century, it was in places also accessible to the public.

Orchestra (Gk. *orcheistrai*, "dance"), large circular dance space in the center of the Greek theater.

Pagoda, Chinese or Japanese temple in the form of a tower with successively diminishing storeys and artistically structured curved roofs on each level.

Panel (Fr. *panneau*, "panel"), recessed wooden plate used to fill in the gap between the mouldings and frames of paneling.

Paso (Sp.), colorful figure or group of figures carved from wood, usually in life size, depicting scenes from the Passion and carried through the streets during processions.

Patio (Old Sp. *patu*, *pati*, "leased land, meadow"), closed inner courtyard of a building, usually with ambulatories.

Pediment, the classical flat triangular or segmental arch pediments were imitated during the Renaissance, Baroque and Neoclassical periods and, as in the originals, can be broken or have a cornice continuing through it, in other words the central part can be missing or projecting to a greater or lesser extent. The tympanum (area within the pediment) can be decorated.

Pegasus, winged horse in Greek mythology which sprang from Medusa's neck when Perseus cut her head off.

Pendentive (Fr. "suspended arch"), the curved triangular area used to link a square ground plan with the round dome above it.

Peripteral temple (Gk. *peripteros*, "winged all around"), form of Greek temple with a simple arrangement of columns surrounding it.

Peristyle (Gk. *peristylon*), colonnade surrounding a courtyard or square.

Personification (Lat. *persona*, "person", and *facere*, "make"), representing gods, ideas or objects as human beings.

Pietà (It. "mercy, sympathy"; from Lat. *pietas*, "piety"), representation of the sorrowing Virgin Mary holding the dead Christ in her arms.

Pilaster (It. *pilastro*; from Lat. *pila*, "pillar"), rectangular pillar which usually only projects a short way from the wall which it structures, with a base, shaft and capital. It is frequently fluted (vertical grooves on the shaft).

Pillar (Lat. *pila*), vertical supporting element with a square, rectangular or polygonal cross-section. It can be subdivided into a base, shaft and capital. Depending on its position and formation, it can be a free-standing, wall or corner pillar or a pier buttress (pillar placed outside a building to help the wall bear the pressure of the vault and weight of the roof).

Pinnacle, small tower used as a Gothic architectural ornament. It usually has four or eight sides, a tall pointed roof, and is frequently located on the ornamental pediments of windows or portals or as the crown of pier buttresses (supports built outside the building to help the wall bear the force of the vault and weight of the roof).

Piscina (Lat.), 1. fishpond, 2. swimming pool in public Roman baths; also the font in a baptistery (separate sacred building for baptism).

Plateresque style (Sp. *platero*, "silversmith"), stylistic term for Spanish architectural and decorative art of the first two thirds of the 16th century, and using stone ornaments carved so delicately and elaborately that they are reminiscent of fine filigree work with precious metals.

Pliny the Elder (23/24 – 79 A.D.), born Gaius Plinius Secundus, Roman writer. The only one of his works to have survived is his *Historia Naturalis* (Natural History) in 37 volumes, in which Pliny for the first time collected all natural phenomena in an encyclopedic form.

Podium temple (Lat. *podium*; from Gk. *podion*, "step, step-like rise"; and Lat. *templum*, "holy place"), in Etruscan and Roman architecture a temple with a front on a high base (podium) entered by way of a broad staircase at the front.

Pointed arch, arch with a pointed top which was particularly popular during the Gothic period.

Polyphemus, famous Cyclops in Greek mythology, son of Uranus and Gaea, with a single round eye in the middle of his forehead; he was made drunk by Odysseus and then blinded with a stake.

Pompey (106–48 B.C.), Roman general and statesman; political opponent of Julius Caesar.

Portal (Med. Lat. *portale*, "entrance hall"), artistically structured entrance to a building. The model for Western portals was the Roman triumphal arch, a free-standing arch which was usually built in honor of an emperor or general.

Portico (Lat. *porticus*, "arcade, hall"), usually open structure, carried by columns or pillars, in front of the main entrance to a building.

Piscina, San Pedro

Often supports a pediment.

Predella (It. "footstool, altar-step"), socle-like base of winged altar-pieces which on occasion is used to house relics (venerated objects or parts of a saint's body). It is frequently decorated with pictorial representations.

Presbytery (Gk. *presbyterion*, "council of the elders") or choir, raised section at the end of a church which is reserved for the clergy and houses the high altar.

Prostyle temple (Gk.), Greek temple with a *cella* (main room) and entrance hall supported by columns.

Pulpit, raised structure which the preacher uses in a church; derived from the ambo, which in the early Christian basilica was set up next to or in front of the chancel screen, and a reading platform raised several steps above it. The pulpit leans against a pillar in the crossing or nave; the foot of the pulpit can have one or more columns or be shaped as a figure, usually has a polygonal broken pulpit rail and is reached via a staircase with a balustrade. Above it is a sounding board in the shape of a baldachin. During the Late Gothic and Renaissance periods, the balustrades and sounding boards were given an architectural structure and lavish sculptural ornamentation.

Pyx or monstrance, container for the Host in Catholic churches; in Spain, specifically a processional tabernacle for the monstrance; an ornamental container usually several layers high, up to 9 feet (3 m.) tall and made of precious metals.

Quadriga (Lat.; from *quattuor*, "four", and

iugum, "bay"), team of four horses before an open two-wheeled war or triumphal chariot. In architecture the quadriga has been used since the 4th century B.C. to crown buildings.

Qibla (Arab.), term for the direction of prayer facing Mecca – indicated within the mosque by the qibla wall – towards which the mosque is pointed.

Reconquista (Sp. "reconquest"), reconquest of those parts of Spain occupied by the Moors in 711 by the Christians from the 8th to the end of the 15th centuries.

Refectory (Med. Lat. *refectorium*; from Lat. *reficere*, "remake"), dining room in a monastery.

Reja (Sp.), railing, window grille.

Relief (Fr.; from Lat. *relevare*, "raise"), a composition or design made so that all or part projects from a flat surface. The degree of relief is indicated in terms such as alto rilievo ("high relief", deeply carved sculpture almost detached from its support), mezzo rilievo (figures seen in the half-round) and bas-relief (figures projecting less than half their true depth from the background).

Portal, Iglesia Santa Marina, Córdoba

Renaissance (Fr.; It. *rinascimento*, "rebirth"), progressive epoch in the arts and intellectual life of southern, western and central Europe, originating in Italy and lasting from the 14th or 15th till the 16th century. The late period, from about 1530 to 1600, is also called Mannerism. The term derives from the word *rinascità* coined by Giorgio Vasari (1511–1574) in 1550; Vasari meant it to refer to progress beyond mediaeval art. Humanism aimed for a new image of humanity, the world and nature and took antiquity as its model. The Renaissance evolved the concept of the "uomo universale", the person of universal learning and all-round intellectual and physical capacity. The visual arts emerged from their status as crafts, and with their new independence artists found that their social status had risen too. The arts and sciences were closely tied and

Reticulated vault, Granada Cathedral

influenced each other (in the discovery of mathematical perspective, for example, or in the anatomical knowledge that now went into the portrayal of the human form). Renaissance architecture took its bearings from the theories of Vitruvius (c. 84 B.C.) and adopted classical features; its major achievements were in palace and church architecture, and centrally planned buildings were characteristic of the period.

Retable (Fr. *retable*; Lat. *retabulum*, "rear wall") or **altar-piece**, sculptural or painted altar decoration usually mounted behind the altar or over its rear wall. It can consist of a single work of art or several panels.

Reticulated vault, late Gothic vault form in which the ribs (weight bearing sections of the ribs (weight-bearing sections of the roof) form a network disguising the division of the bays.

Rib, girder-like projecting moulding, frequently shaped, designed to strengthen the groin of a vault. Between the ribs are the cells, which are not load-bearing.

Rib vault, the intersection of two barrel vaults (semicircular and segmental arch roofs) of equal size at right angles. The intersections are called ribs.

Rococo (from Fr. *rocaille*, "scree, grotto shells"), European period of art from 1720/30 to 1770/80, characterized by a decorational style which favors lightness, playfulness and small scales. In painting, this is underlined by a brightening of the color palette.

Rotunda (Lat. *rotundus*, "round"), a round building or room.

Round arch, semi-circular arch.

Rustication (Lat. *rusticus*, "rural"), stonework consisting of ashlars whose exterior has been roughly dressed.

Early Christian sarcophagus from Martos, Jaén

Sacristy (Med. Lat. *sacristia*; from Lat. *sacer*, "holy, consecrated"), side room of a church used as a storeroom for religious objects and vestments, and for priests to dress them selves.

Sagrario (Sp.), tabernacle, housing for the sacrament, also a chapel for the tabernacle.

Sanctuary (Lat. *sanctus*, "holy"), 1. in all religious buildings the holy place, 2. in Christian churches where the altar is housed, usually identical with the chancel or choir.

Sarcophagus (Gk. *sarcophagos*, "flesh-eater"), a coffin made of wood, metal, clay or stone and usually lavishly decorated with figural representations and ornaments.

Scipio, Publius Cornelius Africanus (235–183 B.C.), Roman general, famous for his victory over Hannibal in the Second Punic War which gained him the honorary title Africanus.

Sebka, diamond-shaped, grid-like surface decoration of the Almohads; popular and frequentlyl used in Mudéjar art.

Seneca, Lucius, Annaeus (c. 4 B.C.–5 A.D.), Roman politician, Stoic philosopher and poet; born in Córdoba.

Shaft-ring or annulet, a stone ring placed around the shaft of a column which originally had a structural function.

Sphinx, Egyptian and Greek mythic creature with the body of a lion and human head; in Greek mythology, she sat before one of the gates of Thebes and killed anyone who could not solve her riddle, "What is it that has four feet in the morning, two at noon and three at night?" – answer: "Man".

Stalactite (Gk. *stalaktos*, "dripping"), hanging dripstone formation growing downwards from the roof (of a cave).

Stellar vault, Late Gothic form of vault in which the ribs (load-bearing parts of the ceiling) form star shapes.

Stone inlay, cladding of walls and floors with colorful, polished stone slabs, usually of marble or porphyry, which are arranged in patterns thus structuring the surfaces and bringing them to life in a decorative fashion.

Stucco (It. "plaster"), mixture of gypsum, lime and sand which can be moulded into any shape when wet, but dries rapidly and cannot then be altered.

Synagogue (Gk. *synagoge*, "place of gathering"; from *synagein*, "bring together"), place of worship, Jewish temple.

Tracery, Capilla Real, Granada

Tabernacle (Lat. *tabernaculum*, "little tent, little hut"), in architecture, an ornamental niche consisting of columns and a pointed roof, frequently used for statues and sometimes found on Gothic buttresses; shrine for containing the consecrated Host.

Taifa kingdom (Sp. *taifa*, "division"), term for the small kingdoms (*taifas*) created during the last two decades, and following the demi-se, of the Caliphate of Córdoba (1031).

Telamones (Gk. "support"), Roman term for atlantes, usually over life-size male stone figures which support an entablature or vault in place of columns. The counterpart of female caryatids.

Thermae (Gk. *thermos*, "warm, hot"), public baths in the Roman Empire; the central parts of the baths were the *frigidarium* and *piscina* (cold swimming pool), the lukewarm *tepidarium* and the hot *caldarium*, which were heated by hypocausts (spaces or channels beneath the floors). Adjacent to them were dressing and massage rooms, saunas and leisure rooms, even libraries.

Titus (39 – 81), Roman emperor (79 – 81).

Tracery, geometrical Gothic ornamental stonework, measured with a compass, used to subdivide the tops of the arches of large windows, and later used to structure pediments, gables, walls and other surfaces.

Trajan (53 – 117), Roman emperor (98 – 117).

Triclinium (Lat.), 1. dining room in Roman houses, 2. dining hall for pilgrims in a monastery.

Triptych (Gk. *triptychos*, "in three parts"), a picture made up of three panels, in particular

Armored statue, Museo Arqueológico Provincial, Seville

a mediaeval winged altar-piece, consisting of a fixed center and two movable side panels.

Triumphal arch (Lat. *triumphus*, "victory procession"), since the 2nd century B.C. a freestanding gateway with several openings in honor of an emperor or general.

Tympanum (Lat.; Gk. *tympanun*, "drum"), the triangular area enclosed by a classical pedi-ment, often decorated with sculptures; in mediaeval architecture, the area over the lintel of a portal, enclosed by an arch.

Valens (328 – 378), Roman emperor of the East (364 – 378), brother of Valentinian.

Valentinian I (321 – 375), Roman emperor of the West (364–375).

Valerian (c. 185 – after 260), Roman emperor (253 – 260).

Vanitas (Lat. "vanity, transience"), complaint about transience and, hence, the triviality of all earthly things which was derived from the Old Testament phrase *vanitas vanitatum* (everything is futile). The saying was a particularly popular subject of pictures during the Baroque period, especially in combination with the warning "memento mori" (remember you are mortal). Typical symbols of Vanitas include the skull, hour-glass and burning candle.

Vault, curved roof above a space, usually composed of wedge-shaped stones. In contrast to a dome, it can also be found above long interior spaces. The abutments, such as the walls or pillars, carry the force and pressure of the vault.

Venus, Roman goddess of Spring and gardens, closely connected with the concept of grace and charm; later equated with the Greek goddess of love, Aphrodite.

Vestibule (Lat. *vestibulum*, "forecourt, entry"; Fr. *vestibule*, "entry hall, forecourt), entry room of a house.

Yesería (Sp. "plaster"), stucco work placed on the surface in a pattern.

Andalusian Architectural Forms

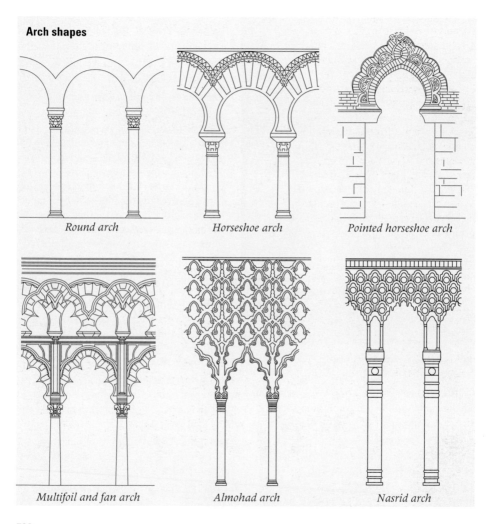

Arch shapes

Round arch

Horseshoe arch

Pointed horseshoe arch

Multifoil and fan arch

Almohad arch

Nasrid arch

Domes

A characteristic feature of the domes of the Mezquita of Córdoba is the blurring of the tectonic relationships between the supports and their load. The domes are supported by a system of arcades whose round arches are braced with multifoil arches that intersect each other. The weight of the dome is carried by an artistic network of ribs, a system in which the individual ribs rest on demi-columns standing on consoles that project from the wall. The ribs structure the vault into small areas that are decorated with mosaic pictures.

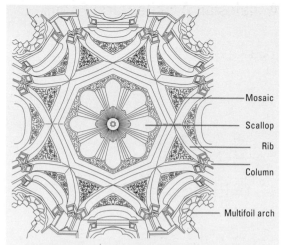

Mosaic

Scallop

Rib

Column

Multifoil arch

Córdoba, Great Mosque, dome before the mihrab

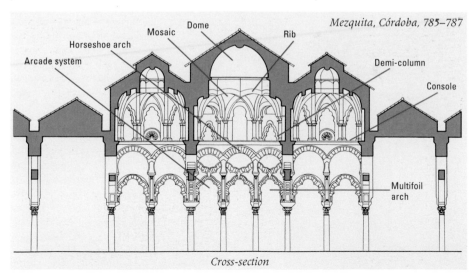

Mezquita, Córdoba, 785–787

Dome

Mosaic

Horseshoe arch

Arcade system

Rib

Demi-column

Console

Multifoil arch

Cross-section

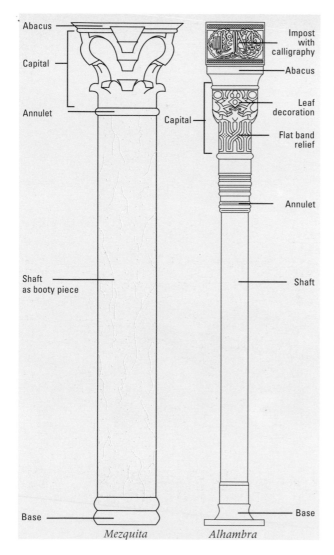

Abacus	
Capital	
Annulet	
	Impost with calligraphy
	Abacus
Capital	Leaf decoration
	Flat band relief
	Annulet
Shaft as booty piece	Shaft
Base	Base

Mezquita　　*Alhambra*

Columns

During the age of the caliphate of Córdoba, Roman and Visigoth booty pieces were frequently used for columns and capitals. In contrast to Roman ones, Visigoth capitals were not bound to their classical models. During the late period of the Emirate, copies of classical capitals were also produced. An independent type of column did not develop until the period of Nasrid architecture in Granada. The slender column shafts are visually connected with the usually basket-shaped capital by means of several annulets above each other. The capital is then divided into a lower zone which has roughly the same diameter as the column shaft and is usually decorated with a band or network in bas-relief, and a wider upper part decorated with lavish leaf ornaments or stalactites. On top of the capital are artistically decorated impost blocks which serve not only to enlarge the surface of the capital but mainly to give more height to the arcades and their short columns.

Ornamentation

Due to the fact that pictures were forbidden by Islam, decoration was entirely limited to ornamentation. However, the combination of geometric, floral, and calligraphic motifs, contained in a strictly symmetrical system and enriched by colorful azulejos decorations, created an exceedingly rich style of wall decoration.

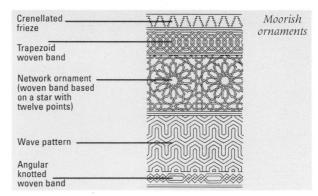

Moorish ornaments

Crenellated frieze

Trapezoid woven band

Network ornament (woven band based on a star with twelve points)

Wave pattern

Angular knotted woven band

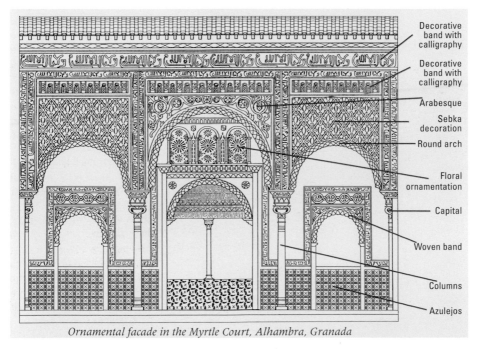

Decorative band with calligraphy

Decorative band with calligraphy

Arabesque

Sebka decoration

Round arch

Floral ornamentation

Capital

Woven band

Columns

Azulejos

Ornamental facade in the Myrtle Court, Alhambra, Granada

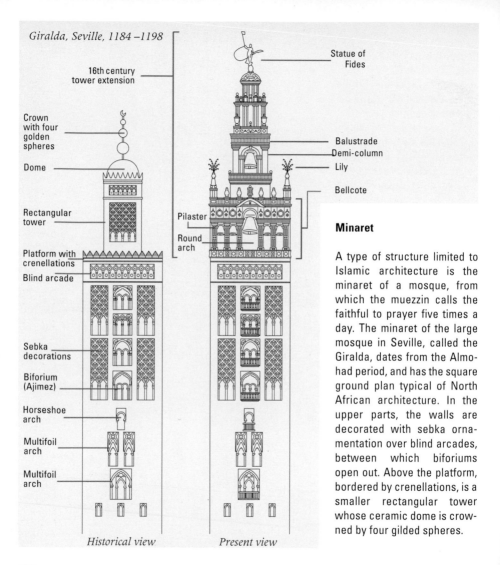

Giralda, Seville, 1184–1198

16th century
tower extension

Statue of
Fides

Crown
with four
golden
spheres

Dome

Balustrade
Demi-column

Lily

Bellcote

Rectangular
tower

Pilaster

Round
arch

Platform with
crenellations

Blind arcade

Sebka
decorations

Biforium
(Ajimez)

Horseshoe
arch

Multifoil
arch

Multifoil
arch

Historical view

Present view

Minaret

A type of structure limited to Islamic architecture is the minaret of a mosque, from which the muezzin calls the faithful to prayer five times a day. The minaret of the large mosque in Seville, called the Giralda, dates from the Almohad period, and has the square ground plan typical of North African architecture. In the upper parts, the walls are decorated with sebka ornamentation over blind arcades, between which biforiums open out. Above the platform, bordered by crenellations, is a smaller rectangular tower whose ceramic dome is crowned by four gilded spheres.

506

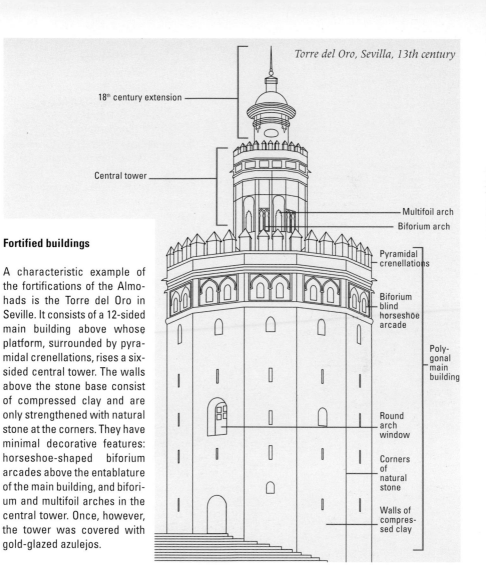

Torre del Oro, Sevilla, 13th century

18th century extension

Central tower

Multifoil arch

Biforium arch

Pyramidal crenellations

Biforium blind horseshoe arcade

Polygonal main building

Round arch window

Corners of natural stone

Walls of compressed clay

Fortified buildings

A characteristic example of the fortifications of the Almohads is the Torre del Oro in Seville. It consists of a 12-sided main building above whose platform, surrounded by pyramidal crenellations, rises a six-sided central tower. The walls above the stone base consist of compressed clay and are only strengthened with natural stone at the corners. They have minimal decorative features: horseshoe-shaped biforium arcades above the entablature of the main building, and biforium and multifoil arches in the central tower. Once, however, the tower was covered with gold-glazed azulejos.

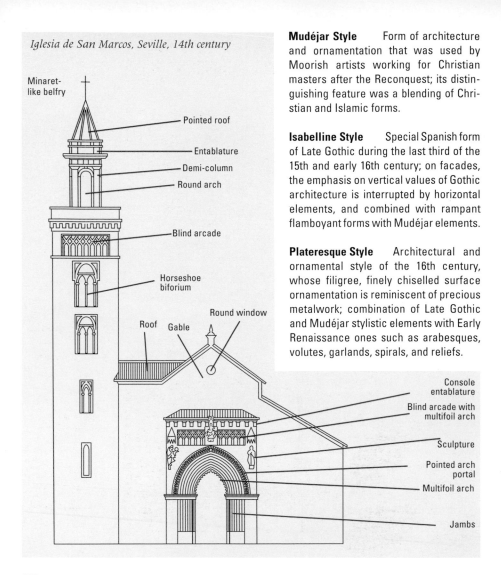

Iglesia de San Marcos, Seville, 14th century

Minaret-like belfry

Pointed roof

Entablature

Demi-column

Round arch

Blind arcade

Horseshoe biforium

Round window

Roof

Gable

Console entablature

Blind arcade with multifoil arch

Sculpture

Pointed arch portal

Multifoil arch

Jambs

Mudéjar Style   Form of architecture and ornamentation that was used by Moorish artists working for Christian masters after the Reconquest; its distinguishing feature was a blending of Christian and Islamic forms.

Isabelline Style   Special Spanish form of Late Gothic during the last third of the 15th and early 16th century; on facades, the emphasis on vertical values of Gothic architecture is interrupted by horizontal elements, and combined with rampant flamboyant forms with Mudéjar elements.

Plateresque Style   Architectural and ornamental style of the 16th century, whose filigree, finely chiselled surface ornamentation is reminiscent of precious metalwork; combination of Late Gothic and Mudéjar stylistic elements with Early Renaissance ones such as arabesques, volutes, garlands, spirals, and reliefs.

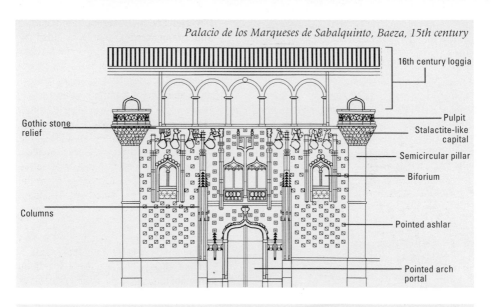

Palacio de los Marqueses de Sabalquinto, Baeza, 15th century

16th century loggia

Gothic stone relief

Pulpit

Stalactite-like capital

Semicircular pillar

Biforium

Columns

Pointed ashlar

Pointed arch portal

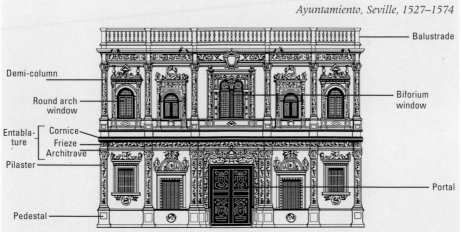

Ayuntamiento, Seville, 1527–1574

Balustrade

Demi-column

Round arch window

Biforium window

Entablature — Cornice
Frieze
Architrave
Pilaster

Portal

Pedestal

Artists' Biographies

Acero, Vincente (first half of 18th century), Spanish architect; works: facade of Guadix Cathedral (1714); new building of Cádiz Cathedral (1720 – 1722); extension of the tobacco factory in Seville (from 1725); design of the facade of Málaga Cathedral (executed between 1724 and 1756 by José de Bada and Antonio Ramos).

Álvarez y Cubero, José (1768 – 1827), Spanish Neoclassical sculptor; with Canova in Rome in 1805; director of the Academy in Madrid in 1826; built the Fuente del Rey in Priego de Córdoba.

Angelico, Fra (c. 1395 – 1455), main representative of the Italian Early Renaissance; in the

Fra Angelico, The Preaching of St. Stephen and the Dispute, 1447–1449
Fresco, 322 x 412 cm, Cappella Niccolina, Musei Vaticani, Rome

Dominican monastery in Fiesole from 1420; from 1436 to 1445, painted the frescoes in San Marco in Florence, was in Rome in 1445, Orvieto in 1447, then in Fiesole and back in Rome from 1452 to 1455. His main works include the *Madonna of the Linen Weavers*, 1433, Museo di San Marco in Florence, and the frescoes for the Chapel of St. Nicholas in the Vatican until 1455.

Aranda, Martín de (first half of 17th century), Spanish sculptor; created the twelve figures of the Apostles made of gilded bronze in the choir of Granada Cathedral (1612).

Arce, José de, (died before 1667), Flemish sculptor; active in Seville from 1636. His works, above all the retable for San Miguel in Jerez de la Frontera, stand out due to their dynamic forms and considerable compositional dramatic quality, which finally enabled the Baroque style to make its breakthrough in Seville.

Arfe y Villafañe, Juan de (1535 – 1603), member of the famous family of goldsmiths that originally came from Germany; main representative of the Spanish High Renaissance; from 1596 in Madrid with Philip II. He created silver pyxes in the classical style of the High Renaissance as influenced by Italy, including the famous pyx in Seville Cathedral; in addition, he produced church furnishings, statues and portrait busts made of bronze. At the same time, he was an important art theoretician based on his major work *On Proportions*, 1585.

Bada, José de (1691 – 1755), Spanish architect; chief architect of Granada Cathedral; in 1719 took over the task of directing the building of Málaga Cathedral, where he built the facade according to the plans of Vicente Acero.

Bartolomé de Jaén, Master (first half of 16th century), Spanish art smith; active in Granada and Jaén amongst others, where due to his creative work an important art school developed. He conceived *rejas* not merely as decorations and functional necessities but as objects of reverence in the manner of a retable with religious scenes. Works: Tenebrario and Easter candelabra in the museum of the Jaén Cathedral; *reja* in the Capilla Real in Granada (1520s); *reja* before the high altar in Seville Cathedral (1524).

Bazán, Lucas (18th century), Spanish architect; in 1745, together with Antonio Corrales, built the belfry of the church of San Juan in Écija.

Benjumeda, Torcuato (1757 – 1836), Spanish architect; pupil of Torcuato Cayón, with whom he collaborated later in life; in 1779 he was appointed as the representative of architecture at the Academia de las Tres Nobles Artes in Cádiz; buildings in Cádiz: royal prison (1764); San José (1787); collaboration on the facade of the town hall.

Berruguete, Alonso (c. 1489 – 1561), Spanish sculptor, painter and architect; son of the painter Pedro Berruguete; from 1504 training in Florence and Rome, where he learned much from the works of Michelangelo; c. 1517 returned to Spain, active in Zaragoza, Valladolid, Salamanca and, from 1539, as the court sculptor of Charles V in Toledo. He was considered by his contemporaries to be one of the greatest artists in Spain and was particularly famous as a sculptor and decorative artist in the Plateresque style. He created altars, choir stalls and decorations; works: parts of the choir stalls in Toledo Cathedral (from 1537); wooden retable in the Sacra Capilla del Salvador in Úbeda.

Bigarny, Felipe de, Bïguerny in Spanish, also called Felipe de Borgoña (c. 1475 – 1542), Spanish sculptor and architect; evidence of his work from 1498; main master of the transition from Gothic to the Renaissance (Early Plateresque style). His chief works in Andalusia include his reliefs with scenes of the Passion of Christ in the choir of Granada Cathedral, and the wooden retable in the Capilla Real, 1520 – 1522.

Bilbao y Martínez, Gonzalo (1860 – 1938), Spanish painter; trained with Francisco and Pedro de Vega in Seville; study journeys to Paris and Italy; from 1888 to 1890 in Morocco, where Oriental themes entered his painting; in 1903 chair at the Escuela de Artes ye Indústrias in Seville. The majority of his work is landscapes and portraits. He was also, however, known for his genre paintings, such as the *Cigarette Workers*, 1915, Museo de Bellas Artes in Seville.

Borcht, Sebastian van der, Dutch 18th-century fortifications architect; built the royal tobacco factory in Seville, 1728 – 1771.

Borromini, Francesco (1599 – 1667), Swiss-Italian architect and sculptor; main representative of the Roman High Baroque; student of Carlo Maderna and Giovanni Lorenzo Bernini. His art, which met the requirements of the Baroque (avoidance of straight lines, sweeping facades, broken pediments, merging of several spaces), served as a model for Rococo architecture in France and Germany amongst others.

Botticelli, Sandro, actually Alessandro Filipepi (c. 1444 – 1510), Italian painter; main representative of the Florentine Early Renaissance; student of Fra Filippo Lippi. Influenced by Antonio del Pollaiuolo and Andrea del Verrochio, but developed his own style. First commissions came from the Medicis. In 1480 he was summoned to Rome by Pope Sixtus IV in order to collaborate on the painting of the Sistine Chapel. His best-known works include the *Primavera*, c. 1478, Galleria degli Uffizi in Florence, and the *Adoration of the Magi* with the portraits of the Medicis, c. 1477, Galleria degli Uffizi in Florence.

Bouts, Dieric (c. 1415 – 1475), main representative of the Old Dutch school of painting; in 1457 he can be proven to have been the town painter in Löwen. Stylistically his work resembled that of Rogier van der Weyden. His works (main works: large altar of the Last Supper, 1464 – 1467, Church of St. Peter in Löwen; the *Arrest and Resurrection of Christ*, 1464, Alte Pinakothek in Munich) excel due to their meticulous depictions, rich colors and fine landscapes.

Campaña, Pedro de, actually Peter de Kempeneer (1503 – 1580), Flemish painter; active in Seville and member of the school of painting; had a great influence on Andalusian painting; works: *Bearing of the Cross*, Museo de Cádiz,

Caravaggio, The Martyrdom of St. Matthew, 1599–1600.
Oil on canvas, 323 x 343 cm, San Luigi dei Francesi, Rome

cathedrals of Seville and Granada. His architectural achievements are reflected by the main facade of Granada Cathedral (plan 1667).

Caravaggio, Michelangelo Merisi da (1571 – 1610), Italian painter; studied in Milan and Venice; from 1588 was in Rome where he briefly worked in the workshop of Giuseppe Cesari. The naturalistic objectivity and hard realism of his early genre pictures at first met with resistance, but finally conquered Baroque painting and created a new genre. His religious paintings (two paintings for the side walls of the Contarelli Chapel in San Luigi dei Francesi, Rome, 1599, and the altar painting of *St. Matthew with the Angel*, 1602, same location) brought about a change in church painting. Caravaggio's works distinguish themselves by their characteristic light-dark painting, sharply lit from the side, which had a great influence on several painters.

Cádiz; *Descent from the Cross*, 1548, Sacristía Mayor, Seville Cathedral; *Candlemass*, 1553, Capilla del Mariscal, Seville Cathedral; high altar painting in Santa Ana, Seville (mid-16th century).

Cano, Alonso, called el Grenadino (1601 – 1667), Spanish painter, sculptor and architect; student of sculpture with Juan Martínez Montañés in Seville, student of painting with Francisco Pacheco. As a painter, an eclectic influenced by Titian, Correggio and Paolo Veronese, as a sculptor the forerunner and architect of the Spanish Baroque. His works can be found in the

Carducho, Vicente (1578 – 1638), Italian painter and art theoretician; representative of the Spanish school of Mannerism; in 1585 came to Spain with his brother Bartolomé (1560 – c. 1608), where he became the court painter in 1609; works: paintings in the chapterhouse of the Granada Cartuja.

Carlone, Michele (traceable 1489 – 1518), Italian architect and sculptor from Genoa; from 1512 active in Andalusia; took on the direction of a group of craftsmen with several members who were responsible for the architectural conception and sculptural decoration of the feudal Castillo of Lacalahorra. He brought the architectural forms of the Renaissance to Spain.

Castillo y Saavedra, Antonio del (1616 – 1668), Spanish painter, drawer, sculptor and poet; son and student of Agustín Castillo; from 1631 to 1634 student of Ignacio Aedo Calderón, from whom he learned polychrome painting on Baroque wooden sculptures; from 1635 can be traced in Córdoba, where he was the most important painter of his age. His three-dimensional light-dark painting is influenced by Zurbarán and José de Ribera; works: *Martyrdom of St. Pelagius*, 1645, Capilla de San Pelagio, Córdoba Cathedral; *Entombment* and *Pietà*, San Andrés, Córdoba; *Crucifixion*, *Archangel Raphael*, *St. Ferdinand*, *St. Catherine*, Museo Provincial de Bellas Artes, Córdoba.

Castillo, Juan del (c. 1590 – 1658), Spanish painter; one of the precursors of the Seville school of painting; teacher of Alonso Cano and Bartolomé Esteban Murillo; active in Granada, Seville and Cádiz; works: *Birth of St. John the Baptist*, *Young St. John*, *The Good Shepherd*, by the high altar of the Convento de Santa Isabel in Seville.

Cayón de la Vega, Torcuato (1727 – 1784), Spanish architect; from 1753 master builder and after the death of his uncle Gaspar Cayón *maestro mayor* of Cádiz Cathedral, whose plans by Vicente Acero he redesigned along classical lines; other buildings in Cádiz: Puerta de Tierra, 1755; Casa de Misericordia; Hospital San José.

Córdoba, Pedro de (2nd half of 15th century), Spanish painter of the Hispano-Flemish style; works: *Annunciation*, 1475, Córdoba Cathedral; *St. Nicholas of Bari*, Museo Provincial de Bellas Artes, Córdoba.

Cornejo, Pedro Duque (1678 – 1757), Spanish sculptor of the Baroque; student of Pedro Roldán; works: choir stalls in Córdoba Cathedral (1748 – 1757).

Corrales, Antonio (18th century), Spanish architect; in 1745, together with Lucas Bazán, constructed the belfry of the church of San Juan in Écija.

Correggio, Antonio Allegri (c. 1489 – 1534), Italian painter; main master of the Renaissance and the school of Parma. His paintings stand out due to the skill with which he handled light, in which the light-dark (*chiaroscuro*) which was developed by Leonardo da Vinci became the determining element. In addition, the strong emotions of his figures and bold foreshortenings were components of his style, anticipating the Baroque, which had a considerable influence on the school of the Carraccis, on Baroque, and indeed on painting in general.

Dancart, Pieter (died c. 1487), Flemish sculptor; only known for his work in Seville; choir stalls in the cathedral together with Nufro Sánchez (1478).

Dyck, Anthonis van (1599 – 1641), Flemish painter and etcher; one of the greatest masters of Flemish art, and one of the greatest portrait painters ever. He studied in the workshop of the Romanist Hendrik van Balen, worked from 1617 to 1620 in the studio of Peter Paul Rubens, although he was already running his own workshop and training apprentices. From 1620 to 1621 in London, then in Italy, in Antwerp in 1627, court painter to Archduchess Isabella in 1630, from 1632 court painter in London, in Flanders in 1634 and Paris from 1640 to 1641. He further developed Rubens' style to achieve finer nuances of color and slimmer figures with sensitive refinement. Apart from religious works (*Bearing of the Cross*, 1617, Church of St. Paul in Antwerp), from 1635 he almost exclusively painted portraits which show him to be a keen observer, and had a great influence on later portrait painting.

Egas, Enrique de (c. 1455 – c. 1534), Spanish Gothic architect and founder of the Plateresque style; from 1494 to 1534 cathedral architect in Toledo; 1506 – 1517 architect of the Capilla Real in Granada; 1521 – 1528 first cathedral architect of the new cathedral in Granada.

Fancelli, Domenico (1469 – 1519), Italian sculptor; came to Spain in about 1508, where he was an influential representative of the Italian Renaissance. His main works include the tomb of Ferdinand and Isabella in the Capilla Real in Granada (1522).

Fernández, Alejo (c. 1475 – 1545), Spanish painter, probably of German-Dutch descent; master of the school of Seville; probably trained in the Netherlands and Upper Italy, for his work combines Dutch and Venetian elements; founder of Renaissance painting in Andalusia; first in Córdoba (*Flagellation of Christ*, Museo Provincial de Bellas Artes, Córdoba) before going to Seville in 1508 (panels of the altar retable in the cathedral; *Virgen de los Navagantes*, 1531 – 1536, Alcázares Reales).

Fernández, Alemán Jorge (c. 1470 – 1533/53), Spanish sculptor, probably of German descent; at first living with his brother Alejo in Córdoba; summoned to Seville in 1505 by the cathedral chapter in order to continue working on the retable in the cathedral that was started by Pieter Dancart.

Ferrer, Tomás (18th century), Spanish painter; active in Granada; works: dome fresco in the sacristy of the Granada Cartuja (1753); frescoes in the arcade spandrels and ceiling fresco of the Camarín in the Hospital de San Juan de Dios in Granada (until 1759).

Figueroa, Ambrosio de (1700 – 1775), Spanish architect; continued the style of his father Leonardo de Figueroa in Seville (Santa Catalina, 1752 – 1758).

Figueroa, Antonio Matías de (c. 1734 – 1796), Spanish architect; grandson of Leonardo de Figueroa; continued the family tradition in Neoclassicism.

Figueroa, Leonardo de (c. 1650 – 1730), Spanish architect; creator of the Seville Baroque architecture, the first to frame brick buildings with white or yellow unworked stone. His buildings distinguish themselves by their lavish use of *azulejos* as well as twisted and decorated columns: Santa María Magdalena (1691 – 1709), San Luis (1699 – 1731), Palacio de San Telmo (1724 – 1734) in Seville.

Florindo, Alonso Ruiz (18th century), Spanish architect; member of the famous family of architects from Fuentes de Andalucía; works: tower of the Iglesia de la Merced in Osuna (1767 – 1775).

Gaínza, Martin de (died 1556), Spanish architect; cathedral architect of Seville Cathedral, where he built the Capilla Real (from 1522) and the Sacristía Mayor (1530 – 1543).

García de Pradas, Juan (active c. 1520 – 1530), Spanish architect and sculptor; works in Seville include: portal of the Capilla Real (1527); portal of the Lonja (1521); continuation of construction work on the Hospital Real (from 1522).

Gijón, Francisco Antonio (1653 – after 1692), Spanish Baroque sculptor; works: *St. Joseph*, 1678, San Nicolás de Bari, Seville; *Dying Christ*, 1682, Capilla del Patrocinio, Seville.

Gil de Hontañón, Juan (died 1526), Spanish architect; together with his son Rodrigo (1500 – 1577) designed the two last great Gothic cathedrals of Spain located in Salamanca and Segovia (built 1523 – 1577) and the new Gothic – style lantern for Seville Cathedral (1517 – 1519).

Gonzáles Álvarez Osorio, Anibal (1876 – 1929), Spanish architect and town planner; designed the Plaza de España and the Plaza de América in the Seville Parque de María Luisa.

Goya y Lucientes, Francisco de (1746 – 1828), Spanish painter, etcher and lithographer; c. 1766 student of Francisco Bayeu in Madrid, in Italy from 1770 to 1771, Madrid from 1775, working in the carpet factory there from 1776, from 1798 court painter, emigrated to Bordeaux in 1824. Goya was very versatile: during his early period, he created decorative cartoons, in bright colors, influenced by the Venetians, for the Gobelin manufactory. From the mid-90s his art anticipated elements of Romanticism and Impressionism, the colors became darker, influences of Diego de Velázquez, Rembrandt and the old Dutch masters became noticeable (*Dressed Maja, Undressed Maja*, 1797, Museo del Prado, Madrid). Goya developed into an extraordinary painter of portraits whose portraits were mercilessly realistic (*Family of Charles IV*, 1800/01, Museo del Prado, Madrid). The Spanish war of liberation against Napoleon had a considerable effect on his work. He created narratives showing the horrors of war and its hardships (*The Third of May, 1808*, 1814, Museo del Prado, Madrid). His printed works using aquatint achieved light-dark effects which capture the demonic (*Caprichos*, 1796 – 1798, *Desastres de la guerra*, 1810 – 1821).

Guas, Juan (c. 1430 – 1496), Spanish architect and sculptor of French or Dutch origins; from 1453 traceable in Castille; active mainly in Toledo; in Baeza, built the Palacio de los Marqueses de Jabalquinto.

Francisco de Goya, Family of Charles IV, 1800 – 1802, Oil on canvas, 280 x 336 cm Museo del Prado, Madrid

Hernández, Juan (16th century), Spanish architect; built the pavilion of Charles V (1543) in the Alcázares Reales in Seville.

Herrera, Francisco de (1627 – 1685), called el Mozo (the Younger), Spanish painter and architect; spent several years in Rome and Naples; in 1672, became court painter to Philip IV in Madrid; painted religious paintings in the High Baroque style (*Apotheosis of St. Francis of Assisi*, 1656, Capilla de San Francisco, Seville Cathedral).

Herrera, Juan de (c. 1530 – 1597), Spanish architect; in Italy in 1553; became the student, in 1559 the colleague and in 1567 the successor of Juan

Bautista de Toledo in Madrid; from 1571 court architect to Philip II. His style, which starts from the Italian Renaissance and is characterized by soberness, strictness and plainness, is a reaction to the flowery Plateresque style; buildings: El Escorial, Madrid, started in 1563 by Juan Bautista de Toledo, continued in 1567 following Herrera's plans; Casa Lonja, Seville (1583 – 1598).

Hurtado Izquierdo, Francisco de (1669 – 1725), Spanish architect, sculptor and decorator; one of the great Spanish architects of the Baroque period. His works were restricted to imaginative interior decorations which have no equal in Europe: Sagrario of the Cartuja in Granada (1702 – 20), whose walls are clad with marble, jasper and porphyry, and whose marble tabernacle is supported by red and black twisted columns; the design of the even more bizarre and lavishly decorated sacristy there (from 1732) is also attributed to him. Decorations of the Camarín in the Santuario de Nuestra Señora de la Victoria, Málaga.

López, Pedro (active 1512 – 1522), Spanish architect; architect of the old cathedral of Jaén, and Málaga Cathedral together with other well-known architects.

Machuca, Luis (died 1573), Spanish architect; after the death of his father Pedro in 1550 continued the construction work on the palace of Charles V on the Alhambra in Granada.

Machuca, Pedro (c. 1485 – 1550), Spanish architect, sculptor and painter; student of the Italian Giuliano da Sangallo; in 1520 returned to Spain; his buildings (palace of Charles V on the Alhambra, Granada, from 1527) are strongly influenced by the Italian Renaissance, but also include characteristics of the Plateresque style, such as window frames decorated with garlands.

Martín Aldehuela, José de (1719 – 1802), architect and sculptor from Aragon; works: marble portal of the Casa del Consulado (1776); Puente Nuevo in Ronda (1784 – 1793); completion of the Plaza de Toros in Ronda (1785); baldachin altar in San Felipe Neri, Málaga (1795).

Martínez, Alonso (14th century), Spanish architect; cathedral architect in Seville, 1386 – 1394).

Memling, Hans (c. 1433 – 1494), main representative of Old Dutch painting; student of Rogier van der Weyden; particularly influenced by Dieric Bouts; was the main master in Bruges (traceable there from 1466). Memling's paintings distinguish themselves through their feeling for grace and moderation, as well as colors of particular beauty and harmony. Exceptional works are his Madonna pictures and portraits; he often combined these two genres on diptychs.

Mena y Escalante, Alonso de (1587 – 1646), Spanish sculptor; works: equestrian statue of St. Santiago, Granada Cathedral (1640); two reliquary altars, transept, Granada Cathedral (1630 – 1632); *Inmaculada*, Abadía del Sacromonte, Granada.

Mena y Medrano, Pedro de (1628 – 1688), Spanish main representative of Baroque sculpture; son of Alonso de Mena, student of Alonso Cano with whom he collaborated from 1652, active in Granada and from 1658 in Málaga. He created religious works in which he developed Cano's style into a realistic though spiritualized means of depiction, avoiding strong emotions. His main works include the 42 high relief statuettes on the rear side of the choir stalls in Málaga Cathedral (1658 – 1662), the statues of the Inmaculada and St. Francis in Córdoba Cathedral and the figures of the Catholic kings in Granada Cathedral (1675 – 1677).

Meneses Osorio, Francisco (c. 1640 – 1721), Spanish figural painter; student and imitator of Bartolomé Esteban Murillo, whom he accompanied to Cádiz in order to collaborate on the cycle for the high altar of the Capuchin church (now in the Museo de Cádiz).

Mesa, Juan de (1583 – 1627), Spanish sculptor and architect; student of Juan Martínez Montañés; created penetrating figures with naturalistic expressions; works: *Jesús del Gran Poder* in the church of the same name in Seville, 1620; *St. John the Baptist*, *Virgen de las Cuevas*, 1623, Museo Provincial de Bellas Artes, Seville; collaborated on the high altar of the monastery of San Isidoro del Campo in Santiponce (1609 – 1613).

Micael Alfaro, José (died 1649), Spanish sculptor, active in Málaga from 1632 to 1647; works: collaborated on the choir stalls of Málaga Cathedral.

Michelangelo Buonarroti (1475 – 1564), Italian painter, sculptor and architect; main representative of the Italian High Renaissance and precursor of Mannerism; trained with Domenico Ghirlandaio and Bertoldo di Giovanni; more important for his development in painting, however, was his interest in Giotto and Masaccio, and in sculpture his study of Jacopo della Quercia; the Classical Age had the greatest influence on his style. At first, Michelangelo worked in Florence and belonged to the circle of poets and scholars which had formed as a "Platonic Academy" around Lorenzo de' Medici, but from 1496 to 1501 he stayed in Rome (*Pietà*, 1498/99, St. Peter's), and then returned to Florence until 1505 (*David*, Academy). In 1505 he went back to Rome to build the tomb of Pope Julius II in St. Peter's, and from 1508 to 1512 he created his main painted work, the painting of the ceiling of the Sistine Chapel. From 1521 he worked on the funeral monument of the Medicis in San Lorenzo in Florence; In 1534 he finally moved to Rome in order to carry out Pope Clement's commission for the fresco of the Last Judgement in the Sistine Chapel (1534 – 1541). From 1547 he was head of construction of St. Peter's; his main architectural work is the dome there.

Millán, Pedro (c. 1487 – before 1526), Spanish sculptor; one of the last representatives of the Gothic school of sculptors in Seville, influenced by Flemish-Burgundian art; created important sacred sculptures (statues of the Puerta del Nacimiento and the *Virgen del Pilar*, Seville Cathedral; sculptures on the portal of the Convento de Santa Paula, Seville).

Montañés, Juan Martínez (c. 1568 – 1649), main

Bartolomé Esteban Murillo, Moses beating Water from a Rock, 1670–1674.
Oil on canvas, 240 x 590 cm, Hospital de la Caridad, Seville

representative of the Seville school of sculptors in the transitional phase from Mannerism to Baroque; student of Pablo de Rojas; successor of Gregorio Hernández; created important religious works, which amongst others distinguish themselves by their balanced beauty and spiritualization of expression while largely abandoning dramatic elements. His main works are the *Cristo de la Clemencia* (1607) and the *Inmaculada* (1628 – 1631) in Seville Cathedral, *Christ on the Cross* in Granada Cathedral, and the retable in San Isidoro del Campo in Santiponce (1610 – 1612).

Mora, José Gómez de (1642 – 1724), Spanish sculptor; royal court sculptor from 1671; influenced by Alonso Cano, whose sacred art he continued (wooden statues of St. Bruno and St. Joseph, 1712, in the Cartuja, Granada; *Mater dolorosa*, Capilla Real, Granada).

Moreno Meléndez, Diego (2nd half of 17th century), Spanish architect; buildings: Colegiata de San Salvador (from 1695) and tower facade of San Miguel (1672 – 1701) in Jerez de la Frontera.

Muñoz Degrain, Antonio (1840 – 1924), Spanish painter; taught the child Picasso in Málaga; works in the Museo Provincial de Bellas Artes in Málaga and in the Museo de Bellas Artes de la Provincia in Granada.

Murillo, Bartolomé Esteban (1618 – 1682), Spanish painter, representative of the school of Seville and one of the most famous painters of the Spanish High Baroque; student of Juan del Castillo; studied the paintings of Raphael, Correggio, Rubens and van Dyck; in 1660 president of the newly founded academy of painting. Murillo is known amongst other things for his charming depictions of Madonnas and saints, whose warm and hazy colors (*estilo vaporoso*) and soft light-dark take away their harsh contours. His main works include the paintings of saints with works of compassion in the Hospital de la Caridad in Seville, the *Inmaculada* (1668) and the *Vision of St. Anthony* (1656) in the cathedral there.

Niculoso Pisano, Francisco (active 1498 – 1535), Italian ceramist from Pisa; active in Seville; works: *Visitation* on the ceramic altar, Oratory of the Catholic kings, Alcázares Reales; portal, Convento de Santa Paula (1504); tombstone of Iñigo López, Santa Ana (1503).

Ordoñez, Bartolomé (c. 1480 – 1520), Spanish sculptor; stayed in Florence during his youth, in Barcelona from 1515; stylistically influenced by Andrea Sansovino and Michelangelo (tomb of Philip the Handsome and Johanna the Mad, 1519/20, Capilla Real, Granada.

Orea, Juan de (c. 1525 – 1580), Spanish architect and sculptor; worked with Pedro Machuca; head of construction of Almería Cathedral (1550 – 1573) and Granada Cathedral; designed Santa María on the Alhambra in Granada (built posthumously 1581 – 1618).

Ortega, Nufro de (1516 – 1575), Spanish sculptor; works: high altar of Santa María in Carmona (1563).

Pacheco, Francisco (1564 – 1654), Spanish painter; master of Spanish Romanism (art influenced by Italy); from 1625 in Seville, where he collected a circle of artists, humanists, poets and theologians; teacher of Diego de Velázquez; created religious paintings, portraits and wrote definitive art historical treatises (*El Arte de la Pintura*, 1649, in which he made a detailed study both of questions of painting and Christian iconography). His best-known works include *St. Sebastian*, 1616, San Sebastián, Alcalá de Guadaira, and the high altar of San Miguel in Jerez de la Frontera.

Palomino de Castro y Velasco, Antonio Acisclo (1655 – 1726), Spanish Baroque painter; in Madrid from 1678, court painter in 1688; created religious paintings (*Inmaculada*, 1713, Córdoba Cathedral) and was one of the most important Spanish art theoreticians (*Parnaso Español*, published in 1724, history of Spanish painting).

Pedrajas, Francisco Javier (1736 – 1817), Spanish Rococo architect and sculptor; works: El Sagrario (tabernacle) in Santa María de la Asunción, Priego de Córdoba (1784).

Phidias (c. 500 – after 438 B.C.), Greek architect and sculptor; main representative of High Classical Attic art; already famous in classical times as a sculptor of statues of gods (*Athena Parthenos*, 438, Parthenon, Athens; *Zeus of Olympia*, Temple of Zeus, Olympia). Copies made during the Imperial Age give us an idea of his work. In Olympia his workshop was found, and amongst other things it included a clay fragment with the carved inscription "I belong to Phidias".

Picasso, Pablo (1881 – 1973), Spanish painter, sculptor and graphic artist; one of the most important artists of the 20th century; co-founder of Cubism; attended art schools in La Coruña and Barcelona, was in Paris for the first time in 1900 (moved there in 1904), where he was strongly influenced by Toulouse-Lautrec and Cézanne; Blue Period from 1901 – 1905; then Rose Period; in 1906 became acquainted with Georges Braque and Henri Matisse; influenced by tribal art, detachment from natural models, beginnings of Cubism (*Les demoiselles d'Avignon*, 1907, Museum of Modern Art, New York). From 1917 Picasso developed a classicist style; in the 1920s Surrealist influences followed, and a heightened expressiveness with distortions and harsh colors, both of which were definitive as regards his later development (*Guernica*, 1937, Centro de Arte Reina Sofia, Madria, a symbol of the horrors of the Spanish Civil War). In addition, Picasso created numerous graphical works, sculptures from 1928 and ceramics from 1947.

Pineda y Paramo, Bernado Simón (1638 – c. 1702), Spanish architect, sculptor and art carpenter; student of Luis Ortiz; in 1660 co-founder of the Seville Academy; most famous Seville altar sculptor in the last third of the 17th century, and one of the most important artists of Seville Baroque; works: design and direction of the construction of the Hospital de la Caridad, Seville (1664 – 1674); execution of the high altar there (1670); altar in Santa Cruz, Seville (1678); altar of Santa María de la Esperanza, San Sebastián, Antequera (1683).

Poussin, Nicolas (1594 – 1665), French painter; main representative of the French High Baroque Neoclassicism; in 1624 travelled from Paris via Venice to Rome, where he spent his entire life, apart from the years between 1640 and 1642. Poussin joined Italian Baroque painting and studied the masters of the Italian Renaissance and Classical Age; created clear history paintings from Classical mythology and biblical events; moulded the "heroic landscape" type with figures from mythology and history; countered the atmospheric tone of his backgrounds, frequently golden brown, with the finely tuned colors of his figures' clothes (*Parnassus*, Museo del Prado, Madrid; *Inspiration of the Poet* and *Landscape with Diogenes*, Musée du Louvre, Paris).

Raphael, actually Raffaello Santi (1483 – 1520), Italian painter and architect; main representative of the High Renaissance; in 1494, entered Perugino's workshop in Perugia, was in Florence in 1504 and 1506 (*Madonna del Granduca*, 1504/1505, Galleria degli Uffizi, Florence), went to Rome in 1508 (*Sistine Madonna*, c. 1512/1513, Gemäldegalerie, Dresden; *Pope Leo X with Two Cardinals*, 1517/1518, Galleria degli Uffizi, Florence) where in 1514 he was named the chief architect of St. Peter's, in succession to Bramante. After he had dealt with all the contemporary influences in Florence (Leonardo, Fra Bartolommeo), and Michelangelo in Rome, there followed the compositional fulfilment of the High Renaissance ideals, including the painting of the stanzas, the private chambers of Pope Julius II in the Vatican (from 1508). Between 1515 and 1518 he designed the 52 ceiling decorations for the loggias in the Vatican.

Ramos, Antonio (1702 – 1782), Spanish architect and sculptor; in 1755 he took over as head of construction of Málaga Cathedral; further buildings: Palacio Episcopal (1756 – 1776) and plans for the facade of San Felipe Neri (2nd half of 18th century) in Málaga.

Riaño, Diego de (died 1534), Spanish architect; worked in Seville from 1523; buildings: northern alabaster chapels and Sacristía de los Cálices (until 1537) in the cathedral; design of the town hall (from 1527).

Ribera, Andrés de (16th century), Spanish architect; active in Jerez de la Frontera: portal of the Cartuja de Santa María de la Defensión (1571); Casa del Cabildo Vièjo (1575).

Ribera, José (Jusepe) de, also called Spagnoletto (1591 – 1652), Spanish painter; in Italy from 1610, living in Naples from 1616; mediator between Italian and Spanish art; influenced by Caravaggio's light-dark contrasting paintings; in his late period, attempted to mute the light-dark and the Spanish Realism, and brighten his colors (*Crucifixion*, Colegiata, Osuna).

Risueño, José (1665 – 1732), Spanish sculptor and painter; student of José de Mora; well-known Baroque artist and successor of Alonso Cano; works: *Ecce Homo*, *Mater Dolorosa*, 1712 – 1732, Capilla Real, Granada; *St. John the Baptist*, *Virtues*, sculptures on the polychrome marble retable in the Cartuja's tabernacle, Granada.

Rodríguez, Alonso (died 1530), Spanish architect; active in Seville from 1496; designed the Sacristía de los Cálices in the cathedral (1529).

Roelas, Juan de las (c. 1560 – 1624), founder of Seville Baroque painting; in Venice from 1606 to 1609, Madrid in 1616/1617, finally in Seville; took up the art of Tintoretto and was influenced by the light-dark painting of Caravaggio (high altar of the Iglesia de San Salvador; *St. James*, Seville Cathedral).

Roldán, Luisa (1650 – 1704), Spanish sculptress; student of, and worked with, her father Pedro Roldán; from 1695 court sculptress of Charles II; works: *St. Servando* and *St. Germán*, Cádiz Cathedral; sculptures of the Passion, Santa Catalina, Seville.

José de Ribera, Holy Trinity, c. 1636
Oil on canvas, 226 x 118 cm
Museo del Prado, Madrid

Roldán, Pedro (1624 – 1699), Spanish sculptor; student of Alonso Cano. His works testify to the realism of that period, for they do not omit extreme emotions such as pain, grief and death (*Entombment*, 1670, Hospital de la Caridad, Seville).

Romero de Torres, Julio (1874 – 1930), Spanish painter; painted in the style of the bourgeois-public Realism of the early 20th century, with numerous adoptions from Spanish and Italian painting of the past; is respected as the "painter of black-brown girls" as no other could match the considerable vividness with which he depicted the beauty and melancholy of Andalusian women; works: *La Chiquita Piconera* (1930), *El Poema de Córdoba* (1914).

Rubens, Peter Paul (1577 – 1640), main representative of Flemish Baroque painting; in Italy from 1600 to 1608, then active in Antwerp; court painter to the Archduke Albrecht, the governor of the Spanish Netherlands. During his early period, he was moulded by the Italian Renaissance and Mannerism (Caravaggio, Titian) and studied the Classical Age in Italy. After 1608 he developed his own style, and from 1615 this is characterized by the Baroque love of passion. In his history paintings from 1620 the present, mythology and allegory merge with one another; he painted landscapes in which the figures become one with the space. Rubens created religious, historical, allegorical and mythological depictions, portraits, landscapes and animal paintings to an equal degree. In his extremely large workshop there were, in addition to his students, independent painters employed to carry out the paintings from his oil sketches. Some of his numerous works one could mention include: *Triptych of the Raising of the Cross, Descent from the Cross, Assumption of the Virgin*, 1610/11, 1610 – 1614 and 1626, Antwerp Cathedral; 21 paintings on the life of Maria de Médici, 1621 – 1625, Musée du Louvre, Paris.

Ruiz, Diego (traceable in Seville in 1427), Spanish sculptor and art carpenter; works: dome in the Sala de Embajadores, Alcazares Reales, Seville.

Ruiz (el Viejo), Hernán I (died 1558), Spanish architect; chief architect of Córdoba Cathedral (1523 – 1547).

Ruiz, Hernán II (c. 1501 – 1569), Spanish architect; continued the construction work on Córdoba Cathedral after the death of his father Hernán I; other buildings: Palacio de los Villalones (1560) and facade of the Palacio de Páez de Castillejo in Córdoba; belfry story of the Giralda, Seville (1560 – 1568); dome of the Capilla Real, Seville Cathedral.

Ruiz, Hernán III (c. 1559 – 1606), Spanish architect in Córdoba; son of Hernán II; completed the construction work on the cathedral (1607); other works: Puerta del Puente (1571); design and start of work on the cathedral's belfry (1593).

Sánchez Bartolomé (16th century), Spanish architect; works: Antigua Casa of the Cabildo in Jerez de la Frontera.

Sánchez Cotán, Juan (1560 – 1627), Spanish

painter; the master of realistic still lives became acquainted with the art of Caravaggio at an early stage, and he further developed it in his *bodegones*. From 1604 a Carthusian monk, later entering the Carthusian monastery of Granada (Cartuja) for which he created numerous religious paintings.

Sánchez, Nufro (15th century), Spanish sculptor; from 1461 mentioned as a citizen of Seville; created the choir stalls in the cathedral there together with Pieter Dancart (1478).

Siloë, Diego de (c. 1490 – 1563), Spanish architect and sculptor; chief architect of the High Renaissance in Spain; probably studied in Italy; lasting influences from Michelangelo and Leonardo da Vinci; in 1528 appointed as architect at Granada Cathedral (until 1559).

Suárez, Antonio de (active 1648 – 1664), Spanish goldsmith; created the large silver pyx in the cathedral museum, Cádiz.

Susillo, Antonio (1857 – 1896), Spanish sculptor: works: statues of famous citizens of Seville on the north facade of the Palacio de San Telmo in Seville; *Compassion*, Hospital de la Caridad, Seville.

Valdés, Lucas (1661 – 1725), Spanish painter, etcher and copper engraver; son of Valdés Leal; works: paintings (*Entrance of Ferdinand the Saint into Seville*, *Autodafé*) in Santa María Magdalena, Seville; illusionist painted architectural decorations and depictions of the Eucharist in the dome of San Luis, Seville.

Valdés Leal, Juan, actually Juan de Nisa (1622 – 1690), main representative of the Seville school of painting; in Seville from 1656; rival of Bartolomé Esteban Murillo; created large religious works (high altar of the Iglesia del Carmen, 1654 – 1658, Córdoba; *Inmaculada*, 1661, Museo de Bellas Artes, Seville); his allegories of death in the Hospital de la Caridad in Seville (1671/72) are famous.

Vandelvira, Andrés de (1509 – 1575), Spanish architect; worked in Baeza and Úbeda amongst others; buildings: cathedral (from 1568) and Capilla Mayor of Santa María del Alcázar y San Andrés in Baeza, Sacra Capilla del Salvador (consecrated in 1559), Palacio de las Cadenas (mid-16th century), inner courtyard of the Palacio de la Rambla (mid-16th century), Palacio de Vela de los Cobos (mid-16th century) and west portal of San Nicolás (1566) in Úbeda.

Vanderbilt Withney, Gertrude (19th/20th century), American sculptress; created the Columbus memorial near Huelva.

Vargas, Luis de (c. 1505 – 1567), Spanish painter; trained in Rome; from 1550 proven to be back in Seville; works: *Adoration of the Shepherds*, 1555, southern outer side aisle, cathedral; *Inmaculada*, 1561, Altar de la Concepción, cathedral.

Vázquez, Juan Bautista (c. 1510 – 1588), Spanish sculptor; in Seville from 1557; works: *Mary Protrectress* and *Virgen de las Fiebras* on the altars of the northern transept chapels of Santa María Magdalena (1651), and the relief of the Madonna

Diego Velázquez, Surrender of Breda, 1634/35. Oil on canvas, 307.5 cm 370.5 cm, Museo del Prado, Madrid

situated over the church portal of the Old University (1573).

Vázquez Días, Daniel (1882 – 1969), Spanish painter; studied in Paris and Italy. He was teacher of the class on decorative painting at the Escuela Superiora de Pintura in Madrid; his works include: wall paintings in Santa María de la Rábida near Palos de la Frontera (1930).

Velázquez, Diego de Silva y (1599 – 1660), main representative of Spanish painting in the 17th century; student of Francisco de Herrera the Elder and Francisco Pacheco; in 1617 was admitted to the painters' guild of San Luca; in

1623 went to Madrid, where he was made court painter; journeys to Italy in 1629 – 1631 and 1649 – 1651. During his early period, still greatly under the influence of Caravaggio, he mainly painted *bodegones*. On his journeys to Italy he examined the works of old masters, particularly Titian, whose masterly use of fleeting brushstrokes in order to create relief and depth by means of shade and light he admired (*The Forge of Vulcan*, c. 1631, *The Surrender of Breda*, 1634/35, Museo del Prado, Madrid); rose to become the most popular portrait painter at the royal court (*Philip IV*, *Infant Baltasar Carlos*, Museo del Prado, Madrid). After the second Italian journey, his main period began, in which he used light and impressionistic brushstrokes to draw objects in light and color, making him one of the great precursors of Impressionism (*Las Meninas*, 1656, Museo del Prado, Madrid).

Vergara, Diego de (beginning of 16th century – 1582), Spanish architect; left Toledo for Andalusia in 1528, where in 1540 he took over the work on San Sebastián in Antiquera and from 1549 took over from Diego de Siloë as head of construction to continue Málaga Cathedral.

Vilches, Cristóbal de (1st third of 17th century), Spanish architect; active in Granada: completed the Cartuja's church.

Weyden, Rogier van der (c. 1400 – 1464), main representative of the Old Dutch school of painting; student of Robert Campin in Tournai; from 1435 city painter in Brussels; 1449/50 in Italy; working in the tradition of Gothic sacred art, also influenced by Jan van Eyck. His work greatly influenced the further development both of Old Dutch and Old German art. His main works include the *Descent from the Cross*, c. 1435 – 1449, Museo del Prado, Madrid.

Zumáragga, Miguel de, (died c. 1651), Spanish architect; traceable from 1585; works: *trascoro* of the cathedral (1619) and plan of the Iglesia del Sagrario in Seville (from 1617).

Zurbarán, Francisco de (1598 – 1664), main representative of Spanish painting in the 17th century; student of Juan de las Roelas; in Seville from 1629; made court painter to Philip IV in 1638; in 1658 moved to Madrid. Amongst other works, Zurbarán painted religious pictures for monasteries, usually cycles of the lives of monks and portraits of monks. His paintings – whether containing one or more figures – distinguish themselves through their simple, peaceful, almost strict composition, which is frequently combined with strong contrasts of light and dark. His main works include the *Bonaventura* cycle, before 1629, formerly in San Buenaventura in Seville, and the *Apotheosis of St. Thomas Aquinas*, 1631, in the cathedral.

Literary references

Non-fiction

Barrucand, Marianne and Achim Bednorz. *Maurische Architektur in Andalusien*. Cologne: 1999

Bonet Correra, Antonio. *Barock in Andalusien*. Herrsching: 1982

Brentjes, Burchard. *Die Kunst der Mauren*. Cologne: 1992

Burckhardt, Titus. *Die maurische Kultur in Spanien*. Munich: 1970

Defourneaux, Marcelin. *Spanien im goldenen Zeitalter*. Stuttgart: 1986

Cipolla, Carlo M. *Die Odyssee des spanischen Silbers. Conquistadores, Kaufleute, Piraten*. Berlin: 1998

Gibson, Ian. *Lorcas Granada. Ein Stadtführer — Auf den Spuren von Federico García Lorca*. Kassel: 1995

Gladiss, Almut von and Margot Scheffold. *Schätze der Alhambra. Islamische Kunst aus Andalusien*. Tübingen: 1995

Grabar, Oleg. *Die Alhambra*. Cologne: 1989

Hänsel, Sylvaine and Henrik Karge, eds. *Spanische Kunstgeschichte. Eine Einführung*. 2 vols. Berlin: 1992

Hees, Horst van. *Andalusien. Kunstdenkmäler und Museen, Reclam's Kunstführer*. Stuttgart: 1992

Horst, Eberhard. *Die Spanische Trilogie. Isabella – Johanna – Teresa*. Hildesheim: 1989

Hottinger, Arnold. *Die Mauren. Arabische Kunst in Spanien*. Munich: 1995

Kusserow, Mourad. Kulturlandschaft Andalusien. Freiburg: 1991

Marcu, Valeriu. *Die Vertreibung der Juden aus Spanien*. Munich: 1991

Perez, Joseph. *Ferdinand und Isabella. Spanien zur Zeit der Katholischen Könige*. Munich: 1995

Schomann, Heinz. *Kunstdenkmäler der Iberischen Halbinsel, part III*. Darmstadt: 1998

Schubart, Hermanfrid and Walder Trillmich, eds. *Hispania Antiqua. Die Denkmäler der Römerzeit*. Mainz: 1993

Stierlin, Henri and Anne. *Alhambra*. Munich: 1993

von der Ropp, Arved and Inge. *Andalusien. Spaniens maurischer Süden*. Cologne: 1985

Wördemann, Franz. *Die Beute gehört Allah. Die Geschichte der Araber in Spanien*. Munich: 1985

Fiction

Ali, Tariq. *Shadows of the Pomegranate Tree.*
Verso Books: 1993

Baer, Frank. *Die Brücke von Alcantara.*
Munich: 1996

Brandenberger, Erna. *Barocke Erzählungen aus Spanien (Narracciones barrocas).* Munich: 1995

Cyran, Eberhard. *Abend über der Alhambra.*
Heilbronn: 1991

de Cervantes, Miguel. *Adventures of Don Quixote.* Penguin: 1988

de Molina, Tirso. *Don Juan.* Stuttgart: 1983

de Silva, Colin. *Alhambra. Arena of Assassins.*

Feuchtwanger, Lion.*The Jewess of Toledo.*
New York: Messner, 1956

Frisch, Max. *Don Juan or The Love of Geometry.*
New York: Hill and Wang, 1969

Gaertner, Lothar. *Nicolasin und Nicolason. Spanische Volksmärchen.* Munich: 1999

Gala, Antonio. *Granada de los Nazaries*: 1992

García Lorca, Federico. *Four Major Plays. Blood Wedding, Yerma, The House of Bernanda Alba, Dona Rosita the Spinster*
New York: Oxford Univ. Press, 1997

Gautier, Théophile. *Reise in Andalusien.*
Munich: 1994

Guiladi, Yael. *Die schöne Orovida.* Berlin: 1998

Hemingway, Ernest. *Death in the Afternoon.*
New York: Scribner, 1999

Hermary-Vieille, Catherine. *Johanna die Wahnsinnige. Die Geschichte einer Sehnsucht.*
Bergisch-Gladbach, 1996

Irving, Washington. *The Alhambra.*
New York: Sleepy Hollow Press, 1982

Jimenez, Juan Ramon. *Platero and I. An Andalusian Elegy.* Univ. of Texas Press, 1983

Merimée, Prosper. *Carmen.*
New York: Bigelow, 1905

Munoz Molina, Antonio. *El Jinete Polaco.*
Planeta, 1998

Potocki, Jan. *The Saragossa Manuskript.*
London: Cassell, 1962

Rilke, Rainer Maria. *Rilke in Spanien. Gedichte, Briefe, Tagebücher.* Frankfurt, 1993

Rushdie, Salman. *The Moor's Last Sigh.*
New York: Random House, 1997

Sender, Ramon José. *Der König und die Königin.* Frankfurt, 1962

Sinoué, Gilbert. *Der blaue Stein.* Munich, 1997

Index

Photographic and Map Credits

The majority of the pictures are drawn from the Archivo Oronoz i
lishers would like to thank the museums, collectors, archives an
kind permission for their images to be reproduced, and for th
production of this book.

Photo: © AKG Photo, Berlin (18, 22, 23, 37 bottom, 47, 75, 91, 142, 158,
191, 193, 204, 205, 206, 207, 240, 241, 242, 268, 320, 348, 383, 393, ⊿
457, 491); Photo: © Archivo Iconografico S.A., Barcelona (13, 327
Bednorz, Cologne (2, 8, 72, 73, 113 bottom right, 198, 199, 257, 260,
295, 297, 298, 301, 303, 305, 307, 312, 316, 319 bottom right, 328, 331,
365 bottom, 394/395, 398, 399, 414 left, 416, 430, 441, 447, 448, 449,
© BEER, Photography, Barcelona (245); Photo: © Biblioteca Apc
(231); Photo: © Bibliothèque Nationale, Paris (141, 192); Photo: ©
turbesitz, Berlin (232); © Bildarchiv Steffens, Mainz, Photo: A
© Collection VIOLLET, Paris (4/5 and 6/7 background); Photo: ©
5 and 6/7 background); Photo: © G. Dagli Orti, Paris (159, 163); ©
Institut, Abteilung Madrid, Photo: P. Witte (180, 187, 371 bottom);
Library (263); Astrid Fischer-Leitl, Munich; End paper; Peter Fr
168/169, 194/195, 208/209, 224/225, 236/237, 258/259, 308-310, 362/3
G. Lopez, Monteagudo (136); © Foto Strenger, Atelier für Wer
Photo: © Giraudon, Paris (321); © Imagepool, Seville (16/17, 27,
top left, 118, 144, 164/165, 166, 170, 171, 172, 196, 197 bottom right, 2
222, 227, 229, 234, 235, 238, 248, 251, 254/255, 270, 271, 296, 311, 318,
404, 407 top, 411, 420, 425 top, 436, 450, 452, 478, 493); Photo: Manu
Institut Amatller d'Art Hispànic, Barcelona (12, 108, 325, 384); Phc
Roy Miles Esq./Bridgeman Art Library, London (269); Photo: © The
ary, London (78); © Jens Rademacher, Hamburg (Illustration and
(30/31, 54-56, 132/133, 160, 212/213, 278/279, 280, 314/315, 368, 396/3
Photo:
© Sächsische Landesbibliothek – Staats-und Universitätsbiblioth
thek, Photo: Kramer (143); Photo: © SCALA Istituto Fotografico, Fl
121, 210, 239, 253, 272, 288, 290, 299, 300,0302, 304, 306, 317, 319 top l
414 right, 419, 468, 469, 470, 476, 490, 495, 510, 513, 517, 520, 523)
sammlung Dresden (138); Photo: © Henri Stierlin, Genf (61, 385, 43

Photographic and Map Credits

The majority of the pictures are drawn from the Archivo Oronoz in Madrid. In addition, the publishers would like to thank the museums, collectors, archives and photographers for giving their kind permission for their images to be reproduced, and for their friendly support during the production of this book.

Photo: © AKG Photo, Berlin (18, 22, 23, 37 bottom, 47, 75, 91, 142, 158, 161, 174, 175, 177, 178, 179, 190, 191, 193, 204, 205, 206, 207, 240, 241, 242, 268, 320, 348, 383, 393, 426, 427, 433, 435, 442, 446, 456, 457, 491); Photo: © Archivo Iconografico S.A., Barcelona (13, 327, 349, 380, 401); Photo: © Achim Bednorz, Cologne (2, 8, 72, 73, 113 bottom right, 198, 199, 257, 260, 261, 268, 283, 285, 286, 289, 291, 295, 297, 298, 301, 303, 305, 307, 312, 316, 319 bottom right, 328, 331, 340, 341, 343, 347, 358/359, 361, 365 bottom, 394/395, 398, 399, 414 left, 416, 430, 441, 447, 448, 449, 453, 458, 459, 480, 483); Photo: © BEER, Photography, Barcelona (245); Photo: © Biblioteca Apostolica Vaticana, Vatican City, (231); Photo: © Bibliothèque Nationale, Paris (141, 192); Photo: © Bildarchiv Preussischer Kulturbesitz, Berlin (232); © Bildarchiv Steffens, Mainz, Photo: Archephoto (264, 265); Photo: © Collection VIOLLET, Paris (4/5 and 6/7 background); Photo: © G. Dagli Orti, Paris (159, 163); 5 and 6/7 background); Photo: © G. Dagli Orti, Paris (159, 163); © Deutsches Archäologisches Institut, Abteilung Madrid, Photo: P. Witte (180, 187, 371 bottom); Photo: © Edinburgh University Library (263); Astrid Fischer-Leitl, Munich; End paper; Peter Frese, Munich (24/25, 115, 125, 168/169, 194/195, 208/209, 224/225, 236/237, 258/259, 308-310, 362/363, 374/375, 408/409); Photo: © G. Lopez, Monteagudo (136); © Foto Strenger, Atelier für Werbefotografie, Osnabrück (38); Photo: © Giraudon, Paris (321); © Imagepool, Seville (16/17, 27, 34, 35, 57, 65, 84, 111, 112, 113 top left, 118, 144, 164/165, 166, 170, 171, 172, 196, 197 bottom right, 200/201, 203, 215, 217, 220, 221, 222, 227, 229, 234, 235, 238, 248, 251, 254/255, 270, 271, 296, 311, 318, 333, 342, 372, 373, 377 top, 378, 404, 407 top, 411, 420, 425 top, 436, 450, 452, 478, 493); Photo: Manuela Rodriguez (110); Photo: © Institut Amatller d'Art Hispànic, Barcelona (12, 108, 325, 384); Photo: © M. Leffler (60); Poto: © Roy Miles Esq./Bridgeman Art Library, London (269); Photo: © The National Gallery Picture Library, London (78); © Jens Rademacher, Hamburg (Illustration and Photo) (281); Rolli Arts, Essen (30/31, 54-56, 132/133, 160, 212/213, 278/279, 280, 314/315, 368, 396/397, 438-440, 443, 445, 471-474); Photo: © Sächsische Landesbibliothek – Staats-und Universitätsbibliothek Dresden, Deutsche Fotothek, Photo: Kramer (143); Photo: © SCALA Istituto Fotografico, Florence (19, 21, 49, 58, 59, 105, 121, 210, 239, 253, 272, 288, 290, 299, 300,0302, 304, 306, 317, 319 top left, 334, 335, 336, 354, 379, 392, 414 right, 419, 468, 469, 470, 476, 490, 495, 510, 513, 517, 520, 523); Photo: © Staatliche Kunstsammlung Dresden (138); Photo: © Henri Stierlin, Genf (61, 385, 432, 444, 454)

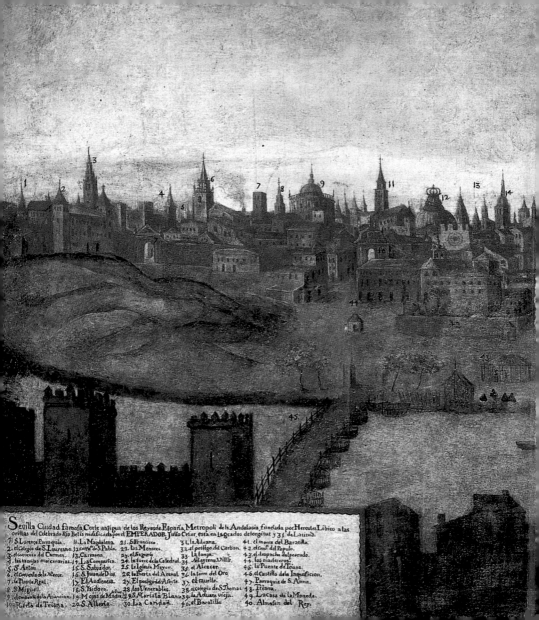

Sevilla Ciudad famosa Corte antigua de los Reyes de España Metropoli de la Andalusia fundada por Hercules Libico a las
orillas del Celebrado Rio Betis redificada por el EMPERADOR Julio Cesar, esta en 19 grados de longitud y 31 de Latitud.

1. S.Lorenzo Parroquia.	11. La Magdalena.	21. S.Francisco.	31. la Aduana.	41. el monte del Baratillo.
2. el colegio de S.Laureano.	12. conv.to de S.Pablo.	22. los Menores.	32. el postigo del Carbon.	42. el conv.to del Populo.
3. el convento del Carmen.	13. Carmona.	23. el Sagrario.	33. La lonja.	43. el despacho del pescado.
4. las monjas mercenarias.	14. La Compañia.	24. la torre de la Catedral.	34. Mayrena Villa.	44. los mataderos.
5. S.Anton.	15. S.Salvador.	25. Iglesia Mayor.	35. el Alcaçar.	45. la Puente de Triana.
6. el convento de Merce	16. S.Juan de Dios.	26. la torre del Arenal.	36. la torre del Oro.	46. el Castillo de la Inquisicion.
7. la Puerta Real.	17. El Audiencia.	27. El postigo del Azeite.	37. el muelle.	47. Parroquia de S.Anna.
8. S.Miguel.	18. S.Ysidoro.	28. los Venerables.	38. el colegio de S.Thomas	48. Triana.
9. convento de la Asuncion.	19. M.ojas de Madre	29. S.Maria la Blanca.	39. la Aduana vieja.	49. La casa de la Moneda.
10. Puerta de Triana.	20. S.Alberto.	30. La Caridad.	40. el Baratillo.	50. Almasen del Rey.